Teaching Modernist Poetry

Edited by

Peter Middleton and Nicky Marsh

First published 2010 by
PALGRAVE MACMILLAN

Palgrave Macmillan in the UK is an imprint of Macmillan Publishers Limited,
registered in England, company number 785998, of Houndmills, Basingstoke,
Hampshire RG21 6XS.

Palgrave Macmillan in the US is a division of St Martin's Press LLC,
175 Fifth Avenue, New York, NY 10010.

Palgrave Macmillan is the global academic imprint of the above companies
and has companies and representatives throughout the world.

Palgrave® and Macmillan® are registered trademarks in the United States,
the United Kingdom, Europe and other countries.

ISBN: 978–0–230–20232–0   hardback
ISBN: 978–0–230–20233–7   paperback

This book is printed on paper suitable for recycling and made from fully
managed and sustained forest sources. Logging, pulping and manufacturing
processes are expected to conform to the environmental regulations of the
country of origin.

A catalogue record for this book is available from the British Library.

A catalog record for this book is available from the Library of Congress.

10 9 8 7 6 5 4 3 2 1
19 18 17 16 15 14 13 12 11 10

Printed and bound in Great Britain by
CPI Antony Rowe, Chippenham and Eastbourne

Teaching the New English

Published in association with the English Subject Centre
Director: Ben Knights

Teaching the New English is an innovative series concerned with the teaching of the English degree in universities in the UK and elsewhere. The series addresses new and developing areas of the curriculum as well as more traditional areas that are reforming in new contexts. Although the series is grounded in intellectual and theoretical concepts of the curriculum, it is concerned with the practicalities of classroom teaching. The volumes will be invaluable for new and more experienced teachers alike.

Titles include:

Gail Ashton and Louise Sylvester (*editors*)
TEACHING CHAUCER

Charles Butler (*editor*)
TEACHING CHILDREN'S FICTION

Robert Eaglestone and Barry Langford (*editors*)
TEACHING HOLOCAUST LITERATURE AND FILM

Michael Hanrahan and Deborah L. Madsen (*editors*)
TEACHING, TECHNOLOGY, TEXTUALITY
Approaches to New Media and the New English

David Higgins and Sharon Ruston
TEACHING ROMANTICISM

Andrew Hiscock and Lisa Hopkins (*editors*)
TEACHING SHAKESPEARE AND EARLY MODERN DRAMATISTS

Peter Middleton and Nicky Marsh (*editors*)
TEACHING MODERNIST POETRY

Andrew Maunder and Jennifer Phegley (*editors*)
TEACHING NINETEENTH-CENTURY FICTION

Anna Powell and Andrew Smith (*editors*)
TEACHING THE GOTHIC

Forthcoming titles:

Gina Wisker (*editor*)
TEACHING AFRICAN-AMERICAN WOMEN'S WRITING

Teaching the New English
Series Standing Order ISBN 978–1–4039–4441–2   Hardback
978–1–4039–4442–9   Paperback
(*outside North America only*)

You can receive future titles in this series as they are published by placing a standing order. Please contact your bookseller or, in case of difficulty, write to us at the address below with your name and address, the title of the series and the ISBN quoted above.

Customer Services Department, Macmillan Distribution Ltd, Houndmills, Basingstoke, Hampshire RG21 6XS, England

Contents

Series Preface

One of many exciting achievements of the early years of the English Subject Centre was the agreement with Palgrave Macmillan to initiate the series 'Teaching the New English'. The intention of the then Director, Professor Philip Martin, was to create a series of short and accessible books which would take widely taught curriculum fields (or, as in the case of learning technologies, approaches to the whole curriculum) and articulate the connections between scholarly knowledge and the demands of teaching.

Since its inception, 'English' has been committed to what we know by the portmanteau phrase 'learning and teaching'. Yet, by and large, university teachers of English – in Britain at all events – find it hard to make their tacit pedagogic knowledge conscious, or to raise it to a level where it might be critiqued, shared, or developed. In the experience of the English Subject Centre, colleagues find it relatively easy to talk about curriculum and resources, but far harder to talk about the success or failure of seminars, how to vary forms of assessment, or to make imaginative use of Virtual Learning Environments. Too often this reticence means falling back on received assumptions about student learning, about teaching, or about forms of assessment. At the same time, colleagues are often suspicious of the insights and methods arising from generic educational research. The challenge for the English group of disciplines is therefore to articulate ways in which our own subject knowledge and ways of talking might themselves refresh debates about pedagogy. The implicit invitation of this series is to take fields of knowledge and survey them through a pedagogic lens. Research and scholarship, and teaching and learning are part of the same process, not two separate domains.

'Teachers,' people used to say, 'are born not made.' There may, after all, be some tenuous truth in this: there may be generosities of spirit (or, alternatively, drives for didactic control) laid down in earliest childhood. But why should we assume that even 'born' teachers (or novelists, or nurses, or veterinary surgeons) do not need to learn the skills of their trade? Amateurishness about teaching has far more to do with university claims to status, than with evidence about how people learn. There is a craft to shaping and promoting learning. This series of books is dedicated to the development of the craft of teaching within English Studies.

Ben Knights
Teaching the New English *Series Editor*
Director, English Subject Centre
Higher Education Academy

The English Subject Centre
Founded in 2000, the English Subject Centre (which is based at Royal Holloway, University of London) is part of the subject network of the Higher Education Academy. Its purpose is to develop learning and teaching across the English disciplines in UK Higher Education. To this end it engages in research and publication (web and print), hosts events and conferences, sponsors projects, and engages in day-to-day dialogue with its subject communities.
http://www.english.heacademy.ac.uk

Notes on Contributors

Peter Barry is Professor of English at University of Wales, Aberystwyth. His most recent books and chapters on contemporary poetry are: *Poetry Wars: British Poetry of the 1970s and the Battle of Earls Court* (2006), *Literature in Contexts* (2007), and 'Contemporary Innovative Poetries in English since 1980' in *The Cambridge History of English Poetry*, ed. Michael O'Neill (2009).

Charles Bernstein is author of *All the Whiskey in Heaven: Selected Poems* (2010) and *My Way: Speeches and Poems* (1999). He is Donald T. Regan Professor of English and Comparative Literature at the University of Pennsylvania.

Alan Filreis is Kelly Professor, Director of the Center for Programs in Contemporary Writing, and Faculty Director of the Kelly Writers House at the University of Pennsylvania. His most recent book is *Counter-Revolution of the Word: the Conservative Attack on Modern Poetry, 1945–60*.

Nicky Marsh is Senior Lecturer at the University of Southampton and her recent publications include *Democracy in Contemporary US Women's Poetry* (Palgrave, 2007) and *Money, Finance, and Speculation in Recent British Fiction* (2007).

Peter Middleton is Professor of English at the University of Southampton, and the author of several books on modern writing including *Distant Reading: Performance, Readership and Consumption in Contemporary Poetry* (2005). He writes extensively on modern poetry, and is currently at work on a book on American poetry and science in the Cold War.

Drew Milne has published essays towards forthcoming studies in contemporary poetics, neo-modernism and performance studies. He edited *Marxist Literary Theory* (with Terry Eagleton), and *Modern Critical Thought*. His books of poetry include *Bench Marks* (1998), *The Damage* (2001), and *Go Figure* (2003).

Peter Nicholls is Professor of English at New York University. His publications include *Ezra Pound: Politics, Economics and Writing*, *Modernisms: a Literary Guide*, *George Oppen and the Fate of Modernism*, and many articles and essays on literature and theory. He has co-edited with

Giovanni Cianci *Ruskin and Modernism* and with Laura Marcus *The Cambridge History of Twentieth-Century English Literature*.

Redell Olsen's publications include *Secure Portable Space* (2004) and *Here Are My Instructions* (co-edited with Susan Johanknect) (2004). She is the course director for the MA in Poetic Practice at Royal Holloway, University of London where she also teaches Creative Writing and lectures on poetry and poetics. She is the editor of How2journal.com.

Robert Sheppard is Professor of Poetry and Poetics at Edge Hill University, where he has particular responsibility for the MA in Creative Writing. He is a poet-critic, and has recently published a volume of poems *Warrant Error* (2009) and a book of criticism, *Iain Sinclair* (2007). He is co-editor of the new *Journal of British and Irish Innovative Poetry* and is working on a critical study of the speculative discourse of poetics. See also www.robertsheppard.blogspot.com.

Carole Sweeney is Lecturer in Modern Literature in the Department of English and Comparative Literature at Goldsmiths, University of London. She has published articles on surrealism and Nancy Cunard's *Negro* anthology. Her book *From Fetish to Subject: Race, Modernism, and Primitivism, 1919–1939* was published in 2004. She is currently working on a book on Michel Houellebecq.

Harriet Tarlo is a poet and academic whose books include *Poems 1990–2003* (2004) and *Nab* (2005). Recent critical and creative work appears in *Pilot, Jacket, Rampike, English,* and the *Journal of Ecocriticism*. Tarlo recently edited a special feature on eco-poetics for *How2* and is currently editing *The Ground Aslant: Radical Landscape Poetry*. She is a Senior Lecturer in Creative Writing at Sheffield Hallam University.

Michael H. Whitworth is a Tutorial Fellow of Merton College, Oxford, and University Lecturer in the University of Oxford. He is the author of *Einstein's Wake: Relativity, Metaphor, and Modernist Literature* (2001), *Virginia Woolf* (2005), and *Reading Modernist Poetry* (forthcoming), and editor of *Modernism* (2006).

Introduction: Pedagogy and Poetics

Nicky Marsh

The pedagogies of modern literary studies and the practices of modernist poetry have shared a long history. Pound and Eliot may have dreaded the 'deadening' life of the academic but the explication of their writing was at the core of the teaching practices that came to dominate the academy for over half a century (McDonald, 1993: 43). 'New Criticism and modernist poetry were', as Alan Golding notes, 'almost literally made for each other' and the institutionalisation of literary studies that took place in the early years of the twentieth century took many of its cues from the emerging principles of high modernism (Golding, 1995: 75). These pedagogical forms were exemplified by the *Practical Criticism* of I. A. Richards and given ideological elaboration by the writing of the Leavises in Britain and of the New Critics in the US. The assumptions supporting this teaching practice were ubiquitous, pervasive, and are still familiar: the close and active reading of the difficult text is a redemptive act, uniquely able to withstand the deforming pressures of an increasingly powerful technocratic and industrialised mass culture. By the early 1950s such assumptions had become commonplace and standardised. 'Every poem', John Guillory asserts, becomes an 'image' of the 'institutional space in which it is read', a means of alerting its well-trained readers to the fact that 'the retreat of literary culture into the university' is a 'transcendence of the conditions of modernity' (Guillory, 1993: 165).

The obvious ironies of this distancing of the perfected modernist poem from the unperfected travails of lived modernity fuelled the revisionist approaches to modernism that came to characterise the field from the early 1980s onwards. The modernist poem could remain the 'unified whole' of Cleanth Brooks' imagination no longer as its repressed social histories, contradictory implications, varied textual manifestations, and complicated political allegiances all began to emerge (Brooks, 1939: 54).

These scholarly developments followed the broader contours of the intellectual transformations of the period, and their milestones are now
relatively familiar. Some critics interrogated the political assumptions
about class, race, gender, and empire that had facilitated the autonomy
of the modernist poem whilst radically expanding the historical and
geographical parameters of the movement.[1] Others responded to the
successive waves of phenomenological criticism, structuralist and post-
structuralist theory that provided a more rigorous vocabulary for understanding modernism's critique of an earlier mimetic. Modernist poetry
was increasingly recognised as both a significant participant in, and com-
mentator upon, wider shifts in culture, aesthetics, and representation.
Its relationship to discourses of psychoanalysis, science, technology, law,
war, democracy, economics, advertising, work, political protest, and consumerism were made increasingly apparent, as was its connection to a
wider range of arts practices, including music, cinema, sculpture, and
the visual arts.[2] The very category of Anglo-American high modernist
poetics upon which New Criticism had been reliant was supplanted, as
a diverse and continually contested range of geographical, political, and
aesthetic modernisms emerged, and scholarly accounts of more complex
genealogies and legacies for poetry began to proliferate.

The effective reading of a modernist poem came to involve both an
awareness of these new cultural histories and a revaluation of the definitions and implications of textuality itself. Critics such as Willard Bohm,
Garrett Stewart, Jerome McGann, Johanna Drucker, and Marjorie Perloff
expanded the critical vocabulary available for discussing the aesthetics
of the typographical marks made on the physical page,[3] whilst others,
such as Lawrence Rainey, Michael Levenson, and Mark Morrison, compiled the material and social histories that had allowed such marks to be
made at all.[4] These changes required a broadening of both the aesthetic
and political methodologies of reading poetry. Renewed attention was
paid to the look of the line and the sound of the syllable in poetry, just
as issues around the cultural production and consumption of the poem
as an artefact – questions of patronage, publication, dissemination, audience, and reception – all became vital components of an active and aware
exegesis.

These new methodologies, critical vocabularies, and cultural histories
demanded far more, from both reader and teacher, than New Criticism's
close reading ever had. As Gerald Graff caustically noted, the new critical
'emphasis on the literary text' had been a 'tactic' that 'made it possible
for literature to be taught effectively to students who took for granted little history' (Graff, 1987: 173). Hence the plurality of critical approaches

towards modernism that have appeared over the past two decades have expanded the possibilities of reading and have also asked much more, from both the reader and the classroom space itself. The expanded possibilities implicit in the resurgence of modernist studies have been made apparent in the burgeoning of new kinds of reading and teaching resources: anthologies that include letters, manifestos, art works, and critical essays alongside less standardised formats for the poems themselves have been produced by editors such as Bonnie Kime Scott, Lawrence Rainey, and, most notably, Jerome Rothenberg and Pierre Joris in their magisterial *Poems for the New Millennium* volumes.[5] From the late 1990s onwards, the dramatically immediate possibilities offered by new technology offered their own counterpart to these resources. Key modernist poems appeared complete with their own annotated hypertexts, and new kinds of electronic archives, such as Cary Nelson's 'Modern American Poetry Project', Brown University's 'Modernist Journals Project', and Buffalo's 'Ubuweb', all began to mature.[6]

Yet there has been relatively little extended reflection on what it means to bring this overwhelming array of new methodologies, resources, and knowledge into relation with the practical exigencies of a pedagogy that is attempting to encourage ten, twenty, or even two hundred students to confidently approach a poem that appears to resist a singular reading.[7] How does a teacher make relevant the register of the small journals that facilitated the appearance of T. S. Eliot's *The Waste Land*, recreate the political and aesthetic discussions about race and empire that were taking place in the salons of expatriate Paris in the 1910s, or stimulate a meaningful conversation about the significance of new forms of scientific knowledge that appeared across the twentieth century? Facilitating the experience of the material or abstract text, allowing students to respond to language as an aural, oral, performed, and visual form, is even more difficult to assimilate readily into a teaching tradition which has so consistently represented writing as the privileged but transparent medium through which meaning can be perceived. It is these difficulties that this collection attempts to explore through a range of pedagogical case studies which encompass the experiences of academics working in both Britain and the US. The collection acknowledges the radically expanded terrain of modernist studies and seeks to offer practical and expert guidance on how this field has been translated into the effective study of poetry and its multiple contexts and manifestations within the classroom. A crucial and founding premise is that these developments should be regarded as part of a broader cultural movement, which incorporates contemporary writing practices alongside recent scholarly, disciplinary, and intellectual innovations. Hence the collection consistently addresses the development of new critical methodologies, histories, and pedagogies alongside developments in contemporary 'late' modernist poetics in its attempt to acknowledge the continually evolving dynamics that teaching modernism needs to maintain if it is not to fall prey to the 'deadening' forces that Pound and Eliot so feared.

This collection can, then, be read through the attempt to provide answers to two kinds of questions. Firstly, the collection offers an engaged debate about the definition and development of modernism as a historical and geographical literary movement, acknowledging a line of influence and contestation amongst poets that stretches from Ezra Pound to Susan Howe, from London to Europe, Africa and the Caribbean. This attempt by many of the essays in the collection to formulate new approaches to teaching and interrogating the Eliotic tradition find frequent and helpful corollaries in the approaches developed for and by more contemporary poetry and poets. Many of the essays thus begin by reflecting again upon the moments of high modernism but find both continuities within, and provisional solutions to, the difficulties that they pose in the aesthetic and theoretical work of more contemporary poets. The second question that the collection seeks to answer concerns the limitations and definitions of dominant models of teaching in the contemporary academy. As the significance and dynamism of the material forms of twentieth-century poetry are increasingly elaborated to scholars and practitioners the necessity for more radical and active forms of both teaching and learning are also being recognised. Many of the essays in the collection suggest that one kind of strategy for producing such sceptical and innovative readers lies in following modernism itself in challenging the boundaries of the categories of the art object and in querying the boundaries between reading and practice, between practice and criticism. Many of our contributors draw upon a critical tradition that has successfully blurred the distinctions between critical reading and creative writing and between poetic writing and poetic criticism. The values and histories of this tradition, which places the disciplinary boundaries between 'creative writing' and 'literary criticism' under increasing pressure, have been carefully delineated and defended by Ben Knights and Chris Thurgar-Dawson.[8]

The opening essays in the collection explore the nature of the relationship between poetic articulation and knowledge. The essays by Peter Nicholls and Drew Milne interrogate the conceptual and pragmatic challenges that reading the modernist text – replete with its multiple histories, materialities, allusions, and references – imply. Both are interested in the possibility of 'training' the reader to become sensitive to the nuances of such pluralities whilst resisting any form of didacticism or singular meaning. Nicholls seeks to contextualise historically the 'excess and complexity' of meaning provided by the movement between reference and allusion in modernist and late modernist poetry; Milne refines the prevalent meanings of the political in modernism and offers the reader strategies for negotiating with the 'impurities of language, literary form, cultural history'. For both critics the cultural distance and difficulties that exist between the poem and the contemporary reader provide a source of productive tension that needs to be explicitly addressed rather than simply overcome or imagined away. Rather than lamenting the loss of the perhaps too easily idealised classically trained reader, for example, Nicholls more usefully considers how knowledge itself functions in a poem and, particularly, how the functions of allusion and reference may themselves have shifted across a century of poetic innovation. Milne urges the reader to supplant the grand political dichotomies of form and history with a sensitivity towards the 'micro-politics of form', one that can be further developed through comparative readings within and without the canon. Many of the theoretical knots unravelled in these two essays find their pragmatic counterparts in other essays in the collection. Peter Barry, for example, describes how he offers his students the opportunity to complete their own 'intertextual tracking' of poems, while a pedagogy capable of disturbing a reader's own assumptions about textuality is central to Charles Bernstein's essay.

The following group of essays, by Michael Whitworth, Harriet Tarlo, Carole Sweeney, and Peter Barry, participate in a critique of the historical parameters and definitions of modernism and highlight the varied political engagements of a wide range of modernist poets. In each case, this engagement is revealed to involve not the reclamation of a singular or unitary notion of identity but an inquiry into the very political forms and languages that modernism could afford and could speak. The essay by Michael Whitworth approaches this question of the relationship between poetry, reference, and knowledge in a historically specific manner. Whitworth's essay strives to equip teachers with the beginnings of a properly chronological and accurate sense of the scientific developments coterminous with the high modernism of 1880–1930 whilst also producing a set of critical questions capable of bringing this chronology to bear on individual poems in a meaningful way. Harriet Tarlo's account of Anglo-American modernist women poets similarly provides a broad framework for understanding the principal canonical, biographical, thematic, and theoretical debates through which women poets continue to be read. Tarlo provides, beyond this, some striking and memorable examples of the particular difficulties and pleasures of reproducing this kind of nuanced knowledge within the classroom. Carole Sweeney's contestation that 'race and colonialism need to be examined, not in isolation from the main strands of modernist activity or as running counter to it, but as part of a complex network of cultural practices both within and outside of Europe and North America' produces new readings of the work of Nancy Cunard and Aimé Césaire. Sweeney draws on both the 'politicised aesthetics and activism of 1930s surrealism' and contemporary developments in the social sciences, particularly ethnography, in order to suggest new ways of thinking about the relationship between race, culture, and art. Peter Barry's essay offers a different interpretation of this need to challenge the historical parameters and definitions of modernism. Barry gives a succinct introduction to the still neglected contributions of British poets to the late modernist experimental scene and provides an exemplary and thorough account of how one might teach these initially resistant texts in a seminar situation.

Another significant continuity in the collection concerns the attempt to approach the materiality of the text and, in so doing, radicalise and open the space of pedagogy itself. An important aspect of this is the recognition of the multiplicity of textuality, a theme taken up in specific ways in the contributions of Alan Filreis, Charles Bernstein, and Redell Olsen. These essays detail the importance of reading the printed text alongside its performed, aural, visual, and digital manifestations. Filreis' essay, for example, searches for the 'non-Euclidean pedagogy' that can accompany a 'new aural consciousness' by aiming for a 'third teaching space' beyond the public classroom and private reading. Filreis finds examples of such a utopian pedagogical possibility in a range of experiments that strive to move beyond the singular emphasis on looking and towards the ethical implications suggested by teaching the multiple and the unknown. Olsen's essay offers models of poetic pedagogy that incorporate 'found material' as a way of developing a 'sense of poetry as a practice in dialogue with visual culture' albeit a 'dialogue in which there are also critical differences'.

The interrogation of New Criticism's tendency to produce abstracted, theoretical readings requires an acknowledgement of the centrality of writing to interpretative practice. This subject is central to the final group of essays, as their authors explore how the reading of modernist poetry requires not simply a respectful attention but its own kind of creative practice. It is in the field of creative writing, of course, that the teaching of poetry has most obviously expanded in the past decade and the essays by Bernstein, Olsen, and Robert Sheppard recount how the experimentations inherent in the modernist tradition can productively unsettle some of the assumptions that have accompanied the expansion of this discipline. Robert Sheppard's essay offers both an account of the specific development of an experimental tradition within the UK context and a practical affirmation of the importance of a 'speculative practice' to the resistant existence of poetics within the academy. Charles Bernstein's writing provides Sheppard with one explicit model for his pedagogy, and in the collection's penultimate essay Bernstein offers insights into the principles which guided the formation of his influential 'creative (w)reading' programme, 'less a workshop than a lab, with experiments in mutant forms conducted on the textual body of the living language'. Bernstein's metaphor, redolent with the dangers and pleasures of manipulating poetry's Frankenstein-like power over language, wittily encapsulates the central tension that motivates the pedagogy for modernist poetry emerging in many of these essays. Our contributors insist on the importance of retaining the vitality of reading and writing, emphasising that experimentation and speculation are at the heart of understanding the continuing legacies of the modernist project. Yet, at the same time, they acknowledge that this permission-giving's seemingly ludic vocabulary is not without its own histories, its own critical debates, its own specific institutional as well as political and cultural contexts. It seems as if it is an understanding of this paradox, the scholarly rigours of literary risk-taking, that is at the heart of this pedagogic programme.

The collection's conclusion, by its co-editor Peter Middleton, explicitly reflects upon the connections between the two limits – the periodisation of modernism and the definition of textual meaning – that so many of our contributors seek to surpass. Middleton suggests that one important way of addressing the 'doubleness' of modernism, rent by the violence of the Second World War, is to emphasise the continuities of modernist poetry's foregrounding of the materiality of the text: we must teach 'our students to see and hear more of what happens in the poem'. Defending this laudable, but now familiar aspiration, leads Middleton to scrutinise what actually constitutes textual meaning, drawing on an alternative tradition of linguistic philosophy to stress that meaning is found not simply in marks and/or signs but in 'a shared, social structuring of the process whereby interpretations, reasons, and questions about them, are connected'. The expansion of modernism, beyond the early twentieth century and beyond the physical page, provides an opportunity for giving significance to poetry's ability to realise these connections. In developing a reader's sensitivities to the possible sites of meaning,

Middleton suggests, we can provide them with a longer and more complex sense of what constitutes both modernism and the 'social fabric' of language itself.

Notes

1. Critics began to look beyond the narrow confines of an Anglo-American elite to the parallel and diverse forms of literary modernism developed in continental Europe, Africa, and the Caribbean as well as within the margins of the metropolitan itself – in Harlem, Scotland, the labour movement, and the domestic sphere. See Houston A. Baker Jr, *Modernism and the Harlem Renaissance* (Chicago: University of Chicago Press, 1989); Marianne DeKoven, *A Different Language: Gertrude Stein's Experimental Writing* (Madison: University of Wisconsin Press, 1983); Rachel Blau DuPlessis, *The Pink Guitar: Writing as Feminist Practice* (New York: Routledge, 1989); Cary Nelson, *Repression and Recovery: Modern American Poetry and the Politics of Cultural Memory* (Madison: University of Wisconsin Press, 1989); Margery Palmer McCulloch, *Scottish Modernism and its Contexts 1918–1959: Literature, National Identity and Cultural Exchange* (Edinburgh: Edinburgh University Press, 2009).

2. Tim Armstrong, *Modernism, Technology, and the Body: a Cultural Study* (Cambridge: Cambridge University Press, 2008); Rachel Bowlby, *Still Crazy After All These Years: Women, Writing and Psychoanalysis* (London: Routledge, 1992); Jed Esty, *A Shrinking Island: Modernism and National Culture in England* (Princeton: Princeton University Press, 2004); Laura Marcus, *The Tenth Muse: Writing about Cinema in the Modernist Period* (Oxford: Oxford University Press, 2007).

3. Willard Bohn, *The Aesthetics of Visual Poetry, 1914–28* (Chicago: University of Chicago Press, 1993); Johanna Drucker, *The Visible Word: Experimental Typography and Modern Art, 1909–1923* (Chicago: University of Chicago Press, 1994); Jerome McGann, *Black Riders: the Visible Language of Modernism* (Princeton: Princeton University Press, 1993); Marjorie Perloff, *The Poetics of Indeterminacy: Rimbaud to Cage* (Evanston: Northwestern University Press, 1981); Garrett Stewart, *Reading Voices: Literature and the Phonotext* (Berkeley: University of California Press, 1990).

4. M. DiBattista and L. MacDiarmid (eds), *High and Low Moderns: Literature and Culture, 1889–1939* (Oxford: Oxford University Press, 1996); Michael Levenson, *A Genealogy of Modernism: a Study of English Literary Doctrine 1908–1922* (Cambridge: Cambridge University Press, 1986); Mark Morrison, *The Public Face of Modernism: Little Magazines, Audiences, and Reception, 1905–1920* (Madison: University of Wisconsin Press, 2000); Lawrence Rainey, *Institutions of Modernism: Literary Elites and Public Culture* (New Haven and London: Yale University Press, 1998).

5. Bonnie Kime Scott, *The Gender of Modernism* (Bloomington: Indiana University Press, 1990); Vassiliki Kolocotroni, Jane Goldman, and Olga Taxidou (eds), *Modernism: an Anthology of Sources and Documents* (Edinburgh: Edinburgh University Press, 1998); Lawrence Rainey (ed.), *Modernism: an Anthology of Sources and Documents* (Oxford: Blackwell, 2005).

6. http://www.english.uiuc.edu/maps/index.htm; http://www.modjourn.org; http://epc.buffalo.edu/poetics/; http:// www.ubuweb.com/

7. An important exception to this is Joan Retallack and Juliana Spahr's recent edited collection *Poetry and Pedagogy: the Challenge of the Contemporary* (New York: Palgrave Macmillan, 2006).
8. Ben Knights and Chris Thurgar-Dawson, *Active Reading: Transformative Writing in Literary Studies* (London: Continuum, 2007); Hazel Smith, *The Writing Experiment: Strategies for Innovative Creative Writing* (London: Allen & Unwin, 2005); Michelene Wandor, *The Author is Not Dead, Merely Somewhere Else: Creative Writing Reconceived* (Basingstoke: Palgrave Macmillan, 2008).

Works cited

Brooks, Cleanth (1939) *Modern Poetry and the Great Tradition*. Chapel Hill: University of North Carolina Press.

Golding, Alan (1995) *From Outlaw to Classic: Canons in American Poetry*. Madison: University of Wisconsin Press.

Graff, Gerald (1987) *Professing Literature: an Institutional History*. Chicago: University of Chicago Press.

Guillory, John (1993) *Cultural Capital: the Problem of Literary Canon Formation*. Chicago: University of Chicago Press.

McDonald, Gail (1993) *Learning to be Modern: Pound, Eliot and the American University*. Oxford: Clarendon Press.

1
The Elusive Allusion: Poetry and Exegesis

Peter Nicholls

Monday morning, and this week's seminar is on Ezra Pound's *Hugh Selwyn Mauberley*. Reponses from the students are punctual and familiar. 'It's impossible to understand!' 'Why so many references to things we've never heard of?' 'If that's what he means, why doesn't he say so?' 'It's elitist.' 'He was a fascist, apparently.' So the annual litany proceeds. Perhaps a broader framing of the problem will help. But: 'How can it be *witty* if I don't know what he's talking about?' 'We don't do the classics anymore! And I can't even pronounce these words you say are in Greek!' 'All these writers' – Lionel Johnson, Ernest Dowson and co. – 'are dead and buried; who reads them?' And the larger question of who and what Mauberley himself might represent in the poem? We never actually get to that, partly because after the work of exegesis has consumed two generally irritable and resentful hours we have managed to construe only the first four pages of the poem. Perhaps the best concluding strategy here is to confront the problem head on: our culture has become increasingly remote from what Pound simply assumed were the principal reference points for any thinking person – Homer, Sappho, Horace . . . The list is long but Pound's network of allusions rarely outstripped a good middle-class education at the time his poem was written. And it is, after all, precisely the *familiarity* of the classics and the ideological work they have done in the recent past ('Dulce et decorum est pro patria mori') that are the principal targets of the poem's ire. Notwithstanding these considerations it is with some relief that we arrive at the denunciation of 'a botched civilisation' propped up by 'a few thousand battered books', though now another awkward question presents itself: why, having got this far – in a mad dash to wind things up we have recklessly moved forward to 'Envoi (1919)' – why does Pound after deriding these 'battered books' suddenly have to go 'old-fashioned' himself ('Hadst thou but song / As thou hast subjects known' and so on)? Here things grind to a halt; the incomprehensibilities of 'Mauberley 1920' ('ANANGKE', 'NUKTIS', 'AGALMA') will fortunately not be visited upon us.

One thing is clear from this rather unsatisfactory seminar: with every generation we move further from the cultural matrix that Pound clearly felt he shared with his readers, a matrix grown by accumulation from centuries of reading and commenting upon the Bible and the Classics. *Mauberley*, of course, testifies to his anxiety that such a tradition was profoundly threatened by the violent embrace of a modernity whose 'accelerated grimace' signalled the rise of consumerism and social uniformity. Mauberley may be an aesthete 'out of key with his time', his hedonism and his propensity to 'maudlin confession' relegating him to the sidelines of the modern age, but Pound still cherishes 'His sense of graduations, / quite out of place amid / Resistance to current exacerbations' (Pound, 1968: 219). For it is nuance and discrimination that the juggernaut of capital crushes, celebrating the 'mould in plaster' – an object made quickly and mechanically – rather than 'the "sculpture" of rhyme', with its semantic and phonic intricacies (206).

Perhaps this throws some light on our seminar's difficulties, for the real problem for these new readers of *Mauberley* goes beyond one of mere reference, and while it is helpful and necessary, of course, for students to know who Penelope and Flaubert were, that knowledge won't in itself explain the allusive habit of mind that finds it attractive to couple them together in this way: 'His true Penelope was Flaubert' (205). The grammar is ostentatiously simple, so much so that it looks at first as if we are being told that 'Penelope' is to be equated with 'Flaubert'. But the two proper names are, of course, logically incommensurable, since Penelope was the fictional wife of the fictional Odysseus, while Flaubert was the actual writer of the nineteenth-century novel *Madame Bovary*. In other words, the references won't in themselves tell us all that we need to understand this highly compressed line because we are also dealing with *allusion*, and as William Irwin notes in one of the few technical discussions of this device, 'allusion is reference that is indirect in requiring more than the mere substitution of a referent' (Irwin, 2001: 288).

What is this 'more' that the line demands? Firstly, perhaps it is the requirement that we recognise the terms of Pound's equation as familiar ones that the poem is wittily drawing into a new relation (that we derive pleasure from this procedure situates allusion on the same ground as Freud's account of jokes[1]). There is an ironic playfulness in *Mauberley*, an epigrammatic hermeticism which, even as it gestures towards a kind of cultural decadence and exhaustion, also celebrates a shared relation to a literary tradition. 'The test of allusion,' writes Earl Miner, 'is that it is a phenomenon that some reader or readers may fail to observe' (Miner, 1993: 39). Some readers will 'get' it, then, while others won't, for the knowledge that allusion assumes will have quite clearly defined social and educational boundaries. This is after all something of a *game* – sometimes, indeed, a game of one-upmanship – between writer and reader (*alludere*, 'to joke, jest, mock, play with' (Perri, 1978: 301)), even if the stakes involved are deadly serious. The rather superior tone of the present essay's opening paragraph may serve to make this point, that we are always either a competent player of the game or a baffled observer of it.

For students grappling with *Mauberley*, then, it often seems that Pound is wilfully esoteric and that he turns his poem into the equivalent of an acrostic. Yet the devices of allusion, citation, and elliptical quotation are deeply ingrained features of poetry as a medium, though they are differently accented and deployed in different periods. Robert Alter, in fact, goes so far as to argue that 'Allusion is not merely a device, like irony, understatement, ellipsis, or repetition, but an essential modality of the language of literature' (Alter, 1996: 111). Early scriptural commentaries provided the original model, but by the time of Dryden allusion had established itself as part of the very fabric of the poetic text (Ricks, 2002: 33). With Dryden, allusion became a complex register of questions of inheritance, influence, and competition, a means by which poets would seek to negotiate the matter of their own newness and originality in relation to a tradition which might be felt as either provocation or constraint. Hence the question, encountered by every generation: is the literature of the past a burden weighing on creative impulse in the present, or is it an enabling, nurturing force? To approach it in the spirit of the latter would be to grasp tradition, as Walter Jackson Bate puts it, not as 'an authority looming over you but . . . as something ancestral rather than parental' (Bate, 1971: 22) and this is just the sense in which modernist writers such as Pound and Eliot sought to activate voices from the past in their own work. Reacting against the Romantic aspiration to poetic originality, Eliot would observe that 'The poem which is absolutely original is absolutely bad; it is, in the bad sense, "subjective" with no relation to the world to which it appeals.' By way of contrast, he concludes, 'Pound is often most "original" in the right sense, when he is most "archaeological" in the ordinary sense' (Eliot, 1928: 10–11). True originality, then, has to do not with 'the expression of personality' (Eliot, 1980: 21), but with the *cultural* origins from which the poet's work derives, with its 'ancestry', as Bate has it. In short, it is hard to separate any form of linguistic expression from the literary past to which a common language binds it: 'The ordinary life of ordinary cultivated people is a mush of literature and life', says Eliot (Eliot, 1928: 10).

We might detect in this strand of modernist thinking a prefiguring of Roland Barthes' distinction between what he calls 'filiation' and 'intertextuality':

> The intertextual in which every text is held, it itself being the text-between of another text, is not to be confused with some origin of the text: to try to find the 'sources', the 'influences' of a work, is to fall in with the myth of filiation; the citations which go to make up a text are anonymous, untraceable, and yet *already read*: they are quotations without inverted commas. (Barthes, 1982: 160)

'Filiation' and reference: these seem easily aligned with Bate's idea of an overbearing 'paternal' tradition which demands passive imitation. Barthes' alternative, 'intertextuality', however, doesn't quite correspond to the looser 'ancestral relation' to the past that Eliot has in mind because, for Barthes, 'intertextuality' is an involuntary and general feature of language (see Miner, 1993: 38–9). Where 'intertextuality' is for this reason generically unmotivated, allusion, whether it is overt or covert, has a definite purpose; it is a literary device. Of *The Waste Land*, for example, Eliot writes: 'I gave the reference in my notes, in order to make the reader who recognised the allusion, know that I meant him to recognise it, and know that he would have missed the point if he did not recognise it' (Eliot, 1965: 128). Eliot is not actually giving very much away when he provides the reference in his notes because when we have the source we still have to puzzle out the allusion. So, for example, the mention in the final section of the poem of 'memories draped by the beneficent spider' (1970: 74) is glossed in the notes (80) with a quotation from Webster's *The White Devil*: '. . . they'll remarry / Ere the worm pierce your winding-sheet, ere the spider / Make a thin curtain for your epitaphs'. Webster's 'curtain' has here become a 'drape', but without Eliot's note we might well have missed its presence in these lines. The allusion is signalled deliberately, however, because it provides a suddenly expanded context: a Jacobean context of violence and death, certainly, but also one in which those who remarry before their husbands are cold in their graves are 'howling wives'. In Eliot's quotation from Webster in his notes, however, the wives are not specifically mentioned, and it is only if we follow out the allusion that we catch the rather cruel and appropriately 'Jacobean' association with the troubled wife of 'A Game of Chess'.[2] Allusion creates an effect of layering, then, and the lines that follow – 'I have heard the key / Turn in the door once and turn once only' – extend these references to deadly loneliness by an allusion to Dante's *Inferno*: 'ed io senti chiavar l'uscio di sotto / all' orribile torre' ('and I heard below the door of the horrible tower locked up'). These words are spoken by Dante's Ugolino who tells of how he and his sons were shut up in the tower and left to starve to death. Eliot's deliberately colourless language here (he is evoking the sadly *common* plight of loneliness in contemporary society) will resonate darkly with the gruesome fate of Ugolino once we have grasped the allusion.

It is this *resonance* which is the issue here: when Eliot simply quotes from another text, the quotation (indicated as such or not) obtrudes in the poem like a piece of foreign matter, its displacement usually registering a satirical sense of cultural degeneration ('When lovely woman stoops to folly' (from Oliver Goldsmith), for example, suggests that, ironically, the modern-day typist, with her 'automatic hand', has no exalted moral position from which to fall or 'stoop'). With allusion, however, the situation is rather different.[3] The echoing of Ugolino's speech in 'What the Thunder Said', for example, is in part direct quotation (*via* translation), though by a kind of elision characteristic of allusion the echoing is as if from within the lines of Eliot's poem. The result is, in Peter Ackroyd's words, 'a continual oscillation between what is remembered and what is introduced, the movement of other poets' words just beneath the surface of his own' (Ackroyd, 1984: 120). It is this kind of interiorisation which is the most significant feature of allusion, with the element taken from the earlier text subtly transformed as we recognise it in a new context. Eliot emphasises this transformative power of allusion in a famous passage of 'Tradition and the Individual Talent':

> Immature poets imitate; mature poets steal . . . The good poet welds his theft into a whole of feeling which is unique, utterly different from that from which it was torn; the bad poet throws it into something which has no cohesion. (Eliot, 1980: 206)

Two things are notable in this passage: first, that good poets *almost always* 'steal' ('A good poet will usually borrow from authors remote in time', Eliot continues); and second, that this 'theft', sanctioned as it is by the very nature of poetic composition, involves a certain violence to the original, the stolen item 'torn' from the first text and 'welded' into the second. Eliot and Pound may seem conservative when they harp on about the values of the tradition, but it is in this creative-destructive act of allusion than they win their modernist spurs. And it is not just because allusion is a deeply ingrained habit of poetic writing that they make it such a distinctive feature of their work; it is also because it seems to provide a necessary complexity of response to modernity itself. Since 'Our civilization comprehends great variety and complexity,' Eliot argues, '[t]he poet must become more and more comprehensive, more allusive, more indirect, in order to force, to dislocate if necessary, language into his meaning' (Eliot, 1980: 289).

Excess and complexity, then, these are what allusion offers us with its particular form of 'indirectness' or elusiveness. We can see this at work even in that short line from Pound's *Hugh Selwyn Mauberley*, 'His true Penelope was Flaubert'. Pound isn't suggesting here that Mauberley wants to marry Flaubert (a reasonable conclusion, though, if we read only at the level of reference, thus taking Penelope as the type of the constant wife), nor is he creating between the two proper names the kind of equivalence we would associate with allegory. With allusion, the operation works the other way round, so that to grasp the linkage between 'Penelope' and 'Flaubert' we have to recover the potentially relevant attributes of each of the two names and then imaginatively combine them.[4] It is here that we can see why allusion has become 'an essential modality' of poetry: not only does it dramatise the poem's relation to the history of which it is part, often permitting a satirical presentation of the modern (as in Pound and Eliot), but its capacity to generate meanings which exceed what is explicitly said allows simple statement to acquire a rich complexity of implication. In fact, when a poet alludes rather than simply refers to an antecedent text it is often difficult to stem the ripple of possible associations (as Ziva Ben-Porat observes (1976: 108), 'the simultaneous activation of the two texts thus connected results in the formation of intertextual patterns whose nature cannot be predetermined').[5] So to return to the example from *Mauberley*, perhaps our first construal of the line is simply that the poet's chief desire is to write like Flaubert, a novelist famous for his absolute commitment to craft and precision. At the same time, though, Pound has already given us a line from the Sirens' speech in the *Odyssey* and the previous stanza has linked the hearing of their song to the linguistic clarity of Homer's Greek. So 'Penelope' does more than name the wife to whom Odysseus is attempting to return, activating a larger complex of allusion which denotes the nature of ancient epic, the sea-voyage, the sound of the 'chopped' sea as rendered in the ancient Greek, the force of desire, and so on. Couple this now with 'Flaubert' and we have some quite complicated contrasts: ancient versus modern, lyric poem versus narrative prose, the world of myth and gods versus the analytic

realism of nineteenth-century fiction and so on, all of which register
that underlying ambivalence towards modernity that the poem tries to
resolve through its gradual exorcism of Mauberley from Pound's career.
And what is even more striking about the way such allusions function
is not just the complexity of association that they can command but
their ability to resonate back and forth across the poem. As we learn
more about Mauberley himself, for example, the fact of his having a
'Penelope' in the first place will become increasingly ironic, for he is certainly not a bold lover like Odysseus (Mauberley only *observes* Circe) and
his purposeless 'drifting' is quite at odds with the wily pragmatism of
Homer's hero.

This capacity of allusion to acquire nuance and meaning as a work proceeds was crucial to Pound's practice, early and late, and might be seen
as a crystallisation of his ambition to 'Make It New' in so far as it works
transformative effects on what would otherwise remain as referent and
quotation. Together, these features of allusion made it a principal device
of *The Cantos* where Pound came increasingly to allude not simply to
other texts but to elements of his own poem. As the long poem gathers
momentum, so the reader increasingly attuned to its methods can activate Pound's allusions to produce hugely extended networks of semantic
and imagistic association. Not surprisingly, then, *The Cantos* in its early
stages is very much what Leonard Diepeveen calls a 'quoting poem' as
Pound introduces materials as 'preparation of the palette' (Pound, 1971:
180). Yet even here Pound is concerned with the propulsive relations he
describes as 'ideogrammic', and with the ways that allusions can connect
and extend thoughts and images. One can already spot that urge in his
thinking in an early letter to his friend and patron Margaret Cravens.
Pound is writing from Sirmione:

> Here I am more or less drowned in beauty, but it isn't the lake, or the
> hills, or even – almost even the olive trees, but the four red leaves of a
> poppy that are the *poetry* simply because they go beyond themselves
> & *mean* Andalucia & the court yard at Cordova. (Pound and Spoo,
> 1988: 27)

'Meaning' is thus for Pound a matter of extension and association, of
things 'go[ing] beyond themselves' to create larger semantic units, the
colour of the poppy leaves here 'alluding' to the red and orange hues
Pound recalled from an early visit to Spain.[6]

Yet *The Cantos*, the work that in many ways would be the embodiment
of this kind of imaginative movement, was also a work in which Pound

invested hugely in the device of quotation, often sticking with his source for page upon page (the so-called Adams Cantos and Chinese Cantos are the most extended cases of the poet's 'writing through' his source texts in this way). Foolhardy as it is to make generalisations about a work of this extent and complexity, we might say that the whole poem therefore oscillates between allusion and reference. The latter pole is governed by Pound's increasing sense of pedagogic urgency which does make him something of the 'village explainer' that Gertrude Stein said he was, a distributor of axioms and verities, a purveyor of the natural and the self-evident. The reader, accordingly, is enjoined to 'study with the mind of a grandson' (Pound, 1994: 564), to become a passive recipient of what has become an avowedly 'parental' tradition. The counter-movement of allusional composition had reached its climax in *The Pisan Cantos* where Pound, deprived of his usual sources of reference, became newly dependent on memory and direct perception. Here the poem moves 'as the winds veer' (Pound, 1994: 457), the mind drawing strength from an 'ancestral' tradition so that the affective properties of things learned by heart and remembered create imaginative spaces in which associations and echoes expand almost infinitely. Such movements become rarer as the poem proceeds, with allusion increasingly curbed by perfunctory reference. To take just one example, this from Canto CVII:

> they had not Magna Charta
> in ver l'estate, Queen of Akragas
> resistent,
> > Templum aedificavit
> > > Segesta (Pound, 1994: 772)

The Latin phrase 'Templum aedificavit' ('He built a temple') quotes from the Commentaries of Pius II and refers to the church constructed in Rimini by Sigismundo Malatesta in the middle of the fifteenth century. Close textual attention has been paid to this monument in Cantos VIII–X where Pound quotes from letters and documents to record the history of its construction. More abbreviated references to the Tempio Mala-testiano abound in subsequent parts of the poem and when we read the Latin words in Canto CVII we expect an elaborate context to be triggered by the phrase. As usual in these late Cantos, the movement is apposi-tional and the Latin phrase does immediately draw the name 'Segesta' into its orbit. Pound is referring to the great unfinished Doric temple in Sicily, yet because we are given only the name (and that for the first time) the best we can do with the connection is to see that two temples were constructed at very different times. The (too) charitable reader may be willing to posit a stronger connection (for example, the rich mytholo-gical iconography of the Tempio made it seem to some a covertly pagan monument, as Segesta obviously was) but this is to try to find a web of allusion where in fact we have only reference and that governed largely by simple nominal equivalence.[7]

If we think of the relation of allusion to quotation and reference as a continuum,[8] then Pound's late Cantos offer an example of a striking swing from the one to the other, and this perhaps explains why the highly fragmented notation of *Thrones* looks formally avant-garde but actually turns out to be rather tiresomely referential, bound in the last analysis to an oppressive 'ideology of accuracy', as Bob Perelman calls it (1996: 88). In some ways, of course, this aspect of Pound's long poem has provided an unfortunate legacy for his critics who can hardly be blamed for reading *The Cantos* referentially. Yet the return to the source text often does little to invigorate the late parts of the poem, simply tying words on Pound's page to words on someone else's. Linguist Michael Leddy takes us closer to the countervailing strength of allusion when he defines it as 'invoking associations and bringing them to bear upon a present context' (Leddy, 1992: 111). There is, to be sure, something elusive and indirect about invocation (the goddess is invoked indirectly and metonymically, by her many names and attributes) and that something is traditionally associated with sound and rhythm. When *The Cantos* truly succeeds it is when Pound has discerned the distinctive rhythm of his materials in rela-tion to the others at work within the poem.[9] This, as poet Robert Duncan realised, was something that lay altogether beyond mere 'reference':

> That one image may recall another, finding depth in the resounding is the secret of rime and measure. The time of a poem is felt as a recognition of return in vowel tone and in consonant formations, of pattern in sequence of syllables, in stress and in pitch of a melody, of images and meanings. It resembles the time of a dream, for it is highly organized along lines of association and impulses of contrast towards the structure of the whole. The same impulse of dream or poem is to provide a ground for some form beyond what we know, for feeling *'greater than reality'*. (Duncan, 1968: 82; his emphases)

Duncan is referring to *The Pisan Cantos* here, but his comments also offer a suggestive way of describing the elusiveness or indirectness of allusion, with its 'lines of association', as something which may inhere in the smallest rhythmic and phonic materials of the poetic line. For Duncan, it is Pound's great achievement to have subordinated the multifarious materials of his poem to complex rhythms of feeling and thought which are generated purely from within the poem itself.

This might give a clue to the way in which younger poets have tried to sidestep the problem of Pound's 'ideology of accuracy', for while a fondness for incorporating 'foreign' material into poems can hardly be said to have diminished, contemporary writers have sought to sever the umbilical cord of reference, and thereby to transform the accuracy of quotation into the suggestiveness of allusion. The Language poet, Bruce Andrews, for example, argues for 'A semantic atmosphere, or milieu, rather than the possessive individualism of reference' (Andrews, 1984: 36), while Michael Palmer describes his own compositional practice like this:

> Occasionally I'll appropriate a source verbatim, but often it will be slightly or radically altered. It becomes altered by the impetus of the poem itself, the demands of the rhythm, the surrounding material, whatever. And so it's not a quotation, exactly. It's a form of citation, but it's layered, covered over. (Palmer, 1999: 286)[10]

Here the 'source' is fully assimilated or interiorised into the poetic text. For the reader, the result of this is something akin to déjà vu, but as an experience now attributable not to some subject as recollection or dream, but rather to a particular mnemic register in the text. '[T]he art of citing without quotation marks', to borrow Walter Benjamin's phrase (1999: 458), is an art of montage in which the punctuality of attribution gives way to an effect of textual 'uncanniness', in which sedimented material seems at once disconcertingly familiar and unfamiliar. While quotation marks conventionally situate the matter they enclose, alerting us to its origin in another time and implying a larger context to which it relates, 'citation' in Palmer's sense 'covers over' and obscures the original location, leaving the matter in a state of tantalising indeterminacy and blurring the difference between (as Jacques Derrida puts it) 'the said and the saying' (1991a: 415). This 'covering over' amounts to a rewriting which encrypts the original material but does so in such a way as to make it lead a kind of ghostly existence in the body of the new (as Derrida observes, 'another language comes to disturb the first one. It doesn't inhabit it, but haunts it' (1991a: 414)). Like allusion, Palmer's 'citation' is constantly elusive, signalling quotation while at the same time seeming to bar access to its original location.

To take a recent example, Lyn Hejinian in her long poem *A Border Comedy* (2001) helpfully provides a list of 'Sources' at the end of the book, though it is only with difficulty that we actually locate their progeny in the text itself. And partly this is because Hejinian's aim is often to produce effects that are quite different from the 'sources' in which they apparently originate. As if to alert us to this, she lists as one of these 'sources' Osip Mandelstam's 'Conversation about Dante', where we read of the poet's work as 'a continuous transformation of the substratum of poetic mate-rial' which demonstrates 'a peculiarity of poetic material which I propose to call its convertibility' (Hejinian, 2001: 213; Mandelstam, 1979: 414). Such 'convertibility' may remind us of Freud's 'dreamwork', and Book 1 of *A Border Comedy* is indeed much concerned with the interrelatedness of dreams, narrative, and hidden secrets. Hejinian also cites her friend Kit Robinson's essay on dreams as another 'source' and there we are told that 'The possibility of a grammar of dreams leads away from the consid-eration of the dream as a code for the analysis of the individual psyche toward a more general view of dreams as problems in perception and description, that is, as problems for writing' (Robinson, 1991: 32–3). This 'grammar of dreams' suggests not just a repetition or citation of dream content in writing but a process by which that writing is itself infected by the modes of dreaming, by those movements of condensation and displacement which Freud had famously described. To which we may add that to consider allusion or citation is also to consider reading and writing as practices that are inextricably linked; indeed, as Antoine Com-pagnon puts it, citation 'is reading and writing; it conjoins the act of reading and the act of writing. To read or write involves an act of citation' (Compagnon, 1979: 34; my translation). Writing in this sense entails a re-writing which articulates the force of desire that governs reading (as Compagnon notes (35), this is how Barthes in *S/Z* defines the '*scriptible*' or 'writerly', as 'what can today be written (re-written)'). To quote with-out quotation marks is, then, to register an extreme of inwardness with another text, the new inhabiting the old in the same movement as it draws it into itself – hence the complex implications of 'learning by heart', as Derrida observes in his 'Che cos'è la poesia?' (Derrida, 1991b). Yet as Derrida also notes there, this echoing of another's words regis-ters not just a 'pure interiority' (231), but an otherness and division that characterise reflection itself.

It is this elusive middle ground that much contemporary poetry has sought to occupy. While we register the 'otherness' of materials within the writing, these have now only a shadowy relation to their original con-text and may be presented in such a way that they function as 'found' materials that are recombined with little attention to the antecedent text as 'source'. The work of Susan Howe offers one of the richest forms of this contemporary way with allusion. Like Pound, Howe is a poet much preoccupied with remote histories and with their complex vibrations in the present in which she writes. Unlike Pound, however, Howe is drawn not to 'luminous details' which light up the past, but with the opacities that block our desire to conform history to an intelligible narrative. The difficulty of her writing in this sense mirrors the 'Cancellations, variants, insertions, erasures, marginal notes, stray marks and blanks' that disfigure any historical record and which make Howe's poetry what she describes as a kind of 'ghost writing' (Howe, 1993: 15). Here 'facts' are highly equivocal and not ultimately of primary importance, for history is grasped not as 'meaning' but as a disruptive force at work in the graphic and phonic materials of the text. 'Letters are sounds we see,' she explains, 'Sounds leap to the eye. Word lists, crosses, blanks, and ruptured stanzas are points of contact and displacement. Line breaks and visual contrapuntal stresses represent an athematic compositional intention' (Howe, 1993: 139).

Howe uses many historical documents to provide the raw materials of her writing, but if we return to them as 'sources' in the way that Pound invites us to do in *The Cantos* we shall usually be disappointed. For Howe will *allude* to an antecedent text in a way that abolishes reference through a paradoxical fascination with its constituent elements. Bruce Andrews' already quoted talk of 'A semantic atmosphere, or milieu, rather than the possessive individualism of reference' seems pertinent here, for even when Howe refers to a particular episode in her source text she may present it in a collage of words drawn from passages that are quite unrelated to it.[11] The historical event is no longer something to which we can simply refer – allusion, we might say, becomes more completely a kind of *e*lusion, a 'nonsense soliloquy' (Howe, 2007: 17) in which the sound of words is 'the telepathic solicitation of innumerable phantoms' (14). In its echoing indirection, poetry, says Howe, is 'A sonic grid of homely minutiae fallen away into posterity [that] carries trace filaments. Tumbled syllables are bolts and bullets from the blue' (13). That 'falling away' is a characteristic motif of her work, confirming that poetry's power of allusion is testament to the insistent presence of what is lost. I have been quoting from Howe's most recent volume, *Souls of the Labadie Tract*, a work too new to have yet yielded up the secrets of its sources. But perhaps even this commonplace statement, with its implicit coveting of hidden 'secrets', runs counter to all I have said of Howe's writing up to this point, namely that its sources may be uncovered but that they live their real life only in the text that transforms them? If that last proposition holds, then a seminar on Howe's work should be free of that irritable reaching after fact and reason which dogged the one on *Mauberley*. But for poetry to work in this way, its reader needs to surrender to a certain fascination, and Howe would probably be the first to admit that such a fascination draws us in two directions at once. In the final analysis, as Robert Alter puts it, 'because of the intrinsically allusive nature of literary expression, there is simply no substitute for careful, retentive reading as a guide to good reading: literature is always its own best teacher' (Alter, 1996: 119). The exegetical itch is not so easily stilled, then, and in Howe's case it is actually induced by her own poetics of erasure and disfigurement. The relation of reference to allusion admits of no easy formulation, we might conclude: for just as Orpheus' compulsion to look back at Euridice finally cost him her presence, so the allusive whispers of 'ghost writing' bespeak our desire for origin even as they convince us of its unavailability.[12] Is Howe suggesting that this elusiveness is ultimately both the condition and the value of poetic expression? That, perhaps, is a question for next term's seminar.

Notes

1. As noted in Perri (1978: 302). Freud famously observes that 'This rediscovery of what is familiar is pleasurable.'
2. The lines that precede those given in Eliot's note are as follows: 'O men / That lie upon your death-beds, and are haunted with howling wives, ne'er trust them, they'll remarry . . .'
3. Eliot is quite aware of the interplay of quotation and allusion as a structural feature of the poem – Elizabeth Gregory (1996: 194 n.3) points out that in his notes to *The Waste Land* Eliot systematically uses 'V[ide].' to indicate quotation and 'cf.' to signal allusions.
4. See Perri (1978: 299) for this distinction: '[in allegory] the referent's attributes must be sufficiently represented in order for the reader to extend the reference, the referent being the tacit part of the allegory. In allusion, conversely, the referent, whether expressed overtly or covertly (but always recognizably) is present in the text and the audience must uncover its attribute(s), the tacit aspect of allusion.'
5. Cf. Diepeveen (1993: viii) on allusion: 'inexactitude lies at its centre'.
6. In an earlier passage in this letter, Pound writes of 'the blazing poppy I found this morning, the first one. It reminds one of what sort of fire there'll be in Andalucia about three weeks from now. By the way do you know the court yard of the mosque in Cordova? – or did you say you didn't know Spain? – that's orangey, the court of the mosque I mean.' The 'fire' refers to the fields of poppies.
7. For a more extended account of this feature of the late Cantos, see Nicholls (2004: 233–50).
8. Diepeveen (1993: 23–47).
9. William Carlos Williams (1969: 108) is finely alert to this aspect of *The Cantos*: 'the material is so molded that it is changed in *kind* from other statement.

It is a *sort* beyond measure. The measure is an inevitability, an unavoidable
accessory after the fact. If one move, if one run, if one seizes up a material –
it cannot avoid having a measure, it cannot avoid a movement which clings
to it – as the movement of a horse becomes a part of the rider also – That is
the way Pound's verse impresses me and why he can include pieces of prose
and have them still part of a *poem*' (his emphases).

10. Claudette Sartilliot (1993: 13) notes the disappearance of quotation marks
in Flaubert's work and takes Derrida's account of quotation as the contami-
nation of one work by another rather than as 'illustration' as the exemplary
mode of postmodern citationality.

11. For an account of this practice, see Nicholls (1996: 594–8).

12. For Howe's use of the myth of Orpheus in *Pierce-Arrow* (1997), see Nicholls
(2002: 455–57).

Works cited

Ackroyd, Peter (1984) *T. S. Eliot*. London: Hamish Hamilton.

Alter, Robert (1996) *The Pleasures of Reading in an Ideological Age*. New York: Norton.

Andrews, Bruce (1984) 'Text and Context', in Bruce Andrews and Charles
Bernstein (eds), *The L=A=N=G=U=A=G=E Book*. Carbondale and Edwardsville:
Southern Illinois University Press.

Barthes, Roland (1982) *Image-Music-Text*, trans. Stephen Heath. London: Fontana.

Bate, Walter Jackson (1971) *The Burden of the Past and the English Poet*. London:
Chatto & Windus.

Benjamin, Walter (1999) *The Arcades Project*, trans. Howard Eiland and Kevin
McLaughlin. Cambridge, MA: Harvard University Press.

Ben-Porat, Ziva (1976) 'The Poetics of Allusion', *PTL: a Journal for Descriptive Poetics
and Theory of Literature* 1: 105–28.

Compagnon, Antoine (1979) *La seconde main ou le travail de la citation*. Paris: Seuil.

Derrida, Jacques (1991a) 'At This Very Moment in This Work Here I Am', in
Peggy Kamuf (ed.), *A Derrida Reader: Between the Blinds*. New York and London:
Harvester Wheatsheaf, 404–39.

——— (1991b) 'Che cos'è la poesia?' in Peggy Kamuf (ed.), *A Derrida Reader:
Between the Blinds*. New York and London: Harvester Wheatsheaf, 221–37.

Diepeveen, Leonard (1993) *Changing Voices: the Modern Quoting Poem*. Ann Arbor:
University of Michigan Press.

Duncan, Robert (1968) 'The H. D. Book: Chapter 4', *Tri-Quarterly* 12: 82–98.

Eliot, T. S. (1928) 'Introduction: 1928', in Ezra Pound, *Selected Poems*. London:
Faber and Gwyer.

——— (1965) *To Criticize the Critic*. London: Faber & Faber

——— (1970) *The Complete Poems and Plays*. London: Faber & Faber.

——— (1980) *Selected Essays*. London: Faber & Faber.

Gregory, Elizabeth (1996) *Quotation and Modern American Poetry*. Houston, TX:
Rice University Press.

Hejinian, Lyn (2001) *A Border Comedy*. New York: Granary Books.

Howe, Susan (1993) *The Birth-mark: Unsettling the Wilderness in American Literary
History*. Hanover, NH: Wesleyan University Press.

——— (2007) *Souls of the Labadie Tract*. New York: New Directions.

Irwin, William (2001) 'What is an Allusion?' *Journal of Aesthetics and Art Criticism* 59(3): 287–97.

Leddy, Michael (1992) 'Limits of Allusion', *British Journal of Aesthetics* 32(2): 110–22.

Mandelstam, Osip (1979) 'Conversation about Dante', in Jane Gary Harris (ed.), *The Complete Critical Prose and Letters*, trans. Jane Gary Harris and Constance Link. Ann Arbor: Ardis.

Miner, Earl (1993) 'Allusion', in Alex Preminger and T. V. F. Brogan (eds), *The New Princeton Encyclopedia of Poetry and Poetics*. Princeton: Princeton University Press, 1993, 38–9.

Nicholls, Peter (1996) 'Unsettling the Wilderness: Susan Howe and American History', *Contemporary Literature* 37(4): 586–601.

—— (2002) ' "The Pastness of Landscape": Susan Howe's *Pierce-Arrow*', *Contemporary Literature* 43(3): 441–60.

—— (2004). 'Two doits to a boodle: Reckoning with *Thrones*', *Textual Practice* 18(2): 233–49.

Palmer, Michael (1999) 'Interview', in Thomas Gardner, *Regions of Strangeness*. Lincoln and London: University of Nebraska Press.

Perelman, Bob (1996) *The Marginalization of Poetry: Language Writing and Literary History*. Princeton: Princeton University Press.

Perri, Carmela (1978) 'On Alluding', *Poetics* 7: 289–307.

Pound, Ezra (1968) *Collected Shorter Poems*. London: Faber & Faber.

—— (1971) *The Selected Letters of Ezra Pound*, ed. D. D. Paige. London: Faber & Faber.

—— (1994) *The Cantos*. London: Faber & Faber.

Pound, Omar and Robert Spoo (eds) (1988) *Ezra Pound and Margaret Cravens: a Tragic Friendship, 1910–1912*. Durham and London: Duke University Press.

Ricks, Christopher (2002) *Allusion to the Poets*. Oxford: Oxford University Press.

Robinson, Kit (1991) 'Time & Materials: the Workplace, Dreams, and Writing', *Poetics Journal* 9: 21–35.

Sartilliot, Claudette (1993) *Citation and Modernity: Derrida, Joyce, and Brecht*. Norman and London: University of Oklahoma Press.

Williams, William Carlos (1969) *Selected Essays*. New York: New Directions.

2
Politics and Modernist Poetics

Drew Milne

Anyone teaching Anglo-American modernist poetry becomes familiar
with resistances to the elitist, authoritarian, or reactionary politics of
prominent modernists. As Michael North puts it, 'The politics of Yeats,
Eliot, and Pound have long been an embarrassment and a scandal'
(North, 1991: 1). The difficulties are confirmed rather than dissipated
by a wider exploration into the poetics of T. E. Hulme, Wyndham Lewis,
D. H. Lawrence or David Jones. T. E. Hulme's pseudonymous 'A Tory Philosophy' sets the tone for much of what came after: 'I believe in original
sin . . . I can't stand romanticism, and . . . I am a certain kind of Tory'
(Hulme, 1998: 157; cf. Levenson, 1984). T. S. Eliot's more famous 1928
declaration of his general point of view as 'classicist in literature, royal-
ist in politics, and Anglo-Catholic in religion' confirms the curiously
unstable compound of interests (Eliot, 1928: 7). Inquisitive students
might seek out the work of more left-wing poets like Joseph MacLeod
or Charles Madge (Milne, 2001). Contrasts can be made with the socialist and communist poetics of Bertolt Brecht, Vladimir Mayakovsky, or
Hugh MacDiarmid. Even if modernists share a sense of socio-political
crisis, for which the antiquated terms of the 'left–right' political spectrum lack historical relevance, the pillars of Anglo-American modernist
poetics nevertheless share attitudes that fall outside the positions now
acceptable within the politics of contemporary capitalism.

The resulting challenges can be read as resistances to the 'progress' of
capitalist modernity, but such challenges force readers to negotiate racial,
gender, and class prejudices, and to engage with anti-democratic or total-
itarian social recipes. Eliot's complicities with anti-Semitism fuel a kind
of ideological back-chat which rumbles on, although Anthony Julius has
put a number of debates to rest, as well as providing a useful discussion
of Pound's anti-Semitism (Julius, 1995). This kind of framing, however,

often leaves students defensively embroiled in attitudes and opinions, as if questions of prejudice and identity politics were the reasons for reading poetry.

A defence of Yeats by W. H. Auden exemplifies the beguiling attempt to snatch virtue from the jaws of error: 'However false or undemocratic his ideas, his diction shows a continuous evolution toward what one might call the true democratic style' (Auden, 1972: 142). Performing such loops, readers cannot easily maintain polite disapproval of the politics while engaging enthusiastically with poetic technique. Cairns Craig suggests, moreover, that for Yeats, Eliot, and Pound, 'the initial effort to maintain a "pure" poetry led them to analyse the problems of poetry as lying in the social world, and solving poetic problems became, therefore, a matter of solving social problems' (Craig, 1982: 20). Like it or not, readers of modernist poetry find themselves in the midst of *both* political *and* poetic problems.

Not so long ago, English teaching was open to more explicitly political approaches. In 'Four Ways with a Reactionary Text', Alan Sinfield observes that 'Most literary texts which the socialist is required by syllabus and convention to teach will be reactionary' (Sinfield, 1983: 81). His essay was published in *LTP,* a journal that sought to connect literature, teaching, and politics, through an informal network of groups committed to radical, theoretical, and socialist approaches. Sinfield argues that, 'for the socialist teacher, the literary text is an embarrassment' (Sinfield, 1983: 83), in part because so many texts established as 'literary' promote a reactionary version of reality, naturalising existing hierarchies and inequalities, and colluding in the suppression of political argument. Modernist texts are more easily perceived as estrangements that provoke arguments, but this hardly stops them being 'reactionary'. Sinfield's four ways are: (i) rejection; (ii) interpretation; (iii) deflection into 'form(alism)'; and (iv) deflection into history (Sinfield, 1983: 83–91). Rejection involves dropping texts from the syllabus or setting materials that denaturalise the canonical emphasis. For Eliot and Pound this might involve making students read *After Strange Gods* (Eliot, 1934), or Pound's Second World War radio broadcasts (Pound, 1978). More sophisticated strategies of rejection involve comparison with rival bodies of writing, foregrounding more progressive or marginalised voices. This informs the ongoing widening of modernism, with new emphases on neglected women (Scott, 1990, 2007) and African-American modernists, such as Melvin B. Tolson (Tolson, 1999). As Sinfield suggests, however, 'this leaves culturally powerful writing to become even more an instrument of conservative influence' (Sinfield, 1983: 84).

Interpretation, Sinfield's second strategy, involves analysing texts 'so as to yield acceptable meanings', from interpretations which neutralise unpalatable politics, to critical interpretations such as those developed by Frankfurt School Marxism and Althusserians. Liberal interpretations often slant readings towards apolitical versions of some universal, humanist, psycho-biographical, or generally anguished human condition. Terry Eagleton, by contrast, directs interpretations towards decoding ideology: 'It is in the blank space between the "form" and "content" of *The Waste Land*, between its cosmic detachment and guilty collusion, that the ideology which produces it is most visibly inscribed' (Eagleton, 1976: 148). Ideological interpretations open up texts, making them newly available for otherwise sceptical readers, but rather evidently impose external categories. Such readings rarely satisfy anyone interested in authorial intentionality or in the detail of literary context and purpose.

Deflection into questions of form and formalism, associated by Sinfield with currents in Marxist criticism through to Derridean deconstruction, focuses on questions that reframe conventional interpretation. This can have the paradoxical effect of allowing reactionary modernists to be read as revolutionaries at the level of form, but, as Sinfield notes, 'there is no intrinsically progressive formal principle' (Sinfield, 1983: 88). This emphasis on formal techniques is, moreover, already characteristic of modernist poetics. Further critical deflection into questions of form usually generalises the question of form, generating yet more 'radical' modes of theoretical formalism. Deflection into history, by contrast, disarms the privilege given to formal construction, focusing on the historical conjunctures in which texts are produced and reproduced. The emphasis on history generates scholarly referentiality that can more easily be legitimated as 'research' than the development of aesthetic appreciation. Cultural materialists and new historicists often offset the conservative effects generated by the emphasis on historical context, by seeking to displace literary study into cultural studies, or by offering syntheses of historicism and theory. Progressive principles may guide approaches to historical research, but there is nothing intrinsically progressive about history. Indeed, historical contextualisation tends to reduce the historical range of arguments articulated by modernist poems to a more domestic, chronological focus, subsuming texts within their immediate context of production. If history is the principal interest, why study modernist texts?

Sinfield's preference for the deflection of texts into history has the paradoxical effect, moreover, of preserving a limited range of texts already deemed worthy of such deflections, rather than offering counter-arguments. Against the weight of history, many texts need to be redeemed from canonical neglect and received ignorance so as to release their unread potential. Historical contextualisation limits the scope for new canonical emphases, new conceptions of ideological interpretation, and new negotiations with the politics of form. Many students of literature, moreover, have only a rudimentary understanding of political history – few know who was American president or British prime minister in 1922, or even who had the right to vote. A good deal of historical work is usually needed, including intellectual and cultural history, before historical analysis can begin. Deflection into history may address one kind of ignorance, then, but teaching historical context, difficult in itself, is usually achieved by neglecting literary and linguistic history, reducing the interest of texts to contexts, rather than addressing their claims as poetic art. Most students and teachers recognise the validity of the work involved, but the politics quickly devolves into tensions between scholarly imperatives and anachronistic projections of contemporary identity politics. There is some irony, then, in the historical imperative so often imposed upon literary texts by leftist criticism, forcing political orientations otherwise addressed to the present and the future to return to the nightmare of history. Karl Marx was fond of quoting Jesus from the gospels: let the dead bury their dead (Marx, 1973: 149; cf. Matthew 8:21–2; and Luke 9:59–60).

Teachers of modernist poetry will explore syntheses of all four approaches, less, perhaps, in the spirit of socialist intervention, than in response to the political insensitivities modernist texts throw up when framed pedagogically. Moreover, anyone teaching *The Waste Land* will encounter students adopting versions of Sinfield's strategies, and is likely to feel the weight of predictability in the resulting responses. Why bother with such reactionary texts anyway, a student might also ask, especially if understanding the poetry is so difficult? Given that many Anglo-American modernists are reactionary, is this also true of the texts they wrote? One obvious response is to ask whether any text can be inherently reactionary, and, if so, what does it mean to be reactionary? Can a text be, or remain, internally reactionary, harbouring within its construction a kind of reactionary poison intrinsic to the writing itself, whatever the writer's intention? If so, are the characteristically difficult texts of modernist poetry especially or perniciously reactionary as compared with more obvious kinds of propaganda or polemic? Is it a defence to note that modernist texts provoke more questions than answers? Such problems arise within modernist poetics. Indeed modernist poetry develops its own versions of Sinfield's approaches. Texts such as *Ulysses, The Waste*

Land, and the *Cantos* prefigure and mediate aspects of their academic appropriation: their authors designed their texts to be resistant to comparison with rival texts, resistant to ideological interpretation, formalist readings, and historical contextualisation. Does this make such texts even more reactionary?

Yeats remains politically controversial (Allison, 2006; Foster, 1997, 2003), but his politics of poetic form excites less interest, perhaps because his forms appear so traditional. His elastic diction and syntax compound public and personal registers in new ways. *A Vision* (1925) brings a new dynamic into relations between prose 'criticism' and poetic practice, and has been read as offering a displaced politics (Cullingford, 1981; Yeats, 1978, 2008). Many consider his collection *The Tower* (1928) to be a major modernist text. Yeats, it could also be argued, is the most significant English language symbolist. His work nevertheless seems less and less central to modernist poetics, assimilated by a conservative ideology of 'lyric' (Vendler, 2007). Yeats' marginality within modernist poetics partly reflects the irrational ideas he entertained. For Yvor Winters 'the better one understands him, the harder it is to take him seriously' (Winters, 1972: 260). Winters' sharp criticisms provide a useful frame for seminar discussion of Yeats. The ideas and traditional forms used by Yeats are masks, consoling disguises. He once acknowledged that, 'Because I need a passionate syntax for passionate subject-matter I compel myself to accept those traditional metres that have developed with the language' (Yeats, 1961: 521–2). The subtlety of his modernist appropriation of traditions help make his work seem belatedly romanticist.

No less engaged in appropriations of tradition, Eliot's *The Waste Land*, along with Pound's *Hugh Selwyn Mauberley* and the *Cantos*, are less reassuring to nineteenth-century tastes. These longer, sequential poems weave layers of short poem forms within structural patterns and extended arguments that decompose conventional lyric forms. Studies of modernism sometimes ignore these poems and their use of sequential decomposition, but without some account of the excitement these texts generate, it is difficult to explain their impact, however negative, on subsequent poetic practices. It may be Eliot's criticism rather than his poetry that is influential, but *The Waste Land* secures and legitimates his critical authority. F. R. Leavis (1932) and Cleanth Brooks (1939) offer paradigmatic readings of *The Waste Land* that remain useful as introductions. Hugh Kenner (1972) offers an exhilaratingly if elusive counter-blast in favour of Pound. Publication of Pound's annotations to the drafts of *The Waste Land* established beyond doubt his importance for Eliot (Eliot, 1971). The facsimile and transcripts of the drafts provide evidence of a

more provisional, collaborative poetics in process, evidence which provides material through which to teach dynamic estrangements of the
canonical forms of the printed poem. The reciprocal influence of *The
Waste Land* on the *Cantos* remains an open question. While the *Cantos*
are less widely taught than *The Waste Land*, and not just for reasons of
scale, Pound's continuing importance is undeniable. The excitement of
Eliot's centrality appears to have waned among modernist enthusiasts.
Marjorie Perloff, for example, has even attempted to reveal a more avant-
garde Eliot, as if to rescue Eliot from his more conservative admirers
(Perloff, 2002).

Despite the weight of associated contexualisations and accumulated
readings, *The Waste Land* continues to resist assimilation, not least by
virtue of the awkward gulf between the 'poem' and Eliot's ambivalent
notes, a gulf between poetry and prose which is critical for modernist poetics more generally. Pound's work breaks down differentiations
between his poetry and his prose writings, with prose citation working
through the texture of the *Cantos*. Maud Ellmann argues that it is impossible to keep Pound's poetry and prose apart: 'His whole opus subverts the
distinction between interpretation and creation' (Ellmann, 1987: 16).
The difference between poetics that maintain a divide between poetry
and criticism, and poetics that subvert such distinctions remains significant: the categories have collapsed, but somehow persist, more as facades
than as foundations. Pound's work continues to inform developments
in poetics as criticism, and criticism as poetics (Bernstein, 1992; Spahr
et al., 1994). Rather than forcing a decision between Eliot and Pound,
Lawrence Rainey's suggestion that the fiction of heroic eras needs to be
retired, points to a mature, if less lively consensus (Rainey, 2007): Pound
and Eliot are central for each other, mutually determining forces in modernist poetry and criticism. Greater prominence can be given to writers
whose work decentres the Eliot–Pound axis, such as Gertrude Stein or
William Carlos Williams. The whole orientation towards modernism
can be made more plural (Nicholls, 1995). Pound and Eliot nevertheless
remain awkward stumbling blocks amid the rubble of sundry polemics.

The more persuasive accounts of Pound and Eliot tend not to provide
expositions of their achieved coherence, so much as reveal historically
contingent revisions and shifts. What emerge are provisional, fragile
compounds that may appear forbiddingly determinate but are loosened
by formal contingencies, opacities, rhythmic resonances, and difficulties of historical intelligibility or recognition. For North, 'the greatest
works of literary modernism – *The Tower*, *The Waste Land*, the *Pisan
Cantos* – are not those that display some triumphant resolution of social

or aesthetic discord, but those that make discord itself into an organizational principle' (North, 1991: 19). The metaphor of discord echoes metaphors of dissonance and disjunction often used to describe critical negativity in the compositional architecture of modernist texts. Rather than generating coherent reconciliations and heroically finished works, the characteristic claim is that compositional practices allow social contradictions to remain unreconciled: a work's form remains in conflict with itself, and thereby resistant to merely formal readings. In the works he highlights, North suggests that a fragmentary freedom remains in play, 'so that their value is finally to keep painfully in view the problems they tried so hard to solve' (North, 1991: 20). There is something unattractive about a model in which a work's value, despite hard work, is a pain-inducing inability to solve problems. Read differently, the craggy qualities of work that acknowledges its fragmented, dissonant musicality is less a heroically positive construction, and more a series of speculative concretions in decomposition. Perloff comments, for example, that: 'one of the special pleasures of reading the *Cantos* is to observe with what agility and grace Pound cuts across the metonymic chains he has created' (Perloff, 1981: 194). North's contextually sensitive readings render the work problematic rather than engagingly radical. The cost of politicised readings appears to be the loss of any pleasure in the poetic text as poetry, or in its differentiation from context. The effect is to engage readers in a politics of criticism which puts as much emphasis on the authority of prose writings – the prose both of the poets discussed and of modernist critics – as on the meaning of modernist poetics as poetics. The politics of modernist poetics, however, disables the categorical differentiation of poetry and prose, and suggests, even if implicitly, a critique of claims for writing's aesthetic autonomy.

North's 'political aesthetic' leans on Theodor Adorno's aesthetics of autonomy and negativity. Adorno, along with Walter Benjamin, is a prominent resource for those attempting to redeem modernist art from its authoritarian tendency to aestheticise politics (Kolocotroni et al., 1998; Rainey, 2005b). For all the radical authority lent by the neo-Marxist aesthetics of Adorno and Benjamin, debates between them, and between Lukács and Brecht, reveal unreconciled differences between aesthetics of production and of reception, differences which point to problems in the aesthetics of autonomy claimed for artworks (Bloch et al., 1977; Lunn, 1985). Generalised claims for formal reflexivity are often translated too quickly across different media, as if musical dissonance were analogous to poetic dissonance, or as if visual techniques involving collage and figurative abstraction could be reproduced in poetic language. The analogies are suggestive, but concrete articulations generate their own problems of medium and content. The politicised formalism of criticism usually puts too much emphasis on the ideology of the aesthetic (Eagleton, 1990), relying on distinctions between form and content which modernism breaks down and renders indeterminate. Emphasising the micro-politics of form provides a necessary antidote to political readings that offer reductively formulaic or formalist accounts of ideological content. The resonance of a quoted metre or social accent can construct and fragment the class determinations of enunciation and social register in ways that dramatise micro-political differentiations, for example the difference between 'goonight' and 'good night' in *The Waste Land* (lines 170–2). Contrast the multiple ironies attending the phrase 'to get the beauty of it hot' from *The Waste Land* (167) with the no less over-determined ironies of the italicised line *'All things save Beauty alone'* from *Hugh Sel-wyn Mauberley* (Pound, 1975b: 106). Articulations of poetic technique in modernist poetics are politically sensitive at the most micro-logical level, and remain resistant to generalisation and abstraction. Even nuanced readings, such as Benjamin's account of Baudelaire, can be criticised, as Adorno suggests, for a reductive parallelism between socio-political con-texts and pragmatic content. However suggestive, Marxist aestheticians, along with what has become known as 'theory', tend to schematise texts, reducing them to conceptual thematics. Theoretical formalism lacks the contextual and historical sensitivity, and tends to neglect poetic tech-niques, linguistic specificities, and concrete particulars of reference and allusion.

While students of modernism are often excited by modernist aestheti-cians such as Adorno and Derrida, they usually struggle to translate the arguments into their own criticism and research, in part because the arguments are difficult to imitate or too abstract, in part because the frameworks of German and French thought translate so awkwardly into English-language modernisms. There are also significant differ-ences between modernist aesthetics and modernist poetics. The poetic significance of language engages different problems of meaning from the visual and performing arts. One important difference is modernist poetry's relation to prose argument and to critical mediation through prose discussion. Although there are problems with theoretical readings of modernism, encouraging students to respond to the text itself, rather than relying on secondary criticism or theory, amounts to a strategy of deliberate blindness that is rarely convincing or successful. Modernist poetics works through differences between poetry and prose in ways that question the received categories of 'art' and the arts: this generates a need for conceptual and theoretical reflection as part of the understanding of poems. It becomes evident, then, that modernist poetics embodies temptations either to put too much emphasis on historical and intellectual contexts, or to develop too quickly into theoretical formalism or conceptual abstraction. Modernist poetics nevertheless seeks to work through and beyond such contextualisation and theoretical paraphrase.

Resulting conflicts can be tested through detailed readings and seminar discussions. *The Waste Land* and the *Cantos* raise questions about religion, mythology, art, and economics, and in ways that go beyond what can be inferred from close reading of immediate textual forms. Whether history is read out of these poems or projected into the text, the resulting articulations are also mediated by poetics whose linguistic, generic, and technical specificities disable existing types of formal description. It is as hard to offer a clear account of the historical arguments offered in *The Waste Land* and the *Cantos*, as it is to summarise their various models of irony, citation, poetic rhythm, or grammar. For all the sustained interest and sensitivity to metre associated with Pound, the *Cantos* continue to resist metrical analysis, in part because metres are continually decomposed by being quoted, translated, fragmented, or aligned with prose. Hugh Kenner's conception of rhythms of recurrence (Kenner, 1971) is echoed by Peter Nicholls' suggestive remarks about rhythm in the *Cantos* (Nicholls, 1984). Marjorie Perloff draws attention to the incorporation of prose tradition in Pound's work (Perloff, 1986). She also suggests construing poetry 'not as "verse" (which is not, in fact, the dominant medium of the poets concerned) but as *language art* or "word-system"' (Perloff, 1981: 43). Relations between syntax and prosody in modernist poetry resist conventional linguistics and verse stylistics, partly because modernist poetics no longer assumes the idea of 'verse', working as much with categories of text, writing, and language, in relation to the poetics of sequences, bookworks, page poetics, and performance.

Resistances to prose paraphrase and formal description also disarm sophisticated political readings, but for most students the possibility of offering any kind of loose paraphrase or prose summary of the poems is sufficiently challenging to produce an anxiety which is not much allayed by consulting student guides (Brooker, 1979; Southam, 1968; Terrell, 1980). Such guides are helpful, but they tend to disable investigations which are a necessary part of responding to poems, as well as neglecting qualities of resonance and meaning that are less determinate than the kinds of referentiality scholarly notes can supply. Allusions are often more elusively suggestive than a gloss can clarify. While seeming indispensable, then, such guides also need to be dispensed with. In his introduction to David Jones' *In Parenthesis*, T. S. Eliot remarks that: 'to study even the best commentary on a work of literary art is likely to be a waste of time unless we have first read and been excited by the text commented upon even without understanding it. For that thrill of excitement from our first reading of a work of creative literature which we do not understand is itself the beginning of understanding' (Eliot, 1963: viii). Students need to be given confidence that commentaries and guides provide only one kind of map, while the more interesting questions of poetic concretion and significance remain open and indeterminate. The resistance of *The Waste Land* and the *Cantos* to paraphrase gives grounds for confidence that readers are not supposed to decipher these poems as if they were elaborate crossword puzzles or academic exercises. As Maud Ellmann suggests, *The Waste Land* is a sphinx without a secret: 'to force it to confession may also be a way of killing it' (Ellmann, 1987: 91). Resistances to formal description and prosaic summary combine to confirm that the kinds of indeterminacy in play are over-determined, rather than some mystified surface opacity readers are supposed to decode. Eagleton, discussing *The Waste Land*, offers a helpful model: 'behind the back of this ruptured, radically decentred poem runs an alternative text which is nothing less than the closed, coherent, authoritative discourse of the mythologies which frame it' (Eagleton, 1976: 150). The priority of terms can be reversed: behind the edifice of structural frames, a radical decentring undermines and ruins the architecture of folly. A centripetal struggle for coherence conflicts with a centrifugal tendency towards fragmentation and the montage of luminous details. Read in either direction, the indeterminacy of what can be reconstituted as the meaning of these poems as poems is sufficiently determinate to undermine summaries of political content.

There are different compounds of determinacy and indeterminacy at work in modernist poetics, then, with different micro-political consequences. If modernist poems inevitably collapsed into a generalised kind of indeterminacy, a determinate incoherence, they would quickly become monotonous. The will to forge new kinds of coherence determines itself through recognition of what is necessarily indeterminate, rather than arbitrarily so, writing through a sense of the failure of traditional meanings and forms. Poetic practices exploring the limits of poetry's conditions of possibility rarely generate reassuringly stable consequences. Radical investigations into fundamental presuppositions undermine the pragmatics of working assumptions, leaving aporetic ruins rather than secured foundations.

Approaching the work of Pound and Eliot as ruined follies rather than as living monuments or institutions highlights the fragmentation and failure their work represents and reflects. Nor does this involve reading against the grain. A concluding line of *The Waste Land* famously acknowledges 'These fragments I have shored against my ruins' (Eliot, 1971: 146). Shored *against* ruins, rather than shored up, that is, with the metaphoricity of shores and shoring in play between morphologies of noun and verb. Levenson comments that: 'In the space of that line the poem becomes conscious of itself. What had been a series of fragments of consciousness has become a consciousness of fragmentation' (Levenson, 1984: 192). Read through adjacent lines, the effect is rather different. A few lines previously, the poem declares: 'I sat upon the shore / Fishing, with the arid plains behind me' (Eliot, 1971: 146). Between land and sea, between rock and water, the ground against which the fragments are shored is hardly firmly rooted, more akin to the stony terrain Hugh MacDiarmid later figured as on a 'raised beach' (MacDiarmid, 1978). These lines from *The Waste Land* are difficult not to read as programme notes to the whole. They follow on, however, from the ruined tower of the Prince of Aquitaine, lost home of the disinherited troubadours also beloved by Pound, and not just ruined but *'abolie'*, but by whom? Similarly, in Canto LXXVI, Pound offers oft-quoted lines which are almost too programmatic: 'As a lone ant from a broken ant-hill / from the wreckage of Europe, ego scriptor' (Pound, 1975a: 458). Lone ants live in denial or in exile from their species. Even as part of what Christine Froula's awkward mix of metaphors calls 'a field of fragments' and 'a mindscape of allegorical ruins' (Froula, 1983: 216) this imagist couplet unsettles conventions of pastoral analogy, just as petals on a wet black bough cannot be made into too exact an analogy for the look of a crowd of faces.

Foregrounded authorially as fragments, ruins, and scenes of wreckage, the architectural metaphors are not those of a heroic new cathedral, temple, or modernist tower, comparable to the iconic Eiffel Tower, Tatlin's Monument to the Third International, or Yeats' more ambivalent poetics of the Tower. Rather than heroically achieved structures, the poetics are those of baroque folly and neo-classical ruins. These texts are more like post-architectural salvage yards, assemblages of rubble and broken scree. Maud Ellmann comments of *The Waste Land*, 'This poem, which has been so thoroughly *explained*, is rarely *read* at all, and one can scarcely see the "waste" beneath the redevelopments' (Ellmann, 1987: 91). Similarly, her discussion of the *Cantos* notes the fragmented lines: 'a sinistra la Torre / seen thru a pair of breeches' (Pound, 1975a: 431; Ellmann, 1987: 1–2). The leaning tower of Pisa does not offer Pound a crow's nest or higher vantage, but generates images seen through power from below the waist or through trousers. The image of Pound in his Pisan cage and subsequently in Saint Elizabeth's hospital suggests the architectural constraints out of which the *Cantos* were written. *The Waste Land*, appropriately, given the poem's interest in the city of London as a financial centre, was written on leave from Eliot's work in Lloyds Bank.

Reading modernist poems as ruined follies, architectures of decomposition, helps to make modernist poems more approachable, less monumental. Fredric Jameson suggests that: 'we must make an assumption that problematizes the very work of textual analysis itself – namely, the presupposition that the works we have canonized as the classics of modernism are in fact not successes, but failures. It is a presupposition that is required for any successful dereification of these now institutionalized texts' (Jameson, 2007: 3; cf. Jameson, 2002). The approach bears fruit in his reading of William Carlos Williams' *Paterson*, though students might struggle with Jameson's characteristically dense syntax and theoretical discourse. Acknowledging the politics as a poetics of ruins helps to articulate the compensating pleasures of archaeological reading. Given the polemical fog associated with inflated claims on behalf of modernism's formal radicalism, a critique of the political illusions involved needs to recognise the excitements of formal radicalism. It is folly, if not political madness, to concede too much to the desire to allow formal critique to stand in for determinate and mediated political articulation. Reactionary opinions and political illusions may go into the making of modernist poems, but the extent to which ruins and follies are themselves reactionary is as much a question of perceptual reconstruction and the perspectives brought to bear. There are confusions involved in most attempts to oppose political orthodoxy, but perhaps the most interesting and most dangerous are those that conflate radical new conceptions of writing with political radicalism. Enthusiasm for 'free verse' requires a degree of free thinking and a willingness to break with literary tradition, but the freedoms associated with modernist forms often plunge writers into the search for new kinds of binding authority, new ways of grounding poetic materials. Modernism's break with the past, its newness, also finds itself thrown by its very radicalism into finding a prehistory for itself or some different vantage from which to respond critically to perceived crises. Joyce's *Ulysses* is paradigmatic, offering both a representation of modern Dublin and an investigation into the resonance of Homer's *Odyssey* for modern life. Modernism projects speculative histories back through

untimely or ahistorical representations of earlier representations or figures: Yeats' Byzantium, Pound's various analogues and personae, and
Eliot's neo-classicism are obvious examples. Archaeological or genealog-
ical projections that generate perspectival shifts also feature in the
work of other modernist poets – from William Carlos Williams, Hugh
MacDiarmid, and Charles Olson, to more recent poets such as Susan
Howe – but with different political entailments. Formal radicalism produces different types of political indeterminacy (Bernstein, 1990), from
fluid aporia to dogmatic fragmentations.

There is nothing inherently or determinately political about different types of formal radicalism, save perhaps a shared sense that existing
modes of writing and representation are inadequate. Using collage and
documentary assemblage, the poetic compounds produced out of factual or highly local kinds of source material often collapse any account
of the mediations and historical processes involved. Political provocations remain active in the folds, gaps, and editing processes, but not
as messages, themes, or content in the traditional sense. The missing
argument – and this is often of deep political significance – is the explanation of how modern Western society became what it is, rather than,
say, realising the potential implicit in some other idealised point of reference. Indeed, many anti-capitalist gestures involve little understanding
of how capitalism works, being motivated more by a kind of aesthetic
distaste for some aspect of modernity. Some of modernism's urgency
reflects the search for ways of not reproducing the wastelands of the
First World War, but it is rare for modernist writers to offer historically
convincing accounts of the socio-political dynamics that led to war.
The more characteristic political gesture involves an implicit polemic
against somewhat arbitrarily selected symptoms of social pathology –
war, technology, disintegration of shared religious values, the decline of
culture – without a sustained account of the pathology generating such
symptoms, and without much clarity as to the political and economic
forces at work. In short, modernist poetry may be generated out of a
reactionary set of attitudes, but the very indeterminacy of modernism's
new forms and unfamiliar perspectives generates political indeterminacy.
There is a politics in play, then, in the poetics of indeterminacy, but not
a determinate politics. To articulate this politics of form requires over-
coming some of the sceptical resistance to abstract categories and mediations which are a necessary part of historical, economic, and political
arguments.

If modernist poetry is not airily dismissed as ideological spam riddled with anti-Semitic and misogynist prejudices, a further well-worn

fault line often opens up. Texts such as *The Waste Land* are accused of being unnecessarily obscure, opaque, difficult, 'academic' in the pejorative sense, or just plain mystified and mystifying, as if all of such qualities could be taken as evidence of scholastic, anti-populist conservatism. These terms need to be differentiated and articulated rather than being left to fester. Obscurity has its uses, while opacity can be a matter of perception that constitutes transparency from another angle. Even if difficulties of various kinds engage readers in hard work, the equation of textual difficulty with authorial elitism and academic authoritarianism is so much waffle. By such logic, a textbook in maths, chemistry, or physics would, at least for the average literature student, be inherently fascistic. In coming to terms with the modern world, anything that makes itself too accessible, too reducible to bullet-point propaganda, is usually peddling truisms with designs on our desires for stupefaction. This is as true for modern poetry as it is for modern education. A shared politics of poetics and pedagogy begins with some recognition that more is involved than making modernism into something easily bought and sold, consumed or enjoyed.

Despite the various publicity strategies and introductory formulae offered by both modernists and academics, then, a minimal condition for political criticism is a willingness to read through and beyond the manifestos and introductory guides, engaging with what Pound called 'the dance of the intellect among words' (Pound, 1954: 25; cf. Perloff, 1996), rather than reductive point-scoring according to some ahistorical conception of political correctness. Modernist poetry does require readers to engage in new and different kinds of work, but then so do the writings of Marx, Nietzsche, and Freud. Difficulty as such provides no index of political virtue. Reluctance to engage with the challenges of modernism may nevertheless take refuge in idle dogma. I fondly recall one student saying to another, in a heated discussion of Eliot's use of languages other than English, 'so some people read Italian and you don't, what exactly is your problem?' Another student pointed out that anyone walking through the streets of central London hears a myriad of languages, and this provides one way into thinking about the layers of language in *The Waste Land*. For those who recognise that the work put into reading modernist poems can be rewarding, there remains the problem of accounting for such rewards when set against the disastrous politics of their authors.

The domestication of modernism into something more reader-friendly often displaces political challenges to the margins, while generating a further set of questions about the politics of academic appropriation implicit in scholarly research. Rainey's recent annotated edition of

The Waste Land (2005a) by no means exhausts the task of reading the poem, but there is something exhausting about the prospect of reading texts already mined with layers of annotation. It was never possible to read *The Waste Land* or the *Cantos* without being aware of layers of referentiality that ask for further research, but the genesis of modernist poetics through poems and prose polemics takes on a very different politics if mediated through the authority of academic criticism. Modernist poetics and its more autonomously autodidactic modes of research need to be distinguished from the philological protocols of research appropriate in a scholarly essay. What, then, does it mean to defend the kinds of intellectual short-cut, unacknowledged citation, reliance on secondary sources, and collaged plagiarism characteristic of modernist poems, while encouraging students not to reproduce such innovative strategies in their essays?

It is possible to question the writing strategies and the historical processes which generated the conservative versions of modernism widely taught in academic institutions, and any political assessment of modernist texts needs to reckon with the extent to which modernist writers are responsible for or complicit with their institutionalised readings. But although ambitious for status and critical acceptance, modernist poetry also challenges the methods and processes of educational assimilation, suggesting the need for radical autodidacticism rather than reliance on existing authorities or educational mediation. Pound suggests, for example, that: 'There is one quality which unites all great and perdurable writers, you don't NEED schools and colleges to keep 'em alive' (Pound, 1951: 45). His bracing prose guides continue to offer more engaging introductions to modernist poetics than the nuanced historical contextualisations of academic criticism. The politics of Pound's autodidactic intellectual self-reliance proves prey, however, to a plethora of random influences and dogma: freedom from received wisdom leaves the door open to conspiracy theories and received ignorance. The excitement of research in autodidactic poetics involves the determination to educate oneself rather than relying on external authorities. This makes it all the more necessary to temper such excitement with an understanding of the potential for mistakes in the short-cuts taken, and of the problems which accrue when texts bypass mediations in favour of nonconformist insights.

Returning to Sinfield's array of strategies, such questions can be explored through consideration of the canonical position of key texts, the status of interpretation, the politics of form, and the historical situation of a text's production and reproduction. What counts as a mistake within a poetics of research? What alternative models are available? An important and useful technique in teaching texts by Eliot and Pound is to set them against contemporary poems that have received less attention, and are, accordingly, less burdened by existing commentaries and more open for new kinds of research. Freedom from extensive secondary criticism, a freedom also evident in comparisons with recent neo-modernist poetry (Mengham and Kinsella, 2004), often troubles students more used to cribs, but can open up the need to read without relying on such props. Mina Loy's 'Love Songs to Joannes' (1917) bears comparison with Eliot's 'The Love Song of J. Alfred Prufrock' (1917); while Loy's ambitious sequence *Anglo-Mongrels and the Rose* (1923–5) bears comparison with *The Waste Land* and *Hugh Selwyn Mauberley* (Loy, 1982). There is a process of dialogue and rivalry between such texts, and even if Eliot and Pound deserve their status as more major poets, comparison allows the values in play to be explored, while juxtaposition produces various kinds of collage and collision between texts. Rather than deflecting *Hugh Selwyn Mauberley* and *The Waste Land* into history, juxtaposition reveals comparable texts produced by friends and rivals of Pound and Eliot. Hogarth Press publications such as Hope Mirrlees, *Paris: a Poem* (1919) and Nancy Cunard, *Parallax* (1925) involve poetics in implicit and sometimes explicit dialogue with both Eliot and Pound. Rather than deflecting *into* history, comparative reading across the networks supporting Eliot and Pound helps to clarify the social formations through which new poetic forms were produced. Such forms are in dialogue with the social formations that both hinder and enable the writing and publication of modernist texts, and the significance of such dialogues at the level of poetic texture is perhaps clearer when contemporary poems of comparable ambition are set against each other.

Such comparisons are made easier by Keith Tuma's *Anthology of Twentieth-Century British & Irish Poetry* (2001). The introductions and glossing are intrusively helpful, but the anthology provides a formal and historical framework for comparative interpretation. Along with Mina Loy and Nancy Cunard, Tuma includes incisive selections from the poetry of Hugh MacDiarmid, David Jones, and Basil Bunting, who offer ample opportunities for critical comparison since so much of their work is explicitly written through sympathetic awareness of Eliot and Pound. Tuma's anthology restores a sense of the range of modernist poetics out of which and through which the modernist ambitions of Eliot and Pound were established. Cary Nelson's *Anthology of Modern American Poetry* (2000) offers comparable opportunities, but the two anthologies have to be read together to understand the Pound–Eliot axis as a transatlantic modernism, perhaps using reading from anthologies which sample poetics (Cook, 2004) and theory (Milne, 2003). Such anthologies become their own kinds of institution, and it remains necessary to keep open the more fragile, pre-institutional formation of modernist poetics, while contextualising the politics of reproduction associated with different institutionalised versions of modernism. Comparison with neglected longer poems is harder to develop as a way of teaching the *Cantos*, but the work of MacDiarmid, Jones, and Bunting, along with William Carlos Williams, Louis Zukofsky, and Charles Olson, provides fruitful and open-ended means for exploring the poetics of long, sequential poems.

The important problems thrown up by the politics of modernist poetry cannot simply be evaded or superseded by claims for the radicalism of form, for the democracy of open or writerly texts, or through claims for the negativity and autonomy of the art work. Recognising that there are real and substantial political entailments engaged by the reading and writing of poetry marks the limits of aestheticism, or 'pure' poetry. As Cairns Craig has argued, 'The purity of poetry could only be maintained in a world that allowed for the existence of a pure art and the effort to discover the failures in the society that prevent the poet's full achievement led to an incorporation of "impure" elements into the poetry itself' (Craig, 1982: 20). Recognition of the limits of pure poetry, and the necessary negotiation with impurities of language, literary form, cultural history, and contemporary sociality helps to make modernist poetics so restless, awkward, and interesting. If the ruins resemble the wasteland of a modern land-fill refuse site, there are nevertheless many baroque pleasures to be recycled.

Works cited

Allison, Jonathan (2006) 'Yeats and Politics', in Marjorie Howes and John Kelly (eds), *The Cambridge Companion to W. B. Yeats*. Cambridge: Cambridge University Press.

Auden, W. H. (1939, reprinted 1972) 'The Public v. the Late Mr. William Butler Yeats', reprinted in W. H. Pritchard (ed.), *W. B. Yeats: a Critical Anthology*. Harmondsworth: Penguin.

Bernstein, Charles (ed.) (1990) *The Politics of Poetic Form: Poetry and Public Policy*. New York: Roof Books.

—— (1992) *A Poetics*. Cambridge, MA and London: Harvard University Press.

Bloch, Ernst, Georg Lukács, Bertolt Brecht, Walter Benjamin, and Theodor Adorno (1977) *Aesthetics and Politics*. London: New Left Books.

Brooker, Peter (1979) *A Student's Guide to the Selected Poems of Ezra Pound*. London: Faber & Faber.

Brooks, Cleanth (1939) *Modern Poetry and the Tradition*. Chapel Hill: University of North Carolina Press.

Cook, John (ed.) (2004) *Poetry in Theory: an Anthology 1900–2000*. Oxford: Blackwell.

Craig, Cairns (1982) *Yeats, Eliot, Pound and the Politics of Poetry*. London: Croom-Helm.

Cullingford, Elizabeth (1981) *Yeats, Ireland and Fascism*. London: Macmillan.

Eagleton, Terry (1976) *Criticism and Ideology: a Study in Marxist Literary Theory*. London: New Left Books.

——— (1990) *Ideology of the Aesthetic*. Oxford: Blackwell.

Eliot, T. S. (1928). *After Strange Gods: a Primer of Modern Heresy*. New York: Harcourt, Brace and Co.

——— (1963) 'A Note of Introduction' (1961), to David Jones, *In Parenthesis*. London: Faber & Faber, 1963.

——— (1971) *The Waste Land: a Fascsimile and Transcript*, ed. Valerie Eliot. London: Faber & Faber.

——— (1972) *For Lancelot Andrewes*. London: Faber & Faber.

Ellmann, Maud (1987) *The Poetics of Impersonality: T. S. Eliot and Ezra Pound*. Brighton: Harvester.

Foster, R. F. (1997, 2003) *W. B. Yeats: A Life*, 2 vols. Oxford: Oxford University Press.

Froula, Christine (1983) *A Guide to Ezra Pound's Selected Poems*. New York: New Directions.

Hulme, T. E. (1998) *Selected Writings*, ed. Patrick McGuinness. Manchester: Carcanet.

Jameson, Fredric (2002) *A Singular Modernity: Essay on the Ontology of the Present*. London: Verso.

——— (2007) *The Modernist Papers*. London: Verso.

Julius, Anthony (1995) *T. S. Eliot, Anti-Semitism, and Literary Form*. Cambridge: Cambridge University Press.

Kenner, Hugh (1971) *The Poetry of Ezra Pound*. Berkeley and Los Angeles: University of California Press.

——— (1972) *The Pound Era*. London: Faber & Faber.

Kolocotroni, Vassiliki, Jane Goldman, and Olga Taxidou (eds) (1998) *Modernism: an Anthology of Sources and Documents*. Edinburgh: Edinburgh University Press.

Leavis, F. R. (1932) *New Bearings in English Poetry*. London: Chatto & Windus.

Levenson, Michael (1984) *A Genealogy of Modernism: a Study of English Literary Doctrine, 1908–1922*. Cambridge: Cambridge University Press.

Loy, Mina (1982) *The Last Lunar Baedeker*, ed. Roger L. Conover. Manchester: Carcanet.

Lunn, Eugene (1985) *Marxism and Modernism: a Historical Study of Lukács, Brecht, Benjamin and Adorno*. London: Verso.

MacDiarmid, Hugh (1978) 'On a Raised Beach', in Michael Greive and W. R. Aitken (eds), *The Complete Poems of Hugh MacDiarmid, 1920–1976*. 2 vols. London: Martin Brian & O'Keefe.

Marx, Karl (1973) *The Eighteenth Brumaire of Louis Bonaparte*, in David Fernbach (ed.), *Surveys from Exile: Political Writings*, vol. II. Harmondsworth: Penguin/New Left Review.

Mengham, Rod and John Kinsella (eds) (2004) *Vanishing Points: New Modernist Poems*. Cambridge: Salt.

Milne, Drew (2001) 'Charles Madge: Political Perception and the Persistence of Poetry', *New Formations* 44 (Autumn): 63–75.

———— (ed.) (2003) *Modern Critical Thought*. Oxford: Blackwell.

Nelson, Cary (2000) *Anthology of Modern American Poetry*. New York: Oxford University Press.

Nicholls, Peter (1984) *Ezra Pound: Politics, Economics and Writing: a Study of* The Cantos. London: Macmillan.

———— (1995) *Modernisms: a Literary Guide*. London: Macmillan.

North, Michael (1991) *The Political Aesthetic of Yeats, Eliot, and Pound*. Cambridge: Cambridge University Press.

Perloff, Marjorie (1981) *The Poetics of Indeterminacy: Rimbaud to Cage*. Evanston, IL: Northwestern University Press.

———— (1986) 'Ezra Pound and "The Prose Tradition in Verse"', in *The Futurist Moment: Avant-Garde, Avant Guerre, and the Language of Rupture*. Chicago and London: University of Chicago Press.

———— (1996) *The Dance of the Intellect: Studies in the Poetry of the Pound Tradition*. Evanston, IL: Northwestern University Press.

———— (2002) *21st-Century Modernism: the 'New' Poetics*. Oxford: Blackwell.

Pound, Ezra (1951) *ABC of Reading*. London: Faber & Faber.

———— (1954) 'How to Read', in T. S. Eliot (ed.), *Literary Essays of Ezra Pound*. London: Faber & Faber.

———— (1975a) *The Cantos*. London: Faber & Faber.

———— (1975b) *Hugh Selwyn Mauberley*, from *Selected Poems*. London: Faber & Faber.

———— (1978) *'Ezra Pound Speaking': Radio Speeches of World War II*, ed. Leonard W. Doob. Westport, CT and London: Greenwood Press.

Rainey, Lawrence (ed.) (2005a) *The Annotated* Waste Land, *with Eliot's Contemporary Prose*. New Haven & London: Yale University Press.

———— (ed.) (2005b) *Modernism: an Anthology of Sources and Documents*. Oxford: Blackwell.

———— (2007) 'Pound or Eliot: Whose Era?' in Alex Davis and Lee M. Jenkins (eds), *The Cambridge Companion to Modernist Poetry*. Cambridge: Cambridge University Press.

Scott, Bonnie Kime (ed.) (1990) *The Gender of Modernism*. Bloomington: Indiana University Press.

———— (ed.) (2007) *Gender in Modernism: New Geographies, Complex Intersections*. Urbana and Chicago: University of Illinois Press.

Sinfield, Alan (1983) 'Four Ways with a Reactionary Text', *LTP: Journal of Literature, Teaching, Politics* 2.

Southam, B. C. (1968) *A Student's Guide to the Selected Poems of T. S. Eliot*. London: Faber & Faber.

Spahr, Juliana, Mark Wallace, Kristin Prevallet, and Pam Rehm (eds) (1994) *A Poetics of Criticism*. Buffalo, NY: Leave Books.

Terrell, Carroll F. (1980) *A Companion to* The Cantos *of Ezra Pound*. Berkeley: University of California Press.

Tolson, Melvin B. (1999) *'Harlem Gallery' and Other Poems*, ed. Raymond Nelson. Charlottesville and London: University Press of Virginia.

Tuma, Keith (2001) *Anthology of Twentieth-Century British & Irish Poetry*. New York: Oxford University Press.

Vendler, Helen (2007) *Our Secret Discipline: Yeats and Lyric Form*. Oxford: Oxford University Press.

Winters, Yvor (1972) 'The Poetry of W. B. Yeats' (1960), reprinted in W. H. Pritchard (ed.), *W. B. Yeats: a Critical Anthology*. Harmondsworth: Penguin.

Yeats, W. B. (1961) *Essays and Introductions*. London: Macmillan, 1961.

—— (1978) *A Critical Edition of Yeats's* A Vision (1925), ed. George M. Harper and Walter K. Hood. London: Macmillan.

—— (2008) *The Collected Works of W. B. Yeats*, Vol XIII: *A Vision, the Original 1925 Version*, ed. Catherine E. Paul and Margaret Mills Harper. New York: Scribner/Simon & Schuster.

3
Science and Poetry

Michael H. Whitworth

Although the New Criticism encouraged a sharp distinction between the language of poetry and the language of science, it has increasingly been recognised that modernist poets took cognizance of scientific developments. What is harder to determine is the nature of the relationship. Science is often mentioned in contextualising introductions to modernism, but many such introductions give students a relatively superficial acquaintance with illustrious names. How can one help students to become knowledge producers rather than passive acquirers, in the face of the real and the perceived difficulties of science? Several problems need to be addressed: problems of the authority of science, problems of knowledge, and problems concerning what counts as knowledge. More mundanely, because the relevant prose texts are not always readily available, and some of the most interesting poets are not canonical, there are problems of resources. In what follows, I have assumed that seminars are the best environment for learning from this material. If lectures are offered in support, it is important that they leave scope for further discussion in seminars. The sometimes arcane nature of the material, and the intimidating authority of science, can leave students more than usually anxious that the poem is a puzzle with only one correct solution, not a space for imaginative exploration.

In spite of the problems, the potential benefits are great. Discussing modernist poetry in relation to science broadens students' contextual knowledge, of course. More importantly it sharpens their awareness of the varieties of specialised discourse in circulation in modernity, and their awareness of specialisation as a crucial feature of modernity. It opens the question of literature as a form of knowledge: the comparison raises the question of the nature of literary knowledge; what can literature know that science cannot? Asking what happens to a scientific idea or term when it is transferred from a scientific context to a poetic one introduces a deeper and more powerful concept of metaphor than is usually encountered in literary studies.

The authority of science

The names of modern scientists sometimes feature in lists of the fore-fathers of modernism dubbed by one critic 'the pantheon' (Herbert, 2001: 50). Einstein rubs shoulders with Nietzsche and Marx, Heisenberg finds his place in the family tree alongside Freud and Frazer. Not always, of course: Freud and Nietzsche are more often cited than their contemporaries in the physical and biological sciences.

When scientists do appear, they are often characterised in sweeping terms: scientific discourses become part of the spirit of the age, and 'the age' is a homogeneous entity in which fine distinctions of chronology are unimportant. Bradbury and McFarlane described modernism as 'the one art that responds to the scenario of our chaos' and 'the art consequent on Heisenberg's "Uncertainty Principle"' (Bradbury and McFarlane, 1976: 27). If consequence implies temporal sequence, then modernism began only in 1928, the date of the *Oxford English Dictionary*'s earliest citations for the 'principle of uncertainty' and the 'principle of indeterminacy'. If Bradbury and McFarlane really meant what they said, then several major works of high modernism – *The Waste Land* and *Ulysses*, for example – merely anticipate the true, post-Heisenberg movement. Of course there is a grain of non-chronological truth in what they say, but if one is to give science a serious place in the culture of modernism, then the chronological facts need to be established, as well as a less specific spirit of the age. It is notable that Bradbury and McFarlane speak of '*our* chaos' as if their culture were identical with that of Eliot and Pound. Though there is a strong case to be made for the continuation of modernism into the late twentieth century, the thirty-plus years that have elapsed since their guide have enabled us to gain a clearer historical perspective on modernism in its best-known phase, 1890–1930, and on its relation to the contemporary sciences.

Science and mathematics have a distinctive place in education: compared to literature, they have sharper definitions of correctness and incorrectness, and, in examinations and tests, sharper criteria for success or failure. To talk about science with literary students one needs to consider their relationship to the authority of science. Are they confident in identifying scientific terminology, and placing it in a larger framework of scientific theory? Do they feel confident in discussing scientific ideas?

Is their confidence well-founded, or misplaced? If misplaced, how well do the students respond to being corrected? One problem that can arise with the discussion of historical phases of science is that students may have acquired some knowledge of the science in a later form, for instance speaking of DNA where modernists might have said 'germ plasm'. However, the outdatedness of the science has the potential to give both tutor and student greater confidence in relation to it: the truth claims of any statements we make about it are to be understood as history, not as science.

Chronologies as contexts

As the example of Heisenberg's Uncertainty Principle demonstrates, the minimal requirement of a historical approach is to establish a chronology of scientific innovations in the period: such a list might include Roentgen's discovery of the X-ray in 1895; Planck's quantum theory of 1900; the foundation of modern genetics through the rediscovery of Gregor Mendel's work in the years 1900 to 1909; Einstein's papers on special relativity in 1905 and on general relativity in 1915; Rutherford's new model of the atom in 1911; Eddington's experimental proof of Einstein's theories in 1919; and Niels Bohr's and Werner Heisenberg's 1925 paper on quantum mechanics. Some student-oriented critical editions of novels, such as the Oxford World's Classics, include scientific events among their chronologies.

From the point of view of bringing students to a critical understanding of science in its relationship to literature, the assumptions behind such a chronology would need to be critiqued, and the chronology supplemented accordingly. Firstly, one might ask, does the need to identify distinct dates privilege certain kinds of discovery over others? It is notable that relativity theory is easier to date than either quantum theory or Mendelian genetics. Secondly, one might ask whether the imperative to identify *innovations* distorts the representation of science. Darwinian evolutionary theory dates back to 1859, but was still influential in the era of modernism. Thirdly, in drawing up such a chronology, one needs to ask what we mean by science. Should developments in the philosophy of science be included? Should the chronology of the popularisation of science be given greater weight than the chronology of discovery? Both questions might alter the status of popular books that discuss scientific method, for example Karl Pearson's *The Grammar of Science* (1892) or A. S. Eddington's *The Nature of the Physical World*

(1928): neither contained original research, but Pearson's was an influential exposition of the emerging descriptionist school of epistemology, and Eddington's was an exposition of recent developments in the physical sciences, framed by speculations on their implications for ideas of natural knowledge.

If one sees the distinctive feature of the literary work as being its linguistic medium, one might argue that the truest chronology is one that identifies linguistic changes. The *Oxford English Dictionary*, especially in its online form, provides a valuable tool. It can be used to supplement an existing chronology: thus a dictionary search on 'relativity', 'uncertainty', 'gene', or 'genetics' reveals when their current scientific meanings came into the language, but also reveals their relations to their earlier senses. There are limitations, however. Although relativity theory's innovative approach to space and time is registered in the *OED*'s entry for 'space-time', its impact on the notion of 'simultaneity' does not warrant a separate entry; although the new physics emphasised the limitations of the observer, and therefore the distinction between the real and *apparent* simultaneity of two events, the concept of simultaneity in itself does not change. Again, popular expositions of relativity had much to say about starlight travelling through space, both in relation to special and general relativity, but a dictionary cannot register the local historical associations of 'light' and 'starlight'.

Science and modernist impersonality

Reading about early twentieth-century science can sharpen students' appreciation of the place of poetry and the role of the poet. The most readily tangible aspects of this topic relate to ideas of impersonality, tradition, and imagination. T. S. Eliot's 'Tradition and the Individual Talent' is widely anthologised, and may be supplemented with a range of contemporary texts. Eliot's analogy of the catalyst is the most explicit appropriation of science in the essay, but is ultimately less interesting to discuss than the larger themes of impersonality and tradition. As has been shown elsewhere, Eliot's essay draws upon an ongoing debate, conducted mostly in the pages of the *Athenaeum* in 1919, about the relation of science and art (Hutcheon, 1984: 52–5; Whitworth, 1996: 149–70). For the purposes of seminar discussion, it could also be framed by a debate of longer duration concerning the role of the imagination in science.

The longer debate could be taken to start with Karl Pearson's *The Grammar of Science*: in the introductory chapter, the shorter sections on 'Science and the Imagination', 'The Method of Science', and 'Science and the Aesthetic Judgment' are readable and stimulating; in the second chapter the sections on 'The Brain as a Central Telephone Exchange' presents a provocative analogy, as does, in the third chapter, 'The Mind as a Sorting Machine'. *The Grammar of Science* was an influential text: Eliot knew it through Josiah Royce's seminar in 1913–14 (Smith, 1963: 93, 107), and T. E. Hulme alludes to the sorting-machine analogy in his 'Cinders' (1994: 13). Alongside it one might use Henri Poincaré's 'The Selection of Facts', and his 'Hypotheses in Physics' (1905: 140–59, 1914: 15–24). The books in which they appear were read widely, both in French and in English translations, in Britain and America.

A significant early document on the literary side is Pound's 'A Few Don'ts for Imagists' (1913). There Pound insists that the poet is like the scientist, and that 'The scientist does not expect to be acclaimed as a great scientist until he has *discovered* something. He begins by learning what has been discovered already. He goes from that point onward' (1954: 6). Eliot essayed a similar idea of tradition in 1918:

> A poet, like a scientist, is contributing toward the organic development of a culture: it is just as absurd for him not to know the work of his predecessors or of men writing in other languages as it would for a biologist to be ignorant of Mendel or De Vries. (1918: 84)

It is worth noting that the idea of impersonality did not appear overnight, and that it had been rehearsed long before 'Tradition and the Individual Talent'.

However, the most valuable cluster of essays appears in the *Athenaeum* in 1919. The scientific context is provided by Einstein's theory of gravitation which, in early 1919, was untested, and so had the curious status of being a scientific theory which was bold in its revision of existing ideas, and elegant in its proposed solution, but which had not been put to experimental proof. The scientific journalist J. W. N. Sullivan wrote many general articles on the nature of science, advancing a position similar to that of Pearson and Poincaré; Sullivan was the deputy editor of the *Athenaeum* and someone well known within London literary circles (for biographical details, see Bradshaw, 1996). The most relevant essays are 'The Place of Science', 'The Justification of the Scientific Method', and 'Science and Personality'. To give a clearer indication of how these discussions relate to the emergence of Einstein's theories into the popular realm, one might turn to Sullivan's expository essays 'The Notion of Simultaneity' and 'The Equivalence Principle', which contain passing remarks on scientific 'genius' and on the beauty of Einstein's theories.

Sullivan's essays on scientific method provoked Roger Fry to write 'Art and Science'. Fry argues that Sullivan had allowed too much to aesthetic criteria, to the extent that he would accept a scientific theory which was elegant but which did not conform to the facts. A full discussion of the debate might also bring in the contemporaneous essays by I. A. Richards and H. W. Crundell. In 'Science and Personality' Sullivan does not engage as directly with Fry as Fry had with him, but he continues the debate about the distinction between science and art. Sullivan's main position is that science 'rests on the obliteration of personality' while art 'is an emphasis and expression of individuality'; the terminological shift from 'personality' to 'individuality' is worth noting and discussing. However, Sullivan is also aware that 'the cultivation of individualities is declining'. Eliot's essay draws on this theme, but questions the presumption that personality and individuality are equivalent: a poem can be both individual and impersonal. The relationship of Eliot's thinking to the context of writers in the *Athenaeum* emerges more directly in 'Modern Tendencies in Poetry', a lecture from October 1919, published in 1920; although at present the text is relatively difficult to obtain, it will become more readily accessible when an edition of Eliot's collected prose appears.

The questions one might put to these prose texts will differ according to the teaching context, but might touch on questions of motivation. Why did Pearson, Poincaré, and Sullivan find it valuable to think about the element of imagination in science? Were they hoping to adjust public attitudes to science, and, if so, why? (J. L. Heilbron's discussion of the institutional context of science is relevant here: though science was culturally powerful, its paymasters in government and the universities were predominantly humanist by background.) On the literary side, what was to be gained by Pound and Eliot in aligning poetry with science? What risks were there in associating poetry with science?

Ideas of poetic form

Considered in broad outline, the fragmentary nature of modernist poetic form seems to stand in some sort of connection to the science of the late nineteenth and early twentieth centuries. Historian of science Gerald Holton summarised the characteristic themes of modern physics as being those of 'disintegration, violence, and derangement': he highlights terms such as 'decay', 'displacement', and 'discontinuity' (Holton, 1973: 95). One might also look beyond the physical sciences: the Mendelian idea of discontinuities in evolution was alluded to approvingly by Hulme when he sought to justify his 'classical' attitude (1994: 61).

However, although the broad territory is promising, closer connections are more difficult to locate; in a pedagogical context, they can be still more difficult to open to productive discussion. The difficulty is that the analogies are almost always impressionistic. Some sort of imaginative effort is needed in order to reconstruct the connections between science and poetic form, but it is difficult to set the parameters for validity: one person's imaginative insight is another's flight of fancy. It is possible to turn these difficulties to advantage, and to discuss the problem at a metatextual level. Initially, one might study not modernist texts, but critical texts that have sought to identify connections between science and modernist form. What counts, for each critic, as a valid explanation or interpretation? What counts as valid evidence, and what counts as irrelevant? As an extreme instance, one might introduce Hugh Kenner's anachronistic association of *The Cantos* with chaos theory. What is to be gained by making anachronistic connections, and what is lost? By opening questions of method and validity, one provides the students with a vocabulary in which to defend their own interpretations.

From here one can turn to modernist texts about literary form that make specific reference to science. The vast majority of texts make scientific references only in passing, and to determine the larger implications of such references is no easy task. A single phrase, such as Eliot's description of Ben Jonson's characters as 'non-Euclidean', requires several contexts. It is productive to contextualise such texts with a more sweeping account of the change in the modernist zeitgeist; for example, Waldo Frank's 'For a Declaration of War', in which the non-Euclidean geometries are given a place in the emergent new culture. Frank's large picture may be used to frame T. S. Eliot's more cryptic and local remark about Jonson. Alongside Frank, one might introduce Poincaré's 'Space and Geometry' (Poincaré, 1905: 51–71); for the complete picture, one also needs to note the importance of 'the fourth dimension' in spiritualist discourse.

Science in the poem

If discussions of form seem too far removed from the linguistic texture of modernist poems, then it is possible to turn to poems where scientific ideas or scientific vocabulary form part of the poem itself. The best known, and the most readily available, are the neo-metaphysical poems of William Empson, but Empson's method of incorporating science into poetry was not the only one. There is an identifiable neo-metaphysical school, beginning with Herbert Read's poems in *The Mutations of the*

Phoenix (1923), and running through to Empson, Michael Roberts, and C. Day Lewis in *Transitional Poem* (1929) and *From Feathers to Iron* (1931). Outside this school there were others, notably Hugh MacDiarmid, using scientific vocabularies and ideas in distinctive ways.

The place of scientific vocabulary in T. S. Eliot's poetry provides a starting point. The scientific concepts are relatively straightforward, and so one can attend to the question of the effect of this vocabulary within each poem. What effect does 'etherised' have in the opening lines of 'The Love Song of J. Alfred Prufrock'? One might ask whether the sound of the technical term is unexpected – and how 'chloroformed' or 'anaesthetised' might sound different – as well as asking about the unexpectedness of the concept. Similarly, one might ask about the effects of 'phthisic' on the texture of 'Burbank with a Baedeker: Bleistein with a Cigar'. And what of 'staminate' and 'pistillate' in 'Mr Eliot's Sunday Morning Service': are their distinctiveness and oddity relatively unobtrusive amidst the poem's other rare words and its opening novel compound?

Poets are diverse in their responses to science and their means of appropriating it. Individual poems raise individual difficulties. However, there are some general questions that may be posed, which help to bring coherence to the field. Firstly, the *utility* of science to the poet: what did the scientific idea allow the poet to do or say that would not otherwise have been possible? Does the scientific idea merely provide a veneer of modernity, or is it doing more serious work? Secondly, is there a first-person speaking voice in the poem, and how authoritative is its presence in relation to science? In the tradition of metaphysical wit deriving from John Donne, the speaking subject dominates and subordinates science to his ends, but in other kinds of science poem, notably those of Michael Roberts, the personal voice has less presence, and the ideas dominate. Thirdly, the presence of other ideas and vocabularies from other intellectual domains: does science dominate, or do other domains also contribute? If so, do they challenge the authority of science, or coexist comfortably? Of course in some poems the answer may not be straightforward: the more open the form of the poem, the less certain the hierarchies of knowledge.

Fourthly, the *temporality* of scientific knowledge. Scientific knowledge is constantly in flux, and science is valued for its ability to produce new knowledge. Does the poem emphasise the relative novelty of its scientific ideas? For example, when in 'Invitation to Juno' Empson remarks that scientists had 'of late' demonstrated that two strips of heart culture could be joined, the novelty of the idea is foregrounded. Of course in many cases the novelty would have been understood without being explicitly tagged. By drawing on sciences in a period of rapid transition, poets were creating works that were at high risk of decay. The difficulty of assimilating science to poetry was remarked upon by Wordsworth in the 1802 Preface to the *Lyrical Ballads*, though Wordsworth was more optimistic than some of his modern successors. Writing in 1941, L. A. G. Strong objected to the language of modern poetry:

> I have felt, in reading certain poems of the last ten years, that many of the abstract terms used by the poets have no overtones. It is as if a painter suddenly stuck on his canvas a piece of actual material, cabbage leaf, corduroy, whatever it might be, instead of painting it. The patch, the abstract word snatched from contemporary life, has not been assimilated. (Day Lewis and Strong, 1941: xviii)

Strong appears strangely ignorant of the use of collage in modernist painting, but his image of a piece of organic material used in a painting conveniently summarises the issue of temporality in the modern science poem. Words, like cabbages, decay.

One approach to poems using scientific language would be to take the poet as the basic unit of study. The prose and poetry of Michael Roberts provide a rich field, particularly if one includes the poems in his first collection, *These Our Matins* (1930), which are not fully represented in the *Collected Poems* (1958). Roberts had studied chemistry at King's College, London, and mathematics at Trinity College, Cambridge, so had a deeper familiarity with science than many of his contemporaries. 'Rocks are Immutable' makes reference to the electron, to chlorophyll, and to the gamete; 'Schneider Cup' brings in the Doppler effect and an asymptotic curve (1930: 39, 49). 'The Goldfish' plays with a less specific vocabulary of time, contemporaneity, and a bounded existence; it suggests Einsteinian cosmological questions, but ends with a reference to the early modern scientist Telesio (1930: 50). Other early poems such as 'Rugged Dawn' deal with epistemological questions (1930: 42). The later poem 'Sirius B' takes as its central image a white dwarf, so dense that light has difficulty escaping its gravitational pull (1958: 65). Roberts' uncollected prose writings often touch upon poetry's relation to science: 'Credo: a Note on Poetry and Science' establishes some philosophical guidelines, drawing on Eddington; 'On Mechanical Hallelujahs' criticises Alfred Noyes' poems for being overawed by the scale of the universe.

However, there are other possible approaches. It is better for students to have understood a small core of scientific ideas clearly than to have been exposed to a wide range of ideas without reaching the point where they feel confident enough to discuss them. When time is limited it is more productive to limit attention to poems that engage with a particular domain of science, or, more specifically, poems that use particular elements of vocabulary. Practically speaking, the range of available poems for such exercises is greatly expanded if one makes comparison between modernist poems and those from earlier or later poetic movements. The most readily available anthology, Riordan and Turney's *A Quark for Mister Mark* (2000) takes a long historical perspective. These practical factors may be turned to pedagogical advantage. Using these resources, one may consider poets who engaged with modern science without being in any sense modernist, and thus may raise larger questions about the definition of modernism and its relation to modernity. For example, 'The Atom' by Thomas Thorneley (1855–1949) dates from the post-Rutherford era, but its mode of address would not have been out of place in the late eighteenth century (Riordan and Turney, 2000: 158). What might a truly modernist poem about the destructive potential of the atom have looked like, between 1910 and 1945? And how might it have been changed by the actual use of atomic weapons at Hiroshima and Nagasaki? Of course, we should not assume that modernism stands in a privileged relationship to scientific modernity: we might also ask whether there is anything to be said in favour of Thornley's poetics.

As well as allowing a contrast with the 'obviously' unmodernist, a broader historical perspective allows the possibility of questioning the modernism of poets closer to the main movement. Poets like Empson and Roberts learned much from the earlier generation of Eliot and Pound, but they do not have all the formal features usually associated with modernism. 'Late modernist' poets have frequently made use of scientific discourse: the introduction of poems in a late modernist mode allows questions about the unity of the speaking self to be raised.

One possible cluster of poems begins with the idea that light takes time to travel. The idea was a commonplace of expositions of relativity, and has become something of a commonplace in lyric poetry. The idea had been known for centuries, but, one might argue, speaks vividly to a modernity in which cognition cannot keep pace with perception, and in which reality, if it is known at all, is known only belatedly. It also contains a potential for sentimentality which needs to be carefully handled. W. J. Turner's 'In Time Like Glass' (c.1921) is one of the earliest poems on this theme; W. W. Gibson's relatively unknown 'Windows' and 'Chambers' groups also make intriguing reference to rays of light. The same phenomenon appears in Louis MacNeice's 'Star Gazer', in the concluding lines of Basil Bunting's *Briggflatts*, in Edwin Morgan's 'At the

Television Set', and in Richard Ryan's 'Galaxy'. One might also introduce Roberts' 'Sirius B', particularly in contrast to 'Galaxy', though Roberts' interest in the massiveness of the star is better placed alongside Empson's 'Letter I'. As well as enabling questions about modernism, the comparative perspective enables questions about different ways of handling the same idea; questions about how it changes depending on whether it is the central conceit, or part of a richer mixture.

'What kind of knowledge is poetry?' asked Heath-Stubbs and Salman in their anthology *Poems of Science* (1984: 36). A comprehensive answer to the question requires not only a comparison of poetry to narrative fiction and drama, but also a consideration of the relation of poetry to science. In the era of modernism both disciplines reflected on the knowability of reality and on the media through which we communicate our knowledge; both became increasingly specialised. To note these similarities is not to imply convergence. Poetry could not know quantifiable reality, nor was it a suitable medium for the formulation of testable predictions. But even the most impersonal poetry 'knows' something of the human scale of existence, especially when by contrast it invokes microscopic and astronomical scales. By appropriating discourses that seemingly ignore the human, modernist poetry could speak of aspects of existence that the idiom of conventionally humanistic poetry could not address. And by placing scientific idioms in unexpected contexts, it forces the reader to be active and, like all modernist poetry, forces the reader to recognise that knowledge is not given, but is produced.

Works cited and further reading

Albright, Daniel (1997) *Quantum Poetics: Yeats, Pound, Eliot, and the Science of Modernism.* Cambridge: Cambridge University Press.

Armstrong, Tim (2000) 'Poetry and Science', in Neil Roberts (ed.), *A Companion to Twentieth-Century Poetry in English.* Oxford: Blackwell, 76–88.

Bell, Ian F. A. (1981) *Critic as Scientist: the Modernist Poetics of Ezra Pound.* London: Methuen.

Bradbury, Malcolm and James McFarlane (eds) (1976) *Modernism, 1890–1930.* Harmondsworth: Penguin.

Bradshaw, David (1996) 'The Best of Companions: J. W. N. Sullivan, Aldous Huxley, and the New Physics', *Review of English Studies* 47: 188–206, 352–68.

Bunting, Basil (1994) *The Complete Poems.* Oxford: Oxford University Press.

Cain, Sarah (1999) 'The Metaphorical Field: Post-Newtonian Physics and Modernist Literature', *Cambridge Quarterly* 28: 46–64.

Crundell, H. W. (1919) 'Art and Science', *Athenaeum* (4 July): 566.

Day Lewis, C. (1957) *The Poet's Way of Knowledge.* Cambridge: Cambridge University Press.

Day Lewis, C. and L. A. G. Strong (1941) 'Introduction' to *A New Anthology of Modern Verse, 1920–1940*. London: Methuen, xiii–xiv.

Eliot, T. S. (1918) 'Contemporanea', *The Egoist* 5(6) (June/July 1918): 84.

—— (1920) 'Ben Jonson', *The Sacred Wood*. London: Methuen.

—— (1920) 'Modern Tendencies in Poetry', *Shama'a* 1: 9–18.

Empson, William (2000) *The Complete Poems*, ed. John Haffenden. London: Allen Lane.

Foster, Steven (1965) 'Relativity and *The Waste Land*: a Postulate', *Texas Studies in Literature and Language* 7: 77–95. [Far from satisfactory, but could be used as a test case in relation to methodology.]

Frank, Waldo (1924) 'For a Declaration of War', *Secession* 7: 5–14.

Friedman, Alan J. and Carol C. Donley (1985) *Einstein as Myth and Muse*. Cambridge: Cambridge University Press. [Gives brief coverage to a wide range of poets and novelists who drew upon Einstein.]

Fry, Roger (1919) 'Art and Science', *Athenaeum* (6 June): 434–5.

Gibson, W. W. (1919) 'Chambers', *Athenaeum* (11 July): 583.

—— (1920) 'Windows', *The Fortnightly Review* n.s. 113: 570–1.

Heath-Stubbs, John and Phillips Salman (eds) (1984) *Poems of Science*. Harmondsworth: Penguin.

Heilbron, J. L. (1982) 'Fin-de-Siècle Physics', in Carl Gustaf Bernhard, Elisabeth Crawford, and Per Sörbom (eds), *Science, Technology and Society in the Time of Alfred Nobel*. Nobel Symposium, 52. Oxford: Pergamon, 51–73.

Herbert, Christopher (2001) *Victorian Relativity*. Chicago: University of Chicago Press.

Holton, Gerald (1973) *Thematic Origins of Scientific Thought*. Cambridge, MA: Harvard University Press.

Hulme, T. E. (1994) *The Collected Writings of T. E. Hulme*, ed. Karen Csengeri. Oxford: Clarendon Press.

Hutcheon, Linda (1984) *Formalism and the Freudian Aesthetic*. Cambridge: Cambridge University Press.

Kayman, Martin A. (1986) *The Modernism of Ezra Pound: the Science of Poetry*. London: Macmillan.

Kenner, Hugh (1988) 'Self-Similarity, Fractals, Cantos', *ELH* 55: 721–9.

MacNeice, Louis (2007) 'Star Gazer', *Collected Poems*, ed. Peter MacDonald. London: Faber & Faber, 607–8.

Middleton, Peter (2007) 'Can Poetry Be Scientific?' in Philip Coleman (ed.), *On Literature and Science: Essays, Reflections, Provocations*. Dublin: Four Courts Press, 190–208.

Morgan, Edwin (1973) 'At the Television Set', *From Glasgow to Saturn*. Cheadle: Carcanet, 22.

Poincaré, Henri (1905) *Science and Hypothesis*. London: Walter Scott.

—— (1914) *Science and Method*, trans. F. Maitland. London: Thomas Nelson.

Pound, Ezra (1954) *Literary Essays of Ezra Pound*, ed. T. S. Eliot. London: Faber & Faber.

Richards, I. A. (1919) 'Art and Science', *Athenaeum* (27 June): 534–5.

—— (1926) *Science and Poetry*. London: Kegan Paul.

—— (1970) *Poetries and Sciences*. London: Routledge. [A significant revision of the 1926 book.]

Riordan, Maurice and Jon Turney (eds) (2000) *A Quark for Mister Mark: 101 Poems About Science*. London: Faber & Faber.

Roberts, Michael (1928) 'Credo: a Note on Poetry and Science', *Poetry Review* 19: 192–6.

—— (1928) 'On Mechanical Hallelujahs, or How Not To Do It', *Poetry Review* 19: 433–8.

—— (1930) *These Our Matins*. London: Elkin Mathews.

—— (1958) *Collected Poems*. London: Faber & Faber.

—— (1980) *Selected Poems and Prose*, ed. Frederick Grubb. Manchester: Carcanet. [Contains a concise bibliography of Roberts' uncollected prose writings.]

Rousseau, G. S. (1978) 'Literature and Science: the State of the Field', *Isis* 69: 583–91. [Outdated, but still an important introduction to the development of the field.]

Ryan, Richard (c.1973) 'Galaxy', in John Heath-Stubbs and Phillips Salman (eds), *Poems of Science*. Harmondsworth: Penguin, 314–15.

Smith, Grover (ed.) (1963) *Josiah Royce's Seminar, 1913–1914*. New Brunswick: Rutgers University Press.

Sullivan, J. W. N. (1919) 'The Place of Science', *Athenaeum* (11 April): 176.

—— (1919) 'The Justification of the Scientific Method', *Athenaeum* (2 May): 275.

—— (1919) 'The Notion of Simultaneity', *Athenaeum* (23 May): 369.

—— (1919) 'The Equivalence Principle', *Athenaeum* (6 June): 433.

—— (1919) 'Science and Personality', *Athenaeum* (18 July): 624.

—— (1923) 'The Interest of Science', *Aspects of Science*. London: Cobden-Sanderson, 9–22. [Incorporates 'The Place of Science' and 'Justification'.]

Turner, W. J. (1921) 'In Time Like Glass', *In Time Like Glass*. London: Sidgwick & Jackson, 1.

Whitworth, Michael H. (1996) *'Pièces d'identité*: T. S. Eliot, J. W. N. Sullivan and Poetic Impersonality', *English Literature in Transition* 39: 149–70.

—— (2001) *Einstein's Wake: Relativity, Metaphor, and Modernist Literature*. Oxford: Oxford University Press.

4
'The New Comes Forward': Anglo-American Modernist Women Poets

Harriet Tarlo

Women's poetry poses a number of additional challenges to the teacher and the student on top of the already demanding job of bringing modernism into the lecture or seminar room. When asked which modernist poets they know, two names will usually be forthcoming (certainly from British students), that of T. S. Eliot and Ezra Pound. It is remarkable that this is still the case, particularly as poets such as H.D. (Hilda Doolittle) and Gertrude Stein shared the international modernist stage in their time. They, like Pound and Eliot, travelled from America to Europe before the First World War where Stein settled in Paris, surrounded by her renowned salon of modernist painters, while H.D., in London, became a key figure in the formation of Imagism (arguably the mother of Anglo-American poetry). Meanwhile British-born Mina Loy moved between the modernist centres of activity (Paris, Florence, and New York) while Marianne Moore, after a brief flurry of travel, remained resolutely at home in New York. These four women are the key first-generation Anglo-American women poets on whom I shall concentrate in this chapter.[1] Many students do not know that experimentation in poetry has continued unceasingly to this day; this essay ends with a discussion of contemporary women poets in the modernist tradition.

Students will be fascinated by the lives of the major modernists and can find riveting accounts of them.[2] It is important, however, to sound a note of caution about over-emphasis on biography. Women writers from Sappho to Plath have been 'prisoners of biography' and modernist women writers are no exception to this (Altman, 1992: 39). Carolyn Burke, herself a celebrated biographer of Mina Loy, stressed the importance of reading the work beyond the biographical and, in particular, avoiding the equation of the lyric 'I' with the author herself in favour of seeking out the 'more impersonal or nonpersonal' voices in women's poetry (Burke, 1985: 132). One element of modernist women's writing lives which *is* worth drawing attention to is the degree to which they persevered with their writing long term, often without publication or critical notice to reward them.[3] Twenty-first-century students, living in a world in which art is increasingly commodified, are impressed by this commitment to revolutionary forms, language, and themes.

Modernist canons and masculinist currents

The fact that students may not have heard of any of these poets is significant and necessitates some discussion of canons and their formation. Traditionally, the modernist writer is expected to conform to three key classifications: writing between c.1890 and 1930, breaking with previous literary conventions to create avant-garde forms, and engaging with modernity in terms of ideas, subject matter, and language. Earlier critical books on modernism do not add, *oh and they should also be male*, but, retrospectively we can see that this was in fact an implicit or, being kinder, an unconscious factor in the selection of canonical modernist writers. The dominance of literary criticism by male academics during the first half of the twentieth century, when 'modernism' was being established, is the most obvious factor.

It could be argued of course that the writers I have mentioned above form a new canon of their own, a canon created quite recently, between the 1980s and the present day, by a highly articulate and dedicated generation of scholars. In the early days, this group consisted, in the main, of American feminist critics such as Rachel Blau DuPlessis, Marianne Dekoven, Margaret Dickie, Susan Stanford Friedman, and Bonnie Kime Scott. They were engaged, not only in producing critical work about these writers, but also in printing, reprinting, and disseminating their work. They have brought to prominence the work of long-neglected writers, but even within this short time, there have been important challenges to this new canon. Perhaps the most significant and welcome has been the reclamation of the women poets of the Harlem Renaissance and of Negritude, two interrelated modernist movements based in New York and Paris (see Carole Sweeney's essay in this volume for further discussion of this).

Certainly, it is important to stress to students that, a hundred years since its inception, the hard edges of modernism, who is in and who is out, are constantly being debated. It gives them an insight into the formation of literary movements, with all the ideological and political debates this entails, as well as making modernism an exciting and

'happening' subject to study. As a teacher of modernism, I find it important to develop my own working definition of modernism if only to
prevent my students becoming totally confused. This does tend to come
down to an argument over what degree of emphasis you place on form
and what degree on content. While I consider formal experimentation
to be the key factor in defining a text as modernist, I also recognise
that gender, as a social construct, cannot be considered without examining modernist writers' engagement with the world around them. For
instance, critics such as Shari Benstock (1987: 26), Janet Wolff (1990:
56), and Angela K. Smith (2000) have argued that the importance of the
First World War to modernism has contributed to the marginalisation of
women writers.[4] Their experience of war is always regarded as secondary,
the masculine bond through suffering in the trenches not being part of
their war experience. This highlights the fact that, despite the emphasis on aesthetics within modernism, the modernist canon is also partly
defined by what is seen as suitable content or at least the reflection of
certain experiences in modern life. Yet, it is not as if women writers did
not write about war, as Trudi Tate's (1998) and Angela Smith's (2000)
scholarship of recovery has shown. When it comes to modernist poetry,
there is a notable example of this in the relative fates of T. S. Eliot's and
H.D.'s war epics. Whereas generations of school and university students
have battled their way through T. S. Eliot's *The Waste Land*, H.D.'s Second
World War epic, *Trilogy*, has only recently become a set text in universities. For many years, this poem was left to the initiates, the largely
female readership of poets and feminists, who championed H.D.'s cause.
The views of the woman poet on war were clearly not seen as relevant.
On the other hand, Stein's rejection of classical and masculine materials
in favour of the everyday objects of the domestic and material world was
equally baffling to male critics for many years.

The male dominance of modernism is not of course solely attributable
to the subsequent development of literary criticism. Other deeper reasons can be traced back to the roots of modernism itself, in particular
the modernist male artists' association of women with the 'mass culture'
that they defined themselves against. The language of the modernist
manifesto is evidence of the masculine force of this 'antagonism', to
invoke Poggioli's term. Working with manifestos in the seminar room
can establish a sense of this. The first task is to create a picture for students of the intensity of these meetings of small groups of men, and the
occasional woman, shaping their convictions into dictatorial announce-
ments to the world. Then, drawing on the resources of Kolocotroni
et al.'s *Modernism: an Anthology of Sources and Documents* (1998), small

groups of students can each be presented with a key modernist manifesto. I have used Futurist, Imagist, Dada, Surrealist, and Vorticist manifestos in the past. To help students access their sometimes alienating language try asking each group to present their own manifesto to the rest of the class in a semi-dramatised form, as if in an attempt to convince them of their perspective. This also involves selecting key passages which exemplify the manifesto as a whole and is therefore a useful close read-ing exercise which does really encourage them to unpick the language and meaning (or, in some cases, lack of meaning) in the manifesto. In some, evident misogyny is written into the actual manifesto statements such as Marinetti's notorious ninth declaration from the 'Manifesto of Futurism':

> 9. *We will glorify war* – the world's only hygiene – militarism, patri-otism, the destructive gesture of freedom-bringers, beautiful ideas worth dying for, *and scorn for woman*. (Kolocotroni et al., 1998: 251)

Perhaps more challenging, and particularly relevant to the Anglo-American scene, is 'Long Live the Vortex', the manifesto of Vorticism, the exclusively male movement co-founded by Ezra Pound after he left Imagism to its fate as 'Amygism' (a characteristic slur on Amy Lowell). From the first declaration, 'Long live the great art vortex that has sprung up in the centre of this town!', this manifesto is characterised by a phallic thrusting or, to use its own language, a 'crude energy flowing through us' (Kolocotroni et al., 1998: 291). The association of biological or sexual energy with the new science of electricity is characteristic of modernist discourse, as Armstrong has shown, and is linked to the idea of the body as a machine.[5] The Vorticist manifesto is also peppered with numerous digs against the Futurists reminiscent of a playground fight between two boys who know they are disturbingly similar. For the student groups studying these texts, it is the close analysis of tone, central metaphors, and language that soon reveals what Andreas Huyssen has called 'the powerful masculinist and misogynist current within the trajectory of Modernism' (Huyssen, 1988: 49).

Modernism, feminism, and beyond

To the contemporary student, feminism seems to be a far more divisive concept than when I took my undergraduate degree in the 1980s. Now I find that some students take a strong line 'for' or 'against' feminism and that to others it is just a rather outdated ideology that their lecturers seem strangely attached to. The study of modernist women's poetry forces them to engage a little more deeply with feminist ideologies and critical readings. Some historical research, particularly on fin-de-siècle feminism, is useful in helping them to appreciate how deeply the lives of women modernists were affected by their experience of living and writing at a revolutionary time for women in the private and public spheres.[6] It can also be helpful to ask students to engage in a little family research into the lives of their own grandmothers and great-grandmothers and how these compare with those of their mothers and indeed their own lives. Once they realise that these poets were part of the era of the 'New Woman' they can understand why women's roles, and in some cases rights, were of such significance to modernist writers.

Were the female modernists feminists? It is not surprising to find that, in the face of masculinist modernism, women modernists did not, for the most part, stride onto the scene declaiming their sex with pride and asserting their defiance of patriarchy These poets have awkward histories, often spending years detaching themselves from their male mentors and their manifestos. H.D., for instance, needed to throw over the model of perfect Imagist in order to write her own (arguably) feminist epics. It could be an interesting research project for groups of students to research and prepare seminar presentations on the complex and ambivalent relationship of women writers to modernist movements: Leonora Carrington's to Surrealism, for instance, or Lorine Niedecker's to Objectivism.

However, it is Mina Loy's feminist highjacking of the polemical techniques of the manifesto that remains the most striking example of rebellion against masculinist modernism and the wider patriarchal culture. Loy was originally excited by Italian Futurism, but was to become disenchanted by the movement's fascism and misogyny. Her first published work, 'Aphorisms on Futurism', already reveals ambivalence towards the movement and to the manifesto form. For instance, the exclusive 'we' of Marinetti's manifesto has been replaced with 'you', an inclusive invitation to Loy's readers to abandon the old bourgeois ways or marvellously termed 'Knick-knacks' (Loy, 1985: 272–3). She is far more concerned with the internal, psychological 'crisis in consciousness' than interventions on the material, external world which would see Marinetti 'destroy(ing)' museums, libraries and feminism in favour of racing cars, factories, and ultimately war (Loy, 1985: 273; Kolocotroni et al., 1998: 251). In subsequent works, she offers 'a critique of Futurism's machine culture, seeing the body-machine coupling as fetishism' (Armstrong, 1998: 114).

Loy's 'Feminist Manifesto' of 1914 is one of the very few interventions into manifesto writing from a woman poet. Beginning with the definitive statement that 'the Feminist Movement as instituted at present is inadequate', Loy goes on to address women directly about the need to look deeper than issues such as the right to work in the public sphere. New Woman politics is not enough for Loy as she takes up rhetorical arms against the association of women with bourgeois capitalism and its ideals. Her interest in the psychological sphere is evident as she calls on women to 'WRENCH' themselves out of their current choices: 'Parasitism, Prostitution, or Negation' (Loy, 1985: 269). Loy's radicalism extends to the realm of sexual morality and marriage as she makes such shocking demands as to call for 'the *unconditional* surgical *destruction of virginity* throughout the female population at puberty' and that 'Woman must destroy in herself the desire to be loved' (270–5).[7] I find the study of Loy's manifesto in class always provokes discussion and, often, admiration for her clear-sighted analysis of, in particular, 'the sexual dependence' and 'parasitism' of heterosexual relationships. Sometimes students need to be reminded that her manifesto is close to a hundred years old. Have all the issues raised been resolved to contemporary young women's satisfaction?

Another excellent example of a woman poet's explicit intervention into gender politics is Marianne Moore's tortuous, yet entertainingly satirical, poem, 'Marriage' (Moore, 1982: 62–70). It is necessary to make full use of Moore's notes, in which she identifies her sources for the network of quotations about women, men, and marriage that weave this poem together. For this reason, this is a fine poem for fairly experienced students to work through in small groups, perhaps selecting their favourite lines and most challenging passages to share with the wider class. The 'most challenging' part is important as it is all too easy to home in on epigrammatic feminist favourites such as the reference to The Fall as 'that invaluable accident / exonerating Adam' (63) or the acerbic statement, 'experience attests / that men have power / and sometimes one is made to feel it' (67). There is so much more to enjoy here. Yet 'tortuous' remains an appropriate epithet, partly in reference to the complexity of philosophical thought Moore brings to the problem of the institution of marriage, but also to the lengthy sentences, riddled with complex punctuation, which students might eventually recognise as an embodiment of the difficulty of marriage itself or even of thinking about it at all![8] There's also a pleasing little example of a female modernist taking on the misogyny of a male modernist in Moore's lines around Ezra Pound's statement that 'A wife is a coffin' (67). The line appears in the latter part

of the poem in which the heat of the debate accelerates as Moore alter-
nates 'She says …' and 'He says …' statements in a mock debate or war
of the sexes. This can be very funny, especially when read aloud in male
and female voices. However, after over eight pages of sentences spanning
up to twenty lines and only one short inset stanza to break up the flow,
we are weary of 'Marriage', as surely and characteristically wittily, Moore
intended when she created this remorseless form for the poem.

The pieces discussed above jump out as modernist feminist poems but
it is important to stress that not all modernist poetry by women can
be defined as feminist, nor of course does it confine itself to 'women's
issues'. There are examples of modernist poems that do tackle specifically female experiences in a strikingly direct *and* formally experimental
way, such as Loy's 'Parturition', one of the first ever poetic treatments
of the physical experience of childbirth. As Jane Dowson has suggested,
however, 'negotiation with stereotyped femininity' was more likely to be
'by denial, rejection, avoidance, parody or transgressive representations'
(Dowson, 2002: 2). Ultimately it is too confining to the poets and their
work to emphasise feminine or feminist subject matter above all else, in
particular above formal experimentation.

Contemporary readings and feminist theories

Retreating then from solely thematic readings, we find that the majority of the poems written by women poets are complex, subtle, and
often dark pieces that require reading strategies that do not attempt
to simplify what is intentionally convoluted or oblique. A gendered
reading of modernist poetry can avoid both the biographical and the thematic approach while remaining interested in how ideas about gender
are conveyed in the *form and language* of the work. It is thus particularly open to contemporary theoretical readings. Many of these readings
prove themselves to be inflected by the ideas associated with the psychoanalytical theories of sexual difference, proposed by writers such as
Luce Irigaray and Julia Kristeva. Such feminist theory is used to read
modernist texts, invoking, for instance, theories associated with fluid,
metonymic writing or abjection. However, the relationship between this
theoretical work and modernism is more complex than this. Some critics have suggested that the avant-garde nature of modernism was such
that it allowed women writers to find ways of writing which had never
been seen before and to produce a female form of writing that is an
ur-text if you like for the idea of *écriture féminine* or writing the body
(see Wolff, 1990 and Jardine, 1986). It is also possible to read modernist

women writers as anticipating the work of Kristeva and Irigaray through their own theories of gender and writing. It is easy for these ideas to become confused in student thinking and writing so they need careful differentiation.

The idea of modernist writers as anticipators of *écriture féminine* is rooted in their interest in Freudian ideas about psychology. All the poets I am discussing here shared this interest. Stein was a student of psychology before she left Pennsylvania. H.D. was analysed by Freud and her *Tribute to Freud* is a deeply ambivalent text worth introducing students to. Mina Loy also met Freud in Vienna and reacted strongly to his ideas, as Tuma has documented. It was often their resistance to Freudian ideas about sexual difference and the workings of the unconscious that caused women poets to develop their own theories. Original, often private, writings tell us much, and this material is now available to students in Bonnie Kime Scott's *Gender of Modernism* anthology (1990). Scott presents a very useful selection of letters, reviews, and essays from female and some male modernists which has much relevance to gender theories current among writers of the time. It is particularly interesting to read H.D.'s writing about levels of consciousness in *Notes on Thought and Vision* alongside Pound's recurring image of the female as 'chaos / An octopus / A biological process' (Bush in Scott, 1990: 353–9). While H.D. struggles to dispel dualistic thinking in which mind and body are separated, Pound confirms this thinking, allying the feminine firmly to the body and the masculine to the mind.

Much of the thinking about gender and consciousness that these woman poets were engaged in led them to ask the same question that their counterparts in fictional writing (Woolf, Richardson, Mansfield, and Rhys) were asking: 'Is there a female form of writing?' The psychological origins of writing in language acquisition and the gendered inflection of this are of course at the heart of feminine *écriture*. Here Stein is the great precursor. She associated certain grammatical structures with patriarchal authority. Her passionate engagement with grammar is demonstrated in this sentence on the sentence from *Tender Buttons*: 'A sentence of a vagueness that is violence is authority and a mission and stumbling and also certainly a prison.' In all her work, Stein seeks another sentence, a sentence seen by critics such as Stimpson (1986) and Rehling (1996) as a fluid and innovative form of writing the body that resists hierarchical language structures at all costs.

It is important for students to realise that reading modernist work is not a decoding exercise in which the poem is reduced to a unitary meaning, one based in psychoanalytical theory or a more materialist alternative.

Perhaps some of the most fascinating poems to read in this light are the studiously ungendered pieces to be found within H.D.'s early collections and the subtle, restrained poems of Marianne Moore.

H.D.'s early poems are not just useful as exemplars of the Imagist aesthetic. The elemental dynamics, the enigmatic questions, and the mysterious ungendered pronouns can open up numerous interpretations of these liminal landscapes. 'The Pool' provides a tiny example:

> Are you alive?
> I touch you.
> You quiver like a sea-fish.
> I cover you with my net.
> What are you – banded one? (H.D., 1984: 56)

We can begin with questions. Who does the speaker address? The pool, a metaphor for the other, or a Narcissus-like image of the self within the pool? What are the dynamics of power in this poem? Are they sinister, erotic, or both? Does the reader assume a masculine or feminine identity for either pronoun here? If so, why? What is the band referred to? The borders of the pool? The net? Could this be an oblique reference to a wedding band? Working outwards from 'The Pool', there is a whole group of poems, most from the aptly named 'Sea Garden' volume, to explore in similar terms. 'Sea-Rose', 'Sea-Lily', 'Sea-Gods', 'Sea Poppies', 'Sheltered Garden', 'Garden', 'Sea Iris', and 'Hermes of the Ways', are longer pieces which, read together, set up oppositions between the wild coast and the stifling garden which we can relate to the choices faced by women in this period. In particular, H.D.'s battered yet resilient flowers resist the image of the female muse or lover as passive object of beauty so often encountered in male poetry. The liminal spaces set up in the sea-poems and the desire to exist in the realms of sea *and* land, can be related to her anti-binarism and her interest in more mobile, polymorphous models of gender and sexuality. H.D's cleanly cut language and her irregular yet deeply rhythmic use of repetition and assonance bears detailed technical analysis. It can also be seen as a simultaneous fulfilment of and resistance to the Imagist aesthetic as propounded by Hulme, Pound, and others.

The image of the flower is particularly important in these poems and can be seen as significant throughout women's modernist poetry. The rose, historic emblem of femininity in lyric poetry, features in all the major women modernist poets' work. One might devote a whole seminar session to rose poems beginning with Stein's 'a rose is a rose is a rose', a phrase recurring in eight of her texts, and going on to consider

H.D.'s 'Sea-Rose', Loy's 'English Rose', and Moore's 'Roses Only'. A session such as this in which a number of writers' work is considered together is usefully placed after the students have studied the poets as individual writers. It brings their common concerns as women poets together whilst allowing students to refine their sense of poets' distinctive styles. Arguably, Loy satirises the rose, while Cristanne Miller's reading of Moore's roses might also apply to H.D.: 'wild, prickly, and ethical rather than iconic, aesthetic, and elite' (Miller, 1995: 115). As Stein herself argued, she brought the rose back to life with her famous 'rose is a rose is a rose': 'I think that in that line the rose is red for the first time in English poetry for a hundred years.'[9] I would argue that Stein is also covertly referring to her radically new use of the rose as a lesbian love signet here.[10]

The modernist long poem

Many of the modernist women poets wrote long poems and it is important to consider these alongside the shorter lyrics which have often represented them in the past, not least because the neo-epic is a quintessential part of the modernist project. Modernist women poets 'take on the epic as cultural symbol' of nationhood and masculinity whilst also seeking their own aesthetic, political, or philosophical voice (Friedman, 1990; Frost, 2003: 36–7). Mina Loy's 'Anglo-Mongrels and the Rose' (which appeared in sections in little magazines in 1923–5, but was not published in full until 1982) has been described as 'a strange combination of satire, didactic commentary, and lyrical mysticism', as well as an 'autobiography and automythology' (Tuma, 1998: 145). It is significant that Loy's alter-ego in 'Anglo-Mongrels' is named 'Ova' and that references to the womb occur at the very start and closing of the sequence. Several critics have drawn attention to the emphasis on the maternal body within Loy's work, as DuPlessis succinctly puts it: 'Maternalist thinking meets free love' (DuPlessis, 1998: 45–74; Kinnahan, 1994: 43–74). As in her (at the time) infamous 'Love Songs to Johannes', Loy's 'Anglo-Mongrels and the Rose' is open about the body, stripping back and satirising dress as a disguise for 'Man that is born of woman'.[11] It is now possible to see how this central theme of the maternal was represented materially in Loy's 'constructions', such as 'Communal Cot', 'Maternity', and 'Teasing a Butterfly'.[12] This is a valuable addition to learning for students attempting ambitious texts. Loy's childbirth, womb, and parenting references are ambivalent, yet there is no doubt that in taking the womb as her central metaphor for creation she presents an alternative or 'opposed aesthetic' to the masculinist modernist metaphor of the seminal machine.

There are some modernist long poems which are best digested whole. It is important with these poems to give students some sense of the overall shape of the piece they are about to embark upon so that, at first reading, they can grasp the rhythm and sweep of the poem without drowning in minutiae. This can only be achieved through reading aloud, preferably in the seminar group. Time may be a problem here, but, if you don't have it, you can encourage students to set up an extra-curricular group in order to read the poem together. Before such a reading session, I would usually give a brief lecture on the poet and text in context: 30–40 minutes or so of condensed summary of biography and critical views. The key here is not to capture the poem too tightly in any one critical net, but simply to suggest ways in which it has been read, for example H.D.'s *Trilogy* as a feminist pacifist work of spiritual reclamation or Stein's *Lifting Belly* as a piece of lesbian erotic poetry. Context is important too: without knowing that Stein wrote *Lifting Belly* in France during the First World War and that H.D. wrote *Trilogy* during the London blitz of the Second World War, much might be missed, not least a discussion of why the war appears to feature so little in Stein's poem, a question that is often raised by students who are used to studying officially canonised 'war poetry'.

Whereas there is abundant critical material on H.D.'s long poems and a whole volume forthcoming on teaching her work, teaching Stein is still seen as a risky endeavour, so I shall say a little more about teaching *Lifting Belly* (written around 1915, but not published until 1957). This text is a particularly entertaining and revealing piece to read aloud, especially when divided into two parts as if it is a dialogue. It needs to be made clear of course that Stein did not formally present her poem as a dialogue, but also that she was, in this period, moving into playwriting. Read aloud, the text comes alive in all its rich eroticism, its surreal humour emerges, the puns and homonyms leap out into the room and the extraordinary effects of Stein's use of repetition are actually felt rather than simply discussed. Students may perceive this as comic, meaningless, or mystical (rather as a mantra). It's important to allow for all these perceptions (critical views are just as diverse) whilst also guiding them to think about what Stein is saying about *language* itself by endlessly repeating a present tense, but non-definitive phrase, such as 'lifting belly' in every line of her poem. Sometimes, with discussions of experimental writing of all kinds, I find it useful to ask very literal, simple questions, such as 'What do you think "lifting belly" is? What does it represent, if anything?' Usually, the ensuing discussion will lead to a discussion of Stein's linguistic play, the encoded lesbian eroticism and the celebration of the domestic sphere (also evident in *Tender Buttons*, a possible companion teaching text). When read as a dialogue, the play on titles (mr, misses, sir, 'Lifting belly is amiss') and references to husband and wife roles or dominance and submission between lovers ('Darling wifie is so good / Little husband would') emerges clearly. Rehling offers a convincing reading of the sexual dynamics in *Lifting Belly* as a parody of gender roles, a demonstration of sexual identity as performance rather than as innate (1996: 85).

Contemporary poets in the modernist tradition

Students need not limit themselves to considering poetry written between 1910 and 1950. As this volume recognises, it is important for students of modernism to realise that the experimental tradition continues within Anglo-American poetry. For many contemporary experimental women poets it was necessary to rediscover their modernist predecessors in order to establish a 'feminist avant-garde', to use Elisabeth Frost's terminology or a 'poetics of the feminine', to employ Linda Kinnahan's term. Read together, Frost's and Kinnahan's ground-breaking volumes trace the modernist heritage down from Stein and Loy, through the transitional figure of Denise Levertov to contemporary writers such as Kathleen Fraser, Susan Howe, and Harryette Mullen.[13] Perhaps more immediately exciting reading for students are the forthright yet radical essays of the poet and feminist academic, Rachel Blau DuPlessis. In *The Pink Guitar* and *Blue Studios* DuPlessis writes about women modernists and contemporaries as well as about her own journey as one of the foremost innovative poets in the US. As shorter pieces of writing, they are more accessible to students than, in particular, the lengthy extended arguments put forward in Kinnahan's book and they also provide examples of radically different approaches to the critical essay for female students who are constrained by the traditional essay form and looking for alternatives.

Turning to the poetry itself, Elisabeth Frost's and Cynthia Hogue's recent anthology, *Innovative Women Poets: an Anthology of Contemporary Poetry and Interviews* (2006), is a useful resource featuring fourteen key contemporary American poets including Mei-Mei Berssenbrugge, Rachel Blau DuPlessis, Harryette Mullen, and Leslie Scalapino, to name four I would recommend for student study. This anthology is also important for its inclusion of African-American work in the feminist avant-garde and performance spheres, also discussed by Frost in her critical volume. Frost and Hogue's anthology could be supplemented with Maggie

O'Sullivan's *Out of Everywhere: Linguistically Innovative Poetry by Women in North America and the UK* (1996) as it is important to introduce students to contemporary British women poets who do not receive as much attention as their American counterparts. O'Sullivan herself is one of the most exciting of these and other notables (again, to select four poets for students to begin with) include Caroline Bergvall, Geraldine Monk, Frances Presley, and Denise Riley.[14]

An exemplary contemporary poet to discuss in pedagogical terms would be the American poet, Kathleen Fraser. Like DuPlessis, Fraser is intimately connected to her modernist foremothers and has discussed the female avant-garde tradition in her readable and autobiographical essays, *Translating the Unspeakable: Poetry and the Innovative Necessity* (2000). Here, she also talks about her own powerful need for female predecessors, a need which caused her, in 1983, to found the journal *HOW(ever)*, a forum for publishing and discussing the feminist avant-garde. *HOW(ever)* has a second incarnation as the internet journal, *How2*, where students can also browse the archives of *HOW(ever)*. This is an invaluable electronic resource of twenty-five years of critical and creative responses to innovative poetry by women in the modernist tradition. For students whose degree involves both the study of modernism and of creative writing, it can draw their critical and creative work together, acting as an inspiration for their own experimentations.

Fraser is a quintessential experimenter whose work has metamorphosed through many phases, each more intriguing than the last. There is a fine selected edition of her poems available, *il cuore: the heart* (1997), which enables readers to trace these phases through from her experimentations with lyric and sonnet to her mid-career prose-poems and finally her recent open form sequences. Easily accessible interviews are a very useful way to explore the work of contemporary writers in this media age. In this case, the internet journal *Cauldron and Net* includes Robert Glück's (2002) interview with Fraser in which she talks about her development as a writer and intersperses this discussion with poems chosen to illustrate her point. Using a transcript of this interview in class is like having Fraser there with you to introduce her own poetry.

This interview also provides perhaps the most succinct description of Fraser's attraction to the 'flaw'. She writes about how teaching writing helped her recognise the importance of 'field composition' (aka open form writing) to the exploration of 'the erased or unacknowledged/ unofficial atonalities & arhythmic imperfections that flooded [the] daily lives' of her students as well as herself. It was thus that the 'psycho/physical conditions of stammer, error, uncertainty and ambivalence began to strike me as primary states to be rendered in poetic diction', she notes. It is useful to set this description alongside an extract from one of the 'narratives' in *Each Next*:

(She was 'in a fury' and she wept in spite of herself. His letter told the usual stories in all the old ways. She swallowed them whole. Then came the nausea. She wanted a 'flow' she thought, but in the translation it was corrected, displacing the *o* and substituting *a*. She could give herself to an accident. She was looking out the window.) (Fraser, 1997: 39)[15]

Many avenues of discussion are opened up by considering this passage and the wider piece alongside Glück's interview: the interplay between the autobiographical and the poetic; the difference the third person makes in this; the sense of language as a shifting act of translation; the use of puns in the feminine avant-garde tradition and, above all, perhaps, the idea that this flawed rather than flowing work might be an alternative to the 'usual stories' told by male poets. Not just stories, but style too perhaps. Gregory notes that Fraser's work is rooted in 'desire, pleasure, emotional difficulty, affection, sensuous response' and that the title of her selected, *il cuore: the heart* distances her from 'conceptually-driven poetic practices' (16–17). Significantly in Fraser's poetry, as in DuPlessis', we find a fascination with the psychoanalytical theories of sexual difference first introduced to the Anglo-American academic community in the early 1980s as they were establishing their careers. In particular they, like their modernist predecessors, sought a new female form of language linked to the body.

As her predecessors did, Fraser turned to the longer poetic sequence to explore these and other ideas in new forms. In her highly regarded poetic sequences from *when new time folds up* (1993) she creates palimpsestic pieces with considerable historical depth. These are reminiscent of H.D.'s work of the 1940s and 1950s, a link Fraser acknowledges.[16] For Fraser, as she explains in her essay on the poetic line, 'the *palimpsest*: writing layered into the before and after of other writing' is crucial to the 'difference' of women's writing and may even unearth 'a spiritual and erotic set of valuing essentially ignored by the dominant culture' (Fraser, 2000: 144–5). Critics have argued that palimpsestic reading strategies are required for this work (Hogue, 2000: 177; Kinnahan, 1994: 215). This is a challenge to the tutor who must somehow create a 'female collective consciousness' (Fraser, 2000: 145) in which students are empowered to read this work. Reading relevant critical and autobiographical work alongside the poetry texts is one way to achieve this. It is fruitful for instance to read Fraser's poetic sequence, 'Etruscan Pages', alongside DuPlessis' famous essay, 'For the Etruscans'. Both poets draw on a fragmented and alternative female tradition which DuPlessis makes explicit through reference to Dickinson, Woolf, H.D., Richardson, Stein, Moore, Loy, Nin, Wittig, and Lessing, as well as numerous feminist thinkers. Both pieces use the image of the lost language and civilisation of the Etruscans in order to mourn and explore (among other losses) the idea of a lost language of women.

As this chapter has shown, contemporary women poets have done much to recreate that lost language, bringing marginal women poets back into the modernist canon as well as consolidating an alternative tradition in women's poetry. More importantly, the modernist and contemporary poets discussed here have, over the last hundred years, produced writing that shimmers with formal innovation, satiric wit, and intelligent reflection on gender, identity, and the body in the private and public spheres. To quote from the first line of Kathleen Fraser's superb sequence, 'WING': 'The New comes forward in its edges in order to be itself' (184).

Notes

1. There were of course many other women involved in the modernist enterprise as editors, artists, novelists, and poets; all contributed to the business of creating new forms of twentieth-century art and living new forms of twentieth-century life. See Miller (2007: 68–71) for a useful summary of this activity and Scott (1990) and Dowson (2002) for more detailed discussion of these groups and their alliances. Of particular significance, if you wish to expand your primary texts, are Djuna Barnes, another Paris-based American more famed for her prose than her poetry, and Lorine Niedecker (born in the twentieth century, she came along a little too late to be seen as first generation).
2. See the works cited below, especially Benstock (1987).
3. Marianne Moore is the exception here. Often regarded as the token female modernist, many critics ascribe her continued popularity to her reticence on any subject which might be linked to her personal gendered life.
4. Although she does not discuss poetry, Angela K. Smith's *The Second Battlefield* is a useful text for understanding women's experience of war and also has a section on H.D.'s novel, *Bid Me to Live*, which may help students studying her poetry.
5. It is notable that all the examples Armstrong quotes are male modernist texts, though he does not discuss the gendered implications of this at this point (1998: 19). There is some interesting reflection, however, later in his study on Remy de Gourmont's idea of the male organ as prosthesis and hence masculinity as a cultural extension of the feminine (89). Pound, H.D., and Eliot

were all interested in de Gourmont and Armstrong could therefore be useful for those teaching modernism in the context of gender studies.

6. DeKoven (1999) provides a very useful summary of the transition between nineteenth- and twentieth-century ideas about gender in relation to women writers whilst Ledger (1997) supplies more detailed analysis.

7. Loy's reclamation of the aggressive lingo of the manifesto is reminiscent of the contemporary poet June Jordan's poems reclaiming the aggressive language of rap.

8. See Lakritz (1996: 171–86) for a valuable and sustained discussion of Moore's use of quotation in relation to the poem 'Marriage'.

9. See http://www2.english.uiuc.edu/finnegan/English%20256/gertrude_stein.htm where a kind lecturer from the University of Illinois has provided all the references for the nine rose lines in Stein.

10. Margaret Dickie has an essay on 'Recovering the Repression in Stein's Erotic Poetry' in *Gendered Modernisms* that is useful for exploring this theme (Dickie and Travisano, 1996: 3–25).

11. Paul Peppis has written about Mina Loy's poetry, in the context of sexology, as part of a wider feminist enterprise to develop 'new idioms of female sexual experience by adapting established vocabularies, conjoining . . . scientific and literary language' (2002: 564).

12. Some are reproduced in *The Last Lunar Baedecker* or, rather more clearly, on websites such as that for 'The Daughters of DADA' exhibition held at the Francis N. Nauman Gallery, New York in 2006 (see http://www.francisnaumann.com/Daughters%20of%20DADA/Loy.html).

13. Interestingly, though less relevant here, Kinnahan (1994) sees this tradition as emerging from the William Carlos Williams stable of American modernist poetry.

14. See the publishing lists of Reality Street Editions, Salt Publishing, and Shearsman Books for easily available selected works of these British poets and more.

15. The notes and afterword to *il cuore* are also relevant here with their references to examples of the 'unplanned "accident" – covert error leading to unimpeded risk' (Fraser, 1997: 197).

16. See also Hollenberg's *H.D. and Poets After* (2000) in which poets and critics discuss the influence of H.D. on contemporary poetry. Fraser has an essay in this book (also published in her own *Translating the Unspeakable*) and there is an essay on H.D. and Fraser by Cynthia Hogue. This is perhaps too specialised a book for the undergraduate reading list, but is very useful for academics who are teaching modernist and postmodernist poetry by women in an interlinked way. See also Fraser's interview in Frost and Hogue's *Innovative Women Poets* anthology (2006: 363–4), a useful teaching text.

Works cited and further reading

[The Electronic Poetry Centre at Buffalo (http://epc.buffalo.edu/authors/) and the Modern American Poetry site at the University of Illinois at Urbana-Champaign (http://www.english.uiuc.edu/maps/poets) feature biographies, chronologies and critical material on many modernist and contemporary American poets.]

[The National Poetry Foundation publishes the MAN/WOMAN AND POET series which includes volumes of biographical and critical essays on H.D., Moore, Loy, and Niedecker.]

Altman, Meryl (1992) 'A Prisoner of Biography' (review of four books on H.D.), *The Women's Review of Books* 9(10–11) (July): 39–40.

Armstrong, Tim (1998) *Modernism, Technology and the Body: a Cultural Study.* Cambridge: Cambridge University Press.

Benstock, Shari (1987) *Women of the Left Bank: Paris, 1900–1940.* London: Virago Press. [Very useful for Barnes, Stein, H.D., and Bryher; en passant a great evocation of the general scene.]

Burke, Carolyn (1985) 'Supposed Persons: Modernist Poetry and the Female Subject', *Feminist Studies* 2(1) (Spring): 131–48.

——— (1996) *Becoming Modern: the Life of Mina Loy.* New York: Farrar, Strauss & Giroux.

Debo, Annette and Lara Vetter (forthcoming) *Approaches to Teaching H.D.'s Poetry and Prose*, MLA Approaches to Teaching World Literature.

DeKoven, Marianne (1983) *A Different Language: Gertrude Stein's Experimental Writing.* Madison: University of Wisconsin Press.

——— (1999) 'Modernism and Gender', in *The Cambridge Companion to Modernism*, ed. Michael Levenson. Cambridge: Cambridge University Press.

Dickie, Margaret and Thomas Travisano (eds) (1996) *Gendered Modernisms: American Women Poets and Their Readers.* Philadelphia: University of Pennsylvania Press.

Dowson, Jane (2002) *Women, Modernism and British Poetry 1910–1939: Resisting Femininity.* Aldershot, UK and Burlington, VT: Ashgate. [Challenges the American critical dominance of this area and broadens the definition of male-defined modernism to foreground previously neglected British women poets such as Charlotte Mew, Alice Meynell, Edith Sitwell, and Anne Wickham and Americans, Laura Riding and Edna St Vincent Millay.]

DuPlessis, Rachel Blau (1990, repr. 2006) *The Pink Guitar: Writing as Feminist Practice.* New York: Routledge; repr. Tuscaloosa: University of Alabama Press.

——— (1998) ' "Seismic Orgasm": Sexual Intercourse and Narrative Meaning in Mina Loy', in Maeera Shreiber and Keith Tuma (eds), *Mina Loy: Woman and Poet.* Maine: National Poetry Foundation.

——— (2001) *Genders, Races, and Religious Cultures in Modern American Poetry, 1908–1934.* Cambridge: Cambridge University Press.

——— (2006) *Blue Studios: Poetry and Its Cultural Work.* Tuscaloosa: University of Alabama Press.

Fraser, Kathleen (1997) *il cuore: the heart – Selected Poems 1970–1995.* Hanover, NH: Wesleyan University Press.

——— (2000) *Translating the Unspeakable: Poetry and the Innovative Necessity.* Tuscaloosa and London: University of Alabama Press. [This collection includes essays on H.D., Mina Loy, Lorine Niedecker, and her own work.]

——— Fraser feature, includes 'Interview of Kathleen Fraser, conducted by Robert Glück, April, 2002', *Cauldron and Net* 4 (http://www.studiocleo.com/cauldron/volume4/features/fraser/index.html).

Friedman, Susan Stanford (1990) 'When a "Long" Poem is a "Big" Poem: Self-Authorizing Strategies in Women's Twentieth-Century "Long Poems"', *LIT* 2: 9–25.

Friedman, Susan Stanford and Rachel Blau DuPlessis (1990) *Signets: Reading H.D.* Madison: University of Wisconsin Press.

Frost, Elisabeth A. (2003) *The Feminist Avant-Garde in American Poetry.* Iowa City: University of Iowa Press.

Frost, Elisabeth A. and Cynthia Hogue (2006) *Innovative Women Poets: an Anthology of Contemporary Poetry and Interviews.* Iowa City: University of Iowa Press.

Grahn, Judy (1989) *Really Reading Gertrude Stein: a Selected Anthology with Essays by Judy Grahn.* Freedom, CA: The Crossing Press. [A useful introductory book which introduces Stein's work through selections and is not reliant on heavily theoretical readings.]

Gregory, Eileen (2002) ' "A Poetics of Emerging Evidence": Experiment in Kathleen Fraser's Poetry', in Laura Hinton and Cynthia Hogue (eds), *We Who Love to Be Astonished: Experimental Women's Writing and Performance Poetics.* Tuscaloosa: University of Alabama Press.

Hanscombe, Gillian and Virginia L. Smyers (1987) *Writing for their Lives: the Modernist Women 1910–1940.* London: Women's Press. [H.D., Lowell, Barnes, and Loy are covered here.]

Hardie, Melissa Jane (2005) 'Repulsive Modernism: Djuna Barnes' *The Book of Repulsive Women', Journal of Modern Literature* 29(1): 118–32.

H.D. (1974) *Helen in Egypt.* New York: New Directions.

—— (1984) *Collected Poems 1912–1944*, ed. Louis L. Martz. Manchester: Carcanet Press. [This volume also contains the text of *Trilogy*.]

—— (1984) *Tribute to Freud.* New York: New Directions.

Hogue, Cynthia (2000) ' "I am not of that feather": Kathleen Fraser's Postmodern Poetics', in Donna Krolik Hollenberg (ed.), *H.D. and Poets After.* Iowa City: University of Iowa Press.

Hollenberg, Donna Krolik (ed.) (2000) *H.D. and Poets After.* Iowa City: University of Iowa Press.

Huyssen, Andreas (1988) *After the Great Divide: Modernism, Mass Culture and Postmodernism.* London: Macmillan.

Jardine, Alice (1986) 'Opaque Texts and Transparent Contexts: the Political Difference of Julia Kristeva', in Nancy K. Miller (ed.), *The Poetics of Gender.* New York: Columbia University Press.

Kinnahan, Linda A. (1994) *Poetics of the Feminine: Authority and Literary Tradition in William Carlos Williams, Mina Loy, Denise Levertov and Kathleen Fraser.* Cambridge, UK, New York, and Oakleigh, Melbourne: Cambridge University Press.

Kolocotroni, Vassiliki, Jane Goldman, and Olga Taxidou (eds) (1988) *Modernism: an Anthology of Sources and Documents.* Edinburgh: Edinburgh University Press.

Lakritz, Andrew M. (1996) *Modernism and the Other in Stevens, Frost and Moore.* Gainesville: University Press of Florida.

Ledger, Sally (1997) *The New Woman: Fiction and Feminism at the Fin-de-Siècle.* Manchester: Manchester University Press.

Loy, Mina (1985) *The Last Lunar Baedecker*, ed. Roger L. Conover. The Jargon Society, 1982, repr. Manchester: Carcanet Press.

Miller, Cristanne (1995) *Marianne Moore: Questions of Authority*. Cambridge, MA: Harvard University Press.
——— (2007) 'Gender, Sexuality and the Modernist Poem', in Alex Davis and Lee M. Jenkins (eds), *The Cambridge Companion to Modernist Poetry*. Cambridge: Cambridge University Press.
Molesworth, Charles (1990) *Marianne Moore: a Literary Life*. New York: Atheneum.
Moore, Marianne (1982) *The Complete Poems of Marianne Moore*. London: Macmillan and Penguin.
——— (1987) *The Complete Prose of Marianne Moore*, ed. Patricia C. Willis. New York: Viking Penguin.
——— (2002) *Becoming Marianne Moore: Early Poems, 1907–1924*, ed. Robin G. Schulze. Berkeley: University of California Press. [Very thorough critical edition which includes many poems not featured in the text above, including 'Roses Only'.]
O'Sullivan, Maggie (1996) *Out of Everywhere: Linguistically Innovative Poetry by Women in North America and the UK*. Hastings, UK: Reality Street Editions.
Peppis, Paul (2002) 'Rewriting Sex: Mina Loy, Marie Stopes, and Sexology', *Modernism/Modernity* 9(4): 561–79.
Poggioli, Renato (1981) *The Theory of the Avant-Garde*, trans. Gerald Fitzgerald. Cambridge, MA and London: Belknap Press.
Rehling, Nicola (1996) 'Taking Patriarchy Out of Poetry: Eroticism and Subversion in Gertrude Stein's *Lifting Belly*', *Gramma* 4: 89–106.
Scott, Bonnie Kime (1990) *The Gender of Modernism: a Critical Anthology*. Bloomington and Indianapolis: Indiana University Press.
Smith, Angela K. (2000) *The Second Battlefield: Women, Modernism and the First World War*. Manchester and New York: Manchester University Press.
Stein, Gertrude (1988) *Lectures in America*. London: Virago Press.
——— (1991) *Tender Buttons (Objects Food Rooms)*. Los Angeles: Sun and Moon Press.
——— (1995) *Lifting Belly*. Tallahassee, FL: The Naiad Press.
Stimpson, Catherine R. (1986) 'Gertrude Stein and the Transposition of Gender', in Nancy K. Miller (ed.), *The Poetics of Gender*. New York: Columbia University Press.
Suleiman, Susan Robin (1990) *Subversive Intent: Gender, Politics and the Avant-Garde*. Cambridge, MA and London: Harvard University Press.
Tate, Trudi (1998) *Modernism, History and the First World War*. Manchester and New York: Manchester University Press.
Tuma, Keith (1998) *Fishing by Obstinate Isles: Modern and Postmodern British Poetry and American Readers*. Evanston, IL: Northwestern University Press.
Warren, Joyce W. and Margaret Dickie (eds) (2000) *Challenging Boundaries: Gender and Periodization*. Athens, GA: University of Georgia Press.
Wolff, Janet (1990) 'Feminism and Modernism', *Feminine Sentences*. London: Polity Press. [A useful general essay which defines its terms, summarising theories and drawing parallels between the world of literary and art history.]

5
Race, Modernism, and Institutions
Carole Sweeney

That aesthetic modernism was a thoroughly heterogeneous set of practices and movements ocurring in diverse urban centres across Europe has become something of a commonplace in post-1960s modernist scholarship. Indeed, the most stimulating and field-defining studies in the last two decades have eloquently insisted upon the inherent heterogeneity of modernism's internationalist impetus.[1] Less constrained by previous intellectual and institutional divisions between an Eliotic-Pound inflected Anglo-American modernism versus a more European avant-gardism, these newer studies of modernism broadened the scope of intellectual inquiry to encompass Czech, Russian, Italian, and French (beyond Proust and Mallarmé) variants of modernism. This increasingly comparative approach to the variegated terrains of modernism has provoked significant changes in the ways in which canonicity in modernist studies has been defined, researched, and taught in the university classroom. While the core of a modernist poetry curriculum remains inevitably, and quite properly, based around the 'men of 1914', new theoretical approaches to what constitutes 'English' as a discipline have altered the ways in which we think about cultural authority and the politics of literary canons. Catalysed by the emergence and subsequent intellectual consolidation of post-structuralism in the 1960s and an accompanying theoretical concern with ruptures and margins, scholarly research in modernism has increasingly concerned itself with defining the movement in a more expansive matrix of production, dissemination, and consumption. Major changes in approaches to modernist studies at this time were primarily concerned with the question of gender and neglected modernist women. It was not until the emergence of post-colonial theory as part of a wider institutional politicisation of the humanities in Britain and the United States in the 1980s that issues of race and ethnicity within modernism began to be closely scrutinised as part of a turn to the politics of cultural representation, which has profoundly shaped new departures in both modernist scholarship and teaching.

This is not to suggest that up until this point race had been entirely ignored as a category in modernist studies but that work in this area was, for the most part, confined to examinations of African-American modernism and the Harlem writers of the 1920s. Exceptional indeed would have been an excursion into modernist poetry that excluded Langston Hughes and Claude McKay, and at the outer limits may have even encompassed Zora Neale Hurston and Jean Toomer. However, the role of the Harlem Renaissance in modernism tended to be taught in isolation from other areas of modernist scholarship that was beginning to place emphasis on questions of race and empire in the study of literature and the visual arts in the years 1920–40. Works putatively seeking to redress the normative 'whiteness' of modernist studies such as Houston A. Baker's groundbreaking *Modernism and the Harlem Renaissance* (1987) confined questions of race to an African-American cultural context that seemingly had little dialogue with simultaneous 'black modernisms' occurring across Africa, Europe, and the Caribbean.

Nevertheless, works such as Baker's valuably pointed up the distinctive nature of history and chronology for African-American modernism, accentuating the need to study this against a mainstream version of modernism that had more or less unproblematically inculcated a 'white' Eurocentric chronology of modernity.

> It seems to me that Africans and Afro-Americans – through conscious and unconscious designs of various Western 'modernisms' – have little in common with Joycean or Eliotic projects. Further, it seems to me that the very histories that are assumed in the chronologies of British, Anglo-American, and Irish modernism are radically opposed to any adequate and accurate account of the history of Afro-American modernism especially the discursive history of such modernism. (Baker, 1987: xvi)

Speaking to this idea of a neglected African chronology, Paul Gilroy's arguments in *The Black Atlantic* posited that modernity, and consequently modernist notions of exile, cannot be apprehended as a homogeneous, universal phenomenon for both black and white writers: 'Whether [African diasporic subjects'] experience of exile is enforced or chosen, temporary or permanent, these intellectuals and activists, writers, speakers, poets, and artists repeatedly articulate a desire to escape the restrictive bonds of ethnicity, national identification, and sometimes even "race" itself' (Gilroy, 1993: 19). Arguing that slavery has been unacknowledged as central to 'the ethical and intellectual heritage of the West as a whole', thereby mounting an intellectual challenge to the defensive discourses of cultural nationalism, Gilroy insists that the importance of racial discourses must be rethought in new conceptualisations of modernity and modernism (49). In many ways, of course, Gilroy's work is heir to the radical transnational perspective of C. L. R. James in *The Black Jacobins* (1938) in which James argues for the importance of the Haitian revolution as integral to notions of European modernity. Both critics assert that questions of periodisation and history require consideration outside a singular European pespective.

The relationship between race, empire, and culture most famously expounded in Edward Said's seminal *Orientalism* (1978), and subsequently developed in *Culture and Imperialism* (1993), informs Fredric Jameson's 'Modernism and Imperialism' (1990) and Raymond Williams' *The Politics of Modernism* (1996). In different ways these works all suggest that traces of imperialism are to be found within the 'inner forms and structures of what new mutations in literary and artistic language to which the term modernism is loosely applied' (Jameson, 1990: 44). A deep-rooted entanglement, benign or otherwise, between race and modernism began to be uncovered as many critical works turned their attention to examine the striking coincidence that the period of modernism occurred alongside first the triumphant apogee, then the slow decline of colonialism.

> Ironically, the 'liberating' possibilites of an international, oppositional, and 'revolutionary' modernism for early-twentieth century 'Third World' writers and artists came into being at a time when modernism was itself recuperating the cultural products of non-western countries within an aesthetic of the fragment. (Sangari, 1987: 182)

In *Modernism and Empire* Patrick Williams recognises the need for a re-evaluation of post-Second World War conceptualisations of modernism, asserting that a 'continuing reaccentuation' of its scope and reach is somehow inherent to modernism's own self-conscious nature as a movement (2000: 13). Resisting calls to simply insert the idea of otherness – whether located in gender, race, or sexuality – into modernist studies, Williams advocates a measured approach to the question of modernism's relationship to empire while cautiously welcoming a critical juxtaposition that admits the complexity of this association. What is required are new spatial and temporal maps for both modernity and aesthetic modernism that move beyond an unexamined Eurocentrism; maps that elude traditional disciplinary divisions that have established an intellectual *cordon sanitaire* around English and language area studies. Spurred on by the insights of post-colonial theory, modernist scholarship began to consider a realignment of the cartography of modernist inter-nationalism that permits complex and sometimes difficult discussions about race, empire, and aesthetics to be more fully explored. Various points on this alternative topography of modernism began to be joined up to produce a new map of modernist poetics stretching from Harlem to Cuba, and Jamaica to Senegal and Martinique, all journeying through the key urban nexus of interwar Paris. By repositioning the artistic and politi-cal matrices of modernist poetics, it is possible to reassess the importance of the smaller institutions of modernist production and dissemination for African and Caribbean writers. The role of literary salons and patron-age in Paris of the 1920s and 1930s and the importance of small presses and magazines has been well documented, with suggestive arguments emerging about the private versus the public spheres of modernist pro-duction and consumption.[2] None of these works however, considers a small but vibrant alliance of writers and artists from Harlem, Senegal, Guinea, Martinique, and Jamaica whose salons and publications formed another piece of the interwar modernist matrix. Recent work from out-side 'English' studies has uncovered new connections and intersections of influence within international modernism that recognises the 'voy-ages in' of a black cultural diaspora whose politicised poetics formed a vital part of what Said calls an 'adversarial internationalization in an age of continuing imperial structures' (1993: 295). Teachers and students exploring these 'alternative' modernist connections may consult a num-ber of works that examine the interwar period in Paris from a broadly inclusive cultural perspective. For example, Christopher L. Miller's *Nationalists and Nomads* (1999) and Brent Hayes Edwards' *The Practice of Diaspora* (2003) both offer succinctly contextualised overviews that may be used to urge students to consider the importance of transatlantic networks of print culture and anti-colonial intellectual activism.[3]

Literary and intellectual networks in Paris gave African-American, African, and Caribbean writers like *New Negro* anthologist Alain Locke and French-African novelist René Maran the opportunity to meet and participate in small, often very short-lived, publications espousing the causes of anti-racism and anti-colonialism. Journals such as *Le Paria, Les Continents, Le Messager Dahoméen,* and *L'Action Coloniale* took up the politics of racial equality in the period immediately after the First World

War but it was the later journals, *La Dépêche Africaine, La Revue du monde noir,* and *Légitime Défense* that advocated culture as a locale of political resistance. The publication of these journals occurred in the interwar years in Paris at a time of cultural fascination with black culture, popularly known as negrophilia or *la vogue nègre,* about which Aimé Césaire sceptically remarked:

> Or else they simply love us so much!
> Gaily obscene, doudou about jazz in their excess of boredom,
> I can do the tracking, the Lindy-hop and the tap-dance.
> And as a last delicacy our muted complaints muffled in wah-
> wah...Wait...
> Everything is in order. My good angel grazes on neon lights. I
> swallow sticks. My dignity wallows in puke. ([1939] 1995: 103)[4]

Tracing these new connections across disciplines, teachers of modernist poetry are encouraged towards a more integrated view of the circuits of cultural production and consumption that takes into account the political contexts of this historical epoch and pays close attention to the issue of race. Crucially, this view suggests that race and colonialism need to be examined, not in isolation from the main strands of modernist activity or as running counter to it, but as part of a complex network of cultural practices both within and outside of Europe and North America. Teaching these new strands of modernism requires not just a fresh approach to notions of chronology and periodisation but also a repudiation of customary disciplinary divides that have prevented a properly comparative appraisal of interwar modernism. I use here examples of two peripheral modernist works, Nancy Cunard's ambitious volume *Negro: an Anthology* (1934) and Aimé Césaire's epic poem of exile and homecoming *Notebook of a Return to a Native Land* (1939) to illustrate how alternative textual topographies of modernism can open up debates on race and representation in the modernist poetry seminar while remaining alert to the complexities of textual aesthetics.

Notebook of a Return to a Native Land

T. S. Eliot's seminal essay 'Tradition and Individual Talent' (1917) stands as the most renowned theoretical departure point in the modernist poetry curriculum in which Eliot argues for the importance of history, myth, and temporality as potent structuring forces in modernist poetics. He suggests that an impassioned 'historical sense' stirs the poet with the 'feeling that the whole of literature from Homer and within it the whole literature of his own country has a simultaneous existence and composes a simultaneous order' (Eliot, [1917] 1950: 761). This compelling historical sense and the centrality of mythopoetics in Eliot's work forms an aesthetic template for Anglo-American and Irish modernism of the 1922 generation. For this branch of modernism the reassurance and influence of a long literary tradition from the ancient to the modern assumes a continuous cultural chronology in which epochs and movements can be viewed in a *longue durée* of succession and affiliation. In contrast, for black modernism history is not so unproblematically sustaining and immediately accessible as inspiration because the historical disarticulation and trauma of the African diaspora renders the relationship to the past one of rupture and dislocation, thus lacking a stable mythopoetics. Caribbean writer and critic Edouard Glissant's arguments in *Poetics of Relation* (1997) suggest that this notion of discontinuity and rupture is the marker of Caribbean cultural production:

> The French Caribbean is the site of a history characterised by ruptures that began with a brutal dislocation, the slave trade. Our historical consciousness could not be deposited gradually and continuously like sediment . . . but came together in the context of shock, contradiction, painful negation, and explosive forces. The dislocation of the continuum, and the inability of the collective consciousness to absorb it all, characterise what I call nonhistory. (Glissant, 1997: 61–2)

Glissant also argues that for the Caribbean '*Collective memory* is our urgent task . . . Not "historical" detail from our lost past (not only that) but the eruptions from the depths' (187). These thoughts on history and memory are apposite for the ways in which the epic poem of the negritude movement and of an African-inflected modernism, *Notebook of a Return to a Native Land* by Aimé Césaire, can be pertinently integrated into a modernist poetry curriculum. Broader questions may be posed here that draw students' attention to the relationship between history and text, as well as between ideology and aesthetics. What problems, for example, might have existed for a Caribbean poet like Césaire in writing – and to a certain degree interpellating himself – within a European aesthetic while simultaneously delivering a coruscating indictment of European colonial politics? Can we regard Césaire's poem as a 'vernacular cosmopolitanism'?[5] Also might we be able to talk about an *anti-colonial modernism* drawing upon the politicised aesthetics and activism of 1930s surrealism? Surrealism, a vital coordinate in the teaching of 'alternative' maps of modernism, may be brought in here by way of an introductory lecture. This can lead into seminar material where students are asked to consider, through scholarly articles and primary material, the distinctive nature of surrealism within the wider contexts of modernism and how it offered more complex ways of thinking about race, culture, and art via contemporary social sciences and in particular ethnography.[6]

Aimé Césaire, born in Martinique in 1913, came as a student to Paris in the 1930s where he met Léopold Sédar Senghor from Senegal with whom he became involved in a network of artistic and political activity that brought together writers, students, and painters from North America, West Africa, and the Caribbean.[7] Black writers, artists, and intellectuals met at the weekly Clamart literary salons run by three sisters, Jane, Andrée, and Paulette Nardal, also from Martinique. While it is reported that Césaire found these salons too bourgeois for his tastes they can be credited with stimulating a nascent black artistic consciousness that would generate the modernist poetics of the negritude movement. As suggested above, for many black poets and writers at this time, language, culture, and history were not culturally and aesthetically to hand as a smooth poetic arc from the ancient to the modern. The modernist quest for origins thus assumes a markedly different character for negritude modernism, as James Arnold observes:

> their relation to history and myth was to prove the decisive intellectual problem . . . For Césaire, what mattered was the poetic grasp of history and culture in terms of birth, death, and rebirth – essentially an optimistic version of the eschatological imagination that occurs so prominently in modernist thought from Yeats to Toynbee and from Spengler to Sandburg. (Arnold, 1981: 50, 52)

For African and Caribbean modernist poets history was not a dependable repository for tradition and order but rather something to be wrested back from its victorious authors requiring urgent revision in order to make sense of their central invisibility. As a cultural politics then, negritude attempted to repossess a history that recognised the ruptures of the past to construct in order to create a poetics of the future, a project Glissant describes as

> related neither to a schematic chronology nor to a nostalgic lament. It leads to the identification of a painful notion of time and its full projection forward into the future, without the help of those plateaus in time from which the West has benefited, without the help of that

collective density that is the primary value of an ancestral cultural heartland. That is what I call a prophetic vision of the past. (Glissant, 1989: 64)

History in this sense can be understood not simply as an absence and lack but rather as a space of immanence and becoming. As Sartre remarks of negritude: 'the *race* has transmuted itself into historicity: the Present black explodes and temporalizes himself; Negritude inserts itself into its Past and its Future in the universal History; it is no more a *state*, neither even an existentialist attitude; it is a Becoming.'[8] Thus, rather than lamenting a lack of cultural continuity, negritude placed this lacuna – initiated by the catastrophe of slavery and perpetuated by colonialism – at its poetic centre as a collective subject of a history in process. Glissant's play *Monsieur Toussaint* points up this redemptive possibility of discontinuity; 'For those who know, of their own history, only that obscure and diminished portion to which they have been relegated, the recovery of the near or distant past which has been deformed and obliterated by others may sometimes give us a better sense of the meaning of the present' (Glissant, 1961: 7–8).

For Césaire, European history is a pernicious narrative; an invention to uphold a concept of civilisation based upon a rapacious desire to conquer and loot; 'the slave-ship cracks everywhere . . . Its belly convulses and res/onates . . . The atrocious tapeworm of its cargo gnaws at the foetid / bowels of the strange suckling of the sea!' (1995: 129). The bitter sarcasm of the exclamation mark here underlines the slave trade's violent theft of an embodied African identity leaving only a grotesquely non-human residue. As a politicised poetic movement negritude formed a mythopoetics out of a yet-unrealised history to create a sense of collective memory that sought to repair the broken chronology of the African diaspora. Glissant describes this as 'Our struggle without witness, the inability to create even an unconscious chronology, a result of the erasing memory in all of us. For history is not only absence for us, it is vertigo. This time that was never ours, we must now possess' (Glissant, 1997: 161). Césaire's *Notebook* testifies to this history with a soaring and indicting political urgency:

And this land shouted for centuries that we are brute beasts;
That the pulsing of humanity stops at the entrance of the slave-compound; that we are a walking manure a hideous forerunner of tender cane and silky cotton, and they used to brand us with red-hot irons and we used to sleep in our excrement and they would

sell us in public and a yard of English cloth and salted Irish meat
cost less than we did and this country was quiet, serene, saying
that the spirit of God was in its acts. (1995: 105)

Students wishing to read beyond and around Césaire's poem may be
guided towards his rewriting of *The Tempest* (*A Tempest*) and his figura-
tion of Prospero as the silver-tongued mouthpiece for colonial discourse.

> Lying is your trademark.
> And you have lied so much to me
> (lied about the world, lied about me)
> that you have ended by imposing on me
> an image of myself.
> underdeveloped, you brand me, inferior,
> That is the way you have forced me to see myself
> I detest that image! ... (1986: 162)

This can be read alongside Césaire's earlier essay, *Discourse on Colonialism*,
an excoriating dissection of the ideological mechanisms of the colonial
project that continues to have powerful political resonations today.[9] The
sense of a violently denied existence reaches from history to the body per-
meating deep into the blighted topography of the Caribbean landscape.

> At the brink of dawn, this flat town – staked out, tripped of its
> common-sense, inert, panting under the geometric burden of its
> forever renascent cross, unresigned to its fate, dumb thwarted in
> every way, incapable of growing along the sap of this soil, bur-
> dened, clipped, diminished, alienated from its own flora and fauna.
> (Césaire, 2000: 73)

In Césaire's long poem (itself a difficult genre) a diasporic history is
forged into being from the ruins of dislocation; the movements – exiles,
returns – to and from the island of Martinique, from slavery to freedom,
are those of the unencumbered free body voyaging back from the exile
of history and language.

The movement of consciousness in the poem turns from the thing
that is bought and sold and measured and observed to the subject and
the history that speaks for itself thus breaking open the objectification
or *chosification* of the black subject. This is a movement away from
Fanon's 'crushing objecthood' of blackness; the 'ugly and comical nigger'

'battered down by tom-toms' to the creation of Caribbean mythopoesis pulled out of the negativity of a non-history (Fanon, 1986: 112). As a way of exploring representations of race in European culture from the eighteenth century to the present, students can be asked to undertake research projects (either in groups or singly) charting the historical and aesthetic evolution of stereotypes within racial discourses. This kind of work clears the ground for a closer examination of race and culture in the period of modernism between 1900 and the 1940s.

Significantly, while Césaire's poem 'represents an exhilarating moment of resistance against the racist and paternalistic European discourse of the 1930s' (Rosello, in Césaire, 1995: 12) it does not fall into the essentialism of the Senghorian version of negritude. The *Notebook* presents African civilisation not as a celebration of an 'essential' blackness – 'We not feel the itch of those / who used to hold the spear in our armpits'; 'No, we've never been amazons of the Kings of Dahomey, nor princes / of Ghana with eight hundred camels . . . ' (Césaire, 1995: 105) – but 'as proud utterances of a speaking subject who has been experimenting with various forms of self-characterization and who has now emerged from the crucible with new insight' (Davis, 1997: 48). Here, students could be encouraged to investigate the dynamics of negritude as a politicised cultural movement emerging out of the 1930s and how this might usefully be read against W. E. B. Dubois and Marcus Garvey and the poetics of the Harlem Renaissance. Research projects leading out of this might include looking at the *Notebook* in the light of subsequent critiques of negritude's inherent but strategic essentialism by Fanon (a former student of Césaire's in Martinique) in *Black Skin, White Masks* (1952), the 'creole' poets Patrick Chamoiseau, Raphaël Confiant, and Jean Bernabé and other critiques by Edouard Glissant, Stuart Hall, and Paul Gilroy.

The *Notebook* has been incorporated into modernist studies as a Surrealist poem *par excellence*; André Breton's preface to the New York edition in 1947 definitively inscribed Césaire into the Surrealist pantheon as Lautréamont's black son. By reading it through the lens of Surrealism students can examine the poetics of the *Notebook* that derives some of its aesthetic energies from an oppositional ethics that marked later Surrealist artistic practices. We can urge them to be attentive to the idea that reading the poem through the lens of Surrealism avoids the potential critical pitfalls of simply glossing the *Notebook* within a reductive postcolonial paradigm that posits a forward movement 'from assimilation to commitment; from colonial to national; from imitation to authenticity' (Dash, 1988: 114). Arnold recognises the two matrices in which Césaire's work has been received and studied; one in which he 'represents the late flowering of a French brand of modernism' and the other, more sociological in orientation maybe, 'the poet of decolonisation and the prosecuting voice of anti-colonialism' (Arnold, 1981: 1). As teachers and scholars of modernism we must remain wary of simply absorbing an iconoclastic work like the *Notebook* into a reductively post-colonial reading. It is perfectly possible, however, to integrate the *Notebook* into a modernist syllabus via a study of Surrealism by accentuating the distinctive anti-colonial poetics and reflecting on the particularity of anti-racist, anti-colonial negritude poetics fed upon the oppositional aesthetics of the Surrealist group.[10] The *Notebook* can be taught as a text that grew out of the smaller extra-institutional modernist practices in interwar Paris, nourished along the way by a diasporic mythopoetics and a Caribbean intertextuality born out of a Parisian encounter between Africa, the Caribbean, and Europe. Both Edwards' and Miller's books (referred to above) are extremely valuable critical maps delineating these intellectual and cultural intersections and can be called upon in the form of reading assignments to keep students mindful of the cross-cultural production of modernist aesthetics.[11] In addition, it could prove a useful exercise to read the poem against one or more contemporary texts, Surrealist or otherwise, to suggest a network of aesthetic and ideological contrasts or continuities with the *Notebook*.

Negro: an Anthology

Considered virtually untouchable by every publishing institution Nancy Cunard approached, the ambitiously sprawling text of *Negro: an Anthology* (1934) was engendered through an act of 'poetic justice', described by Cunard as 'final as a tombstone' ([1934] 1970: xxiii). Logistically and politically contentious, the anthology was eventually accepted by Wishart and Company who agreed to its publication with the proviso that Cunard paid for the costs which rose to a hefty £1,500.[12] This was the exact amount for which she settled a libel action out of court against four British newspapers for their defamatory remarks about her involvement with 'people of color' (xxiii). Only a thousand copies were published on 15 February 1934 but despite the exceptional documentary value of the anthology it was almost entirely ignored at the time of its publication and has subsequently disappeared from modernist studies.[13] Originally 855 pages long with 150 contributors on the subject of 'contemporary race relations' in North America and across the colonised world, Hugh Ford's 1970 edited and abridged edition points up the importance of the work in both its scope and subject matter: '*Negro* does more than recall a past that gave shape to the present. And it can certainly claim to be more than a repository of old ideas and attitudes' (Ford, in Cunard, [1934] 1970: xxvii). Writing to Claude McKay in 1932, Cunard described the anthology as 'a very large symposium indeed with a definite and clearly defined intent: to throw light on the appalling way the entire colour "question" is handled' (Winkiel, 2006: 510). A politically charged ethnographic montage, the anthology proceeds by a methodology characteristic of contemporary Surrealist publications *Documents*, *Cahiers d'art* and *Minotaure*, its pages repelete with prose, poetry, photography, catography, musical scripts, and annotated sketches drawn from every corner of the black world. Many African-American poets presented work in the anthology – Sterling Brown, Zora Neale Hurston, Arna Bontemps, Countee Cullen, Langston Hughes – as did Caribbean negritude poets, the Cuban Nicolas Guillen and Jacques Roumain from Haiti. Despite this extraordinary range of content and contributors, the anthology has been perennially neglected across the disciplines partly because little institutional space exists in which to address the intersections of the poetic and the political. 'Despite some effort to bring order to *Negro*, it continued to push out in all directions' (Ford, in Cunard, [1934] 1970: xxi); pushing out beyond some modernist boundaries, across the disciplines *Negro* enabled 'the articulation of a mood . . . Neither a final thing (a framing of the past) nor a "prophecy" (a prediction of the future), but the space of a "new creation" in the performance of reading that takes place in the subjunctive' (Edwards, 2003: 318). An exhilarating, if slightly unruly, fusion of the documentary, manifesto, and creative text, the anthology can be taught as a particularly productive example of modernist rupture; exemplifying 'what at least some modernist work has done from the outset: namely, says "no"; refuses integration, resolution, consolation, comfort; [it] protests and criticizes' (Lazarus, 2005: 431). Selections from the anthology – now easily available in an abridged paperback format – may be read in thematic groups where students are asked, for example, to discuss how the ethnographic and historical pieces inform the poetry and vice versa.

From the early Dadaist anti-language poetics of the 'Chants Nègres' to the use of black dialect in the works of Eliot, Stein, Pound, and e. e. cummings, modernist poets were sporadically drawn to the representation of black dialect. An imaginary and fabricated sense of black speech was mostly used to signify an aesthetic sense of elsewhere standing in insurrectionary opposition to a normative white bourgeois centre, as Michael North notes: 'Blackness, for all sorts of modernists and in all sorts of ways both reactionary and progressive, represented an aesthetic "outside"; an elsewhere "opposed to the standard"' (North, 1994: Preface). Crucially, the anthology attempts to move away from this tendency to instrumentalise race as a marker of modernist aesthetic estrangement and proposes a more complicated critique of the relationship between race and aesthetics within a stringent political agenda that is vigilant to material and lived contexts.[14] The substantial selection of poetry, arranged into sections under the headings 'Negro', 'White', and 'West Indian' poets may be taught in comparative political and aesthetic contexts setting them within a wider black transnational diaspora of cultural production and dissemination. Racial politics in the United States and the Caribbean can be addressed in 'Florida Road Workers' and 'Goodbye Christ' by Langston Hughes, and 'When the Tom-Tom Beats' by Jacques Roumain. These poems all focus on the violent duress the black body must endure across the world; in 'the cities of Morocco . . . Tripoli . . . the coffee hills of Hayti' [sic], 'the cotton fields of Alabama' and 'the streets of Harlem':

> Black:
> Exploited, beaten, robbed,
> Shot and killed.
> Blood running into
>> Dollars
>> Pounds
>> Francs
>> Pesetas
>> Lire
>> (Hughes, 'Always the Same', in Cunard, [1934] 1970: 263)

Elsewhere, several pieces in the anthology speak to the difficulties and potential of poetic translation. 'Louis Armstrong', by Belgian surrealist Ernst Moerman, adroitly translated from the French by Samuel Beckett, attempts a sketch of Armstrong's trumpet and to capture the visceral 'she-notes' of jazz avoiding the primitivist clichés prevalent in contemporary jazz criticism, such as that of French music critic Hughes Pannassié, on 'le jazz hot'.[15]

> Flurry of lighting in the earth
> sockets for his rootbound song
> nights of Harlem scored with his nails
> snow black slush when his heart rises
> (Moerman, in Cunard, [1934] 1970: 185)

Beckett's translation of Moerman's poem transposes the bodily effects of Armstrong's music; 'his arrows from afar they fizz through the wild horses / they fang you and me / then they fly home'. The voice of Armstrong's jazz trumpet, a multi-modulated articulation, is rendered not as an essentialised or innate aptitude of 'Africanness' but as a historically and technically complex 'confessing': 'the black music it can't be easy / it threshes the old heart into a spin / into a blaze' (Moerman, in Cunard, [1934] 1970: 185). A valuable resource for teachers examining the poetics of modernist translation is also to be found in Beckett's other translations in the *Negro* anthology.[16] In particular René Crevel's 'The Negress in the Brothel' and 'Murderous Humanitarianism' by the Surrealist Group in Paris (as they were calling themselves by that time) both offer withering political critiques indicting France's *soi disant* colonial 'civilising mission'.

Césaire's *Notebook* and Cunard's *Negro* anthology can be read together and incorporated into a modernist poetry curriculum in a comparative approach that is attentive to the contemporary politics of modernist institutional practices of production and dissemination. The lingering notion of modernism as a glacial apolitical movement closed to the disorderly contexts of the lived material world is dispelled in these texts and both works can be taught as examples of a Surrealist inflected 'late' modernism responsive to the politics of race and colonialism. Thoughtful consideration of these texts can place an emphasis on the reconfiguration of historical periodisation and the questioning of disciplinary divides may be fruitfully brought to bear on a discussion of modernist poetics that challenges the normative 'whiteness' of the modernist canon.

Notes

1. See Peter Nicholls (1995) and Kolocotroni et al. (1998) for examples of comparative approaches to literary modernism.
2. See Benstock (1986), Levenson (1999), and Rainey (1993).
3. For those with a reading ability in French Philippe Dewitte's *Les Mouvements Nègres en France 1919–1939* is an extremely valuable historical-political resource.
4. All references to Césaire's poem will be taken from the Bloodaxe bilingual edition (1995).
5. A term used by Homi Bhabha to talk about a seam of intellectual activism encompassing Ghandi, Toni Morrison, Fanon, and Du Bois that derives from a 'grassroots' world view (Goldberg and Quayson, 2002: 24).
6. James Clifford's work on ethnography and surrealism is useful here. See in particular *The Predicament of Culture* and the earlier journal article 'On Ethnographic Surrealism'.
7. See Dewitte (1985), Fabre (1991), and Stovall (1996).

8. Sartre (1948: 57).
9. This has been recently reprinted with an introduction by Robin G. Kelly. *A Tempest* is easily available from online post-colonial resources as an e-text at http://www.cs.usyd.edu.au/~matty/Shakespeare/texts/comedies/tempest .html
10. This is the later incarnation of the Surrealist Group at the time of *Le Surréalisme au service de la révolution.*
11. To this end there are a number of useful publications that could also be used here; for example, Seth Moglen's article on Langston Hughes that explores the relationship between empire and aesthetics in the twentieth century. See also Bennetta Jules-Rosette, *Black Paris: the African Writers' Landscape.*
12. Wishart and Company, a left-wing press, also published the *Communist Manifesto* and Robert Tressell's *The Ragged Trousered Philanthropist.*
13. See Marcus (2002) and Sweeney (2004) on the anthology's virtual disappearance in modernist studies.
14. The political agenda is always in reference to communism. While Cunard never actually joined the party she deeply sympathised with the anti-colonialism of communist politics.
15. See Lane (2005) on the primitivism of 1920s and 1930s jazz criticism.
16. Beckett translated eighteen pieces for the anthology.

Works cited and further reading

Arnold, James (1981) *Modernism and Negritude.* Cambridge, MA: Harvard University Press.
Baker, Houston A. (1987) *Modernism and the Harlem Renaissance.* Chicago: University of Chicago Press.
Benstock, Shari (1986) *Women of the Left Bank: Paris, 1900–1940.* Austin: University of Texas Press.
Booth, Howard J. and Nigel Rigby (eds) (2000) *Modernism and Empire.* Manchester: Manchester University Press.
Césaire, Aimé (1986) *A Tempest: Adaptation for a Black Theatre.* New York: G. Borchardt.
—— ([1939] 1995) *Notebook of a Return to a Native Land [Cahier d'un Retour au pays natal],* trans. Mireille Rosello and Annie Pritchard. Newcastle: Bloodaxe.
—— ([1972] 2000) *Discourse on Colonialism,* trans. Joan Pinkham. New York: Monthly Review Press.
Charney, Maurice (1998) 'Caribbean Shakespeare: Aimé Césaire's *Une tempête',* *Journal of Theatre and Drama* 4: 73–80.
Clifford, James T. (1981) 'On Ethnographic Surrealism', *Comparative Studies in Society and History* 23(4): 539–64.
—— (1988) *The Predicament of Culture: Twentieth Century Ethnography, Literature, and Art.* Cambridge, MA: Harvard University Press.
Cunard, Nancy (ed.) ([1934] 1970) *Negro: An Anthology.* London: Wishart and Co. Reprinted New York: Ungar.
Dash, J. Michael (1988) 'The World and the Word: French Caribbean Writing in the Twentieth Century', *Callaloo* 34: 112–30.
Davis, Gregson (1997) *Aimé Césaire.* Cambridge: Cambridge University Press.

Dewitte, Philippe (1985) *Les Mouvements nègres en France, 1919–1939*. Paris: L'Harmattan.

Edwards, Brent Hayes (2003) *The Practice of Diaspora: Literature, Translation, and the Rise of Black Internationalism*. Cambridge, MA: Harvard University Press.

Eliot, T. S. ([1917] 1950) 'Tradition and Individual Talent', *The Sacred Wood: Essays on Poetry and Criticism*. London: Methuen.

Fabre, Michel (1991) *From Harlem to Paris: Black American Writers in France, 1840–1980*. Urbana: University of Illinois Press.

Fanon, Frantz (1986) *Black Skin, White Masks*. London: Pluto Press.

Friedman, Allan Warren (ed.) (2000). *Beckett in Black and Red: the Translations for Nancy Cunard's* Negro *(1934)*. Lexington: Kentucky University Press.

Gilroy, Paul (1993) *The Black Atlantic: Modernity and Double Consciousness*. London: Verso.

Glissant, Edouard (1961) *Monsieur Toussaint*. Paris: Seuil.

——— (1989) *Caribbean Discourse: Selected Essays*. Charlottesville: University Press of Virginia.

——— (1997) *Poetics of Relation*, trans. Betsy Wing. Ann Arbor: University of Michigan Press.

Goldberg, David Theo and Ato Quayson (eds) (2002) *Relocating Postcolonialism*. London: Blackwell.

James, C. L. R. ([1938] 1963) *The Black Jacobins*. New York: Random House.

Jameson, Fredric (1990) 'Modernism and Imperialism', in Terry Eagleton, Fredric Jameson, and Edward W. Said (eds), *Nationalism, Colonialism, and Culture*. Minneapolis: Field Day Company/University of Minnesota Press, 43–66.

Jules-Rosette, Bennetta (1998) *Black Paris: the African Writers' Landscape*, Foreword by Simon Njami. Urbana and Chicago: University of Illinois Press.

Kolocotroni, Vassiliki, Jane Goldman, and Olga Taxidou (eds) (1998) *Modernism: an Anthology of Sources and Documents*. Edinburgh: Edinburgh University Press.

Lane, Jeremy (2005) 'Jazz as Habitus: Discourses of Class and Ethnicity in Hugues Panassie's *Le Jazz Hot* (1934)', *Nottingham French Studies* 44(3): 40–53.

Lazarus, Neil (2005). 'The Politics of Postcolonial Modernism', in Ania Loomba et al. (eds), *Postcolonial Studies and Beyond*. Durham, NC: Duke University Press.

Levenson, Michael Harry (ed.) (1999) *Cambridge Companion to Modernism*. Cambridge: Cambridge University Press.

Locke, Alain (1925) *The New Negro*. New York: Boni.

Marcus, Jane (2002) 'Suptionpremises', *Modernism/Modernity* 9(3): 491–502.

Miller, Christopher L. (1999) *Nationalists and Nomads: Essays on Francophone African Literature and Culture*. Chicago: University of Chicago Press.

Miller, Tyrus (1999) *Late Modernism: Politics, Fiction, and the Arts between the World Wars*. Berkeley: University of California Press.

Moglen, Seth (2002) 'Modernism in the Black Diaspora, Langston Hughes and the Broken Cubes of Picasso', *Callaloo* 25(4): 1189–1205.

Nicholls, Peter (1995) *Modernisms: a Literary Guide*. London: Macmillan.

North, Michael (1994) *The Dialect of Modernism: Race, Language and Twentieth Century Literature*. New York: Oxford University Press.

Rainey, Lawrence S. (1993) *Institutions of Modernism: Literary Elites and Public Culture*. New Haven: Yale University Press.

Richardson, Michael (1996) *Refusal of the Shadow: Surrealism and the Caribbean*, trans. Krzysztof Fijalkowski and Michael Richardson. London: Verso.

Said, Edward W. ([1978] 2003) *Orientalism: Western Conceptions of the Orient.* Harmondsworth: Penguin.

—— (1993) *Culture and Imperialism.* London: Chatto & Windus.

Sangari, Kumkum (1987) 'The Politics of the Possible', *Cultural Critique: the Nature and Context of Minority Discourse* 2(7): 157–86.

Sartre, Jean-Paul (1948) 'Black Orpheus', in *What Is Literature? and Other Essays.* Cambridge, MA: Harvard University Press, 1988. [Also in Léopold Sédar (ed.), *Anthologie de la nouvelle poésie nègre et malgache de langue française.* Paris: Presses Universitaires de France.]

Stovall, Tyler (1996) *Paris Noir: African Americans in the City of Light.* New York: Houghton Mifflin.

Sweeney, Carole (2004) *From Fetish to Subject: Race, Modernism, and Primitivism, 1919–1935.* Westport, CT: Greenwood Press.

Williams, Patrick (2000) '"Simultaneous Uncomtemporaneities": Theorising Modernism and Empire', in Howard J. Booth and Nigel Rigby (eds), *Modernism and Empire.* Manchester: Manchester University Press, 13–38.

Williams, Raymond (1996) *The Politics of Modernism.* London: Verso.

Winkiel, Laura (2006) 'Nancy Cunard's *Negro* and the Transnational Politics of Race', *Modernism/Modernity* 13(3): 507–30.

6
Contemporary British Modernisms

Peter Barry

Some years ago I was asked by a student to explain what I meant by 'contemporary modernist poetry'. I replied 'Well, it's poetry, but not as we know it.' I was pleased with the phrase, and later used it as the title of an undergraduate course on British poetry since the 1970s, which I still teach. I wouldn't claim that this course is by any means cutting edge, but it has given me a strong awareness of the difficulties involved in venturing out – as a teacher rather than a researcher – beyond the comfort zone of recent British poetry, by which I mean the inner-canonical core of Heaney, Hughes, Harrison, Larkin, Duffy, and so on. In what follows I first explain what I understand by 'contemporary British modernism' in poetry, indicating (mainly through the endnotes) some of the teaching resources now available. I then take three representative poets and try to show what forms classroom discussion and study of them might take.

'Only select' – making a syllabus

The original modernist revolution in literature was famously unfinished – it was swept aside by the crisis years of the 1930s and 1940s when the very continuation of humanity and society was in doubt. The 1950s saw a return to domination by more conservative cultural tastes, but by the 1960s a range of British poets were again experimenting in ways which we can now see as a revival and continuation of that modernist agenda. This generation, coming to prominence in the 1960s and 1970s, might be called the 'new-modernists' (or the 'neo-mods'). Many of them were associated with the so-called 'British Poetry Revival' identified by Eric Mottram in the 1970s,[1] and their work can now be found in a range of anthologies.[2] Representative neo-mod figures include Allen Fisher, Bill Griffiths, Lee Harwood, Maggie O'Sullivan, and Denise Riley, and a certain amount of secondary material is now available on all of these, making them suitable for study on BA and MA courses in twentieth-century literature and poetry.[3] This generation was followed by the 'second-wave' neo-modernists, or the 'new-radicals' (the 'neo-rads'), as I will call them, who emerged in the 1990s and took up a similar (or, at least, cognate) agenda. It could be argued that the experimentation stepped up a gear at this point (hence my term 'neo-radicals'). The neo-rads of the 1990s are newer and younger poets, so there is less specific secondary material available on their work. But they have overlapping allegiances and provenances, and it could be said of them that they seek to *continue the continuation* of the revolution begun in the 'high' modernist period of the 1920s and 1930s. Some indicative neo-rad names would be: Sean Bonney, Andrea Brady, Miles Champion, Jeff Hilson, Ira Lightman, Peter Manson, Helen McDonald, Brigid McLeer, Drew Milne, Redell Olsen, Keston Sutherland, Scott Thurston, and Catherine Walsh.[4]

A single-semester or single-year course could not cover the full range of neo-mod and neo-rad poetry, so difficult choices have to be made. There are four available options for constructing the syllabus for BA or MA modules in this area: we can use either a published anthology as the set text (see note 2), or photocopied materials, or individual volumes, or online material (or, of course, some combination of these four). The anthology option is superficially attractive, but it has several disadvantages; the work of the individual poet is devalued in relation to the work of the individual novelist on equivalent contemporary novel courses – an anthology is a single set book, just like a novel, so the impression given is that one novelist is worth twenty or so poets. Further, anthologies have only a handful of poems by each poet, so an anthology-based module could only provide a series of fragmented tasters, rather than opportunities for sustained study. The second option is to use a photocopied course booklet of material. This too is a very labour-intensive method: you would have to obtain permission from all the poets and presses concerned, then assemble the booklet, and finally sell it to the students at the start of the course. The poets, again, may well seem devalued in contrast with novelists, since this will not be seen as a 'proper' book, but the advantages would be that the course material can be tailor-made to your requirements, and it could include critical material. The third option is to use individual books by individual poets as set texts. This gives a poet parity with a novelist, and encourages

a more serious and sustained kind of study. It gives students the experience – perhaps unique for many of them – of buying a book of poetry by
a contemporary poet whose name does not (necessarily) begin with 'H'.
Finally, there is the 'VLE' option, in which an online compendium of
primary and secondary material is assembled which students can access
through the institution's Virtual Learning Environment. This approach,
though inevitably time-consuming, has many advantages, one of the
greatest being that the material constitutes a tailored or bespoke anthology which is unique to a particular course: it can include audio
recordings of the poet's own performances of the work, and useful contextualising material such as interviews with the poet, and manuscript
images.[5]

'Just looking' at a text

Once the syllabus has been compiled, thought can be given to ways
of handling the material in class. Modernist poetry of whatever generation will confront most students with the 'shock of the new', and
our aim must surely be to help students to understand something about
the material they at first feel shocked and affronted by. In the initial
stages, when the perceived strangeness of the material is greatest, it is
wise to find ways of slowing down the rush to judgement. How can
we do this? One technique I use in discussing this kind of work is to
ask students 'just' to describe it. I ask them to tell me as precisely as
possible what is on the page. Elsewhere, I have identified a natural pro-
gression in academic writing from description, through commentary
and discussion to analysis (Barry, 2003). Like everyone else, I was dis-
paraging about 'mere' description, but in teaching this kind of material
there is much to be said for staying at the level of description for as
long as possible. As a technique of teaching literature this procedure is
recommended in Ezra Pound's *An ABC of Reading,* which begins with the
anecdote of Agassiz, the student, and the fish: the graduating student is
asked by Aggasiz to describe the specimen, a request so rudimentary
that the student feels insulted by it, and merely rattles off the textbook definition. Agassiz again asks him to look at the specimen and
describe it, and again, and again. After several days, says Pound, the
fish is in an advanced state of decomposition, but the student knows
something about it. So I ask students not to make any judgements
about what the poet might or might not be trying to do, and whether

they think those aims are good or worthwhile. I want to keep all that 'critique' mentality 'on hold' for as long as possible, and get them 'just' looking.

So instead of the usual clichéd seminar opener 'What did you think of it, then?' (which is useless at best, and fatal at worst, with these poetries), the opener is 'Tell me what's on the page'. Students might then work in pairs at basic description for five or ten minutes, and with a starter piece like Carlyle Reedy's 'The Bedsits' (see below) I would use an image projected by OHP or PowerPoint rather than paper copy. I have found this technique an excellent way of cleansing the doors of perception, and illustrate below the kind of detail and precision a description of an 'open field' page might entail. I have used this piece as an opener on courses because it is so clearly *not* poetry as we generally know it – it unambiguously marks our entry into a realm of distinctly avant-garde practice. Carlyle Reedy is one of the longest-established of the neo-modernist poets, and undoubtedly one of the most radical and uncompromising of innovators.[6] The words seem to be presented more in a pattern than a sequence, and they are, precisely, just words, not phrases or sentences: the piece gives a strong sense of the page as a 'field', in which there are manifest tensions and juxtapositions and connections between the various lexical items, but these are not marked in the usual syntactical ways (by connections like 'and' or 'but', for instance). The questions I would use in conjunction with this piece would be of the following kind (technically, they are 'closed' questions, not 'open' ones like 'What did you think of it?'): Why are the words grouped as they are on the page? What do you think the poem is 'saying'? How would you describe and classify some of the techniques it is using? Is this a 'visual' poem, and if so, what *is* a visual poem, in your view? Is it intended for performance, and if so, how might it be performed? The poem is printed here in full on the following page, and the reader might like to pause and consider it before looking at my comments.

Though it is not placed in the usual title position (which is at the top of the page), the phrase 'The Bedsits' is presumably the title of the piece, since it is in 'title case'.[7] The page seems to be composed as a symmetrical visual design, with blocks of text arranged above and below the title, all words above being lower case, and all words below being upper case. The symmetry is broken in a minor way by the fact that the four 'corner' blocks in the upper part of the page each have four words arranged in four 'lines', while the corner blocks in the lower part of the page each have five words arranged in five 'lines'. In the centre of both halves of

birds   limbs
tongues   plums
nipples   lobes
jelly   sheets

groaning   blackened   they push
flooding   they crush   they thrust
break   they tickle   dark
licking   slick   hot
dying   juicing   beating
drenched   hard   flesh is

quickening   flying   sweat
tingle   dipping   sweet
heaving   stung   meet

hearts   cries
buttocks   strings
passages   marble
thighs   tender

The Bedsits

CHAIRS   MANTLEPIECES
TABLES   CATS
VASES   PIPES
NEWSPAPER   FACES
LINGERIE   BOOTS

SAT UPON   CLUTTERED   CRACKING
BLUE   FOR EATING   IMMOBILE
RANGED   LINING   OF PORCELAIN

SMOKING   FLUSHED   TALKED
RATTLED   SMILING   KNITTED
BURNING   STARCHY   THEY WOULD WEAR

TO READ IN   BY WIRED   MUSICAL
GRIMY   REFLECTING   DRESSED IN
INK SPATTERED   PADDING BY   SLIPPERY

RUGS   MIRRORS
CHESSMEN   DISHES
PEOPLE   TOILETS
GAS FIRES   ANTIMACASSARS
RADIOS   BOOKS

the page is a larger block of text made up of nine three-line blocks in three horizontal sets of three. This kind of 'structural' or 'architectural' description of the text is difficult to write because it concerns an aspect of words on a page which is usually disregarded in literary criticism. It is also unusual for a poem to direct the reader to take note of such things, as this one self-evidently does, by the simple device of infringing the norms which usually govern the arrangement of words on the page. An example of such norms is the convention that the spaces between words are uniform, though convention has, of course, been much disturbed by the long modernist tradition to the point where there is arguably now in existence another 'bibliographic code', as Jerome McGann calls it, for such variable word spacing (McGann, 1991).

When we turn from the morphological structure of the poem to semantics, a pervasive difference of register between upper half and lower half words is very striking. In the upper half, many of the words seem to connote sexual activity – words, for instance, like: tongues, nipples, jelly, limbs, lobes, sheets, groaning, flooding, they crush, they tickle, they push, they thrust, licking, drenched, etc. In the lower half, many of the words are more mundane, suggesting, perhaps, a daily facade which usually effaces this: CHAIRS, TABLES, VASES, NEWSPAPER, MANTLEPIECES, GAS FIRES, RADIOS, DISHES, etc. There are, however, a few 'stray' words in both halves of the pages which would seem to belong better in the other half, such as 'marble' in the top half, and LINGERIE, FLUSHED, BURNING, and SLIPPERY in the lower half. Both halves have a certain period flavour – the *mis-en-scène* of the lower half doesn't really sound like today – 'Bedsits' is an old-fashioned term, and the epoch evoked by MANTLEPIECES, PIPES, RUGS, CHESSMEN, GAS FIRES, RADIOS, and ANTIMACASSARS is more 1930s or 1950s than the present. There may also be an overall mimetic element, whereby the blocks of text on the page are formally arranged like items of furniture in a room, and the formal division of the page into two distinct realms suggests a dichotomy between the diurnal/social conscious world, represented by the lower half of the page, and the nocturnal/eroticised subconscious world, represented by the top half. The spatial reversal of the most obvious way of arranging the page (that is, the fact that the 'subconscious' is on top) may be part of the point of the poem. In the bedsit, or apartment, the two worlds may occupy the same space, but they exist in separate mental compartments, and negotiation between them is difficult.

Reedy's work is characterised by that 'self-conscious attention to text which above all else puts this poetry in the realm of the "experimental" ', and excludes it from the category of poetry 'that is *obviously* and *accessibly* about women's lives' (Tarlo, 1999: 104, 101). Thus, on the 'open field' page, the language often has an element of 'liminalism', often seeming to be poised on a conceptual threshold or interface, so that the words may seem to poise the reader mid-way between signifier and signified, making us experience sound patterns and the 'rustle' of the signifying process itself, while the world signified by the words becomes in some way subordinated to the words themselves, as if 'mere' referentiality is being to some degree held in abeyance. This is like saying that we are involved as readers in watching language being (re)-*invented*, rather than language being *used* (terms used by Robert Sheppard about Maggie O'Sullivan's poetry). As a way of getting students to reach some such conclusion themselves, I would ask them to list some aspects of normal language use which are 'suspended' or 'de-activated' for the duration of this poem, and likewise, what potential aspects of language which we normally 'de-activate' in reading a page are brought into play here. The question may initially be hard to grasp, and my supplementary prompt would be that in reading a page of prose we 'de-activate' any semantic awareness of line endings – the point at which lines begin and end has no meaning, we (rightly) assume. In reading poetry, by contrast, we 'activate' our awareness of line endings, and are alert to this feature, on the grounds that (crudely speaking) line endings are selected by the poet rather than imposed by the printing process.

In moving from 'just looking' at the piece to 'just thinking' about it, students would be asked to consider how writers like Reedy represent a move away from the 'masculinism' of 'open field' pioneer Charles Olson, whose influence dominated the neo-modernist period. Olson's seminal essay 'Projective Verse' would be part of the set reading on this issue, a piece which envisages a 'body centred' concept of writing based on the notion of 'breath'. It could be juxtaposed with the Hélène Cixous concept of *écriture féminine* (in her essay 'The Laugh of the Medusa', which may well be familiar to students from their literary theory courses). In this piece Cixous insists that 'Women must write through their bodies', just as Olson's phallic triumphalism insists that for a man (a word used countless times in the essay) 'Language is one of his proudest acts', it is 'in his physiology'. Women experimentalists, it could be argued, have taken over and transformed the Olsonian 'open field' method and have become its main protagonists. In her 'Afterword' to *Out of Everywhere* Wendy Mulford draws attention to the nature and provenance of the 'radical form' used by these poets:

> For trust in 'radical form' implies openness to the challenge of meaning-generation wherever it may be accessed, and by whatever strategies – a form not handed down, but arrived at, one which the poet *discovers in and through the process of the work* the logical extension of the inherent capabilities of the so-called 'open-field' composition of earlier post-war American poetries such as those of Olson and Black Mountain. (Mulford, in O'Sullivan, 1996: 239–40)

Although it is perhaps a little surprising to see Olson cited as the over-arching influence on the women writers in the anthology, it constitutes a dramatic claim that the true line of continuity from modernism runs through these women poets, rather than through the male line of experimentation. But Olson is not taken by any means uncritically. The collection begins with the eminent poet and professor (at SUNY Buffalo) Susan Howe. In a letter written some years ago to one of my students, Howe carefully distanced her present poetic self from Olson, while at the same time warmly acknowledging his influence:

> I have some problems (lots of them) with Olson's later writing and with a certain vatic cultic following he encouraged . . . I would say that though he certainly got me started I don't read his work much anymore . . . What I love about Olson is his passion. I love his love for Melville and the way he writes about him. I love his need to go back and back. *I love the way he understands one must enter into the mystery of the violence in the very structure of a sentence or a line break or the space of a blank sheet of paper. Mapping, collage, juxtaposition. Walter Benjamin writes about using quotations in this way. The violence of using quotation etc.* (Private letter to James Putnam, 1998, my italics, quoted with permission)

Olson's notion of the page takes it as space rather than time, so to speak: in other words, it is not just a blank screen down which the lines are scrolled, in time with the sub-vocalised performance in the mind of the reader. Rather, the page space is broken and discontinuous, and contains patterns and juxtapositions; it is always a 'disruptive poetics' in some sense (hence the emphasis on violence in the italicised section of the letter above), even when the resulting page is highly ordered and pat-terned. That structure disrupts the way we usually 'read' a page, 'reading' being generally synonymous with the continuous scrolling down just referred to. In other words, we are distinctly in that 'modernist' realm of 'disjunctive', 'disruptive', 'discontinuous', phrase-based rather than sentence-based writing.[8]

'Just looking' at a complete work

Frequently, criticism which purports to discuss whole poems really just discusses individual words, phrases, or lines within them. Similarly, criticism of books of poetry often seems mainly a discussion of individual poems. At the stage of introducing a new complete work, therefore, I ask students to attempt, not a close *reading* of a single page or poem, but a close *looking* at the whole text. I illustrate what I mean by this kind of whole-book description with the Ken Edwards text, below, where the aim is to get students to realise things about the structure and architecture of the set text, rather than zooming in straightaway to close-up individual phrase-and-page scrutiny. I chose this text for the syllabus because it is 'about' the sonnet form, expanding it and 'radicalising' it, so it represents a kind of interface between the two poetic traditions which Edwards himself identifies in the article cited in note 1. It is also a text which is lively, personal, inventive, and engaging, and hence a good choice for the kind of course under discussion here.

Ken Edwards' collection *eight + six* is a book of one hundred sonnets – or fourteen-line poems – ('mostly for Elaine'). It is in two sections, these being 'i' (pp. 9–64), and 'ii' (pp. 67–108).[9] Each poem has its own capitalised title, though some are what I will call 'composites', meaning a set of poems which are 'clustered' together by using the same title. These include the following: six pieces called 'A Wedding', the first un-numbered, the remainder running 2–6, pp. 81–6; seven pieces called 'Perturbations', the first un-numbered, the remainder running 2–7, pp. 100–6; and three pieces called 'I Go To Sleep', un-numbered and 2, pp. 19–21, plus 3, p. 48, making this a *disguised composite*, in that the component parts do not all appear on successive pages. There are also the following sets: 'His Last Gasp', un-numbered and 2, pp. 60–1, and 'In Lithuania', un-numbered and 2, pp. 95–6, which might be called *composite pairs*, and 'The Panic Museum (*Theory of Poetry*)', p. 14, with 'THE POETS GATHER (*Theory of Poetry 2*)', p. 29, which can be called a *concealed composite pair*, since the pairing of these two separated pieces is indicated in the subtitles rather than the titles; and finally there is a composite set where the title varies, 'One to One', 'One to Many', 'Many to One', 'Many to Many', pp. 88–91. Having identified the 'composites', my questions would be: What are they for? Do they correspond to any aspect of more traditional sonnet sequences? My own response would be that the effect of the composites seems equivalent to the way a set of adjacent poems in a sonnet sequence will provide a series of different 'takes' on a given theme or idea ('marriage', for instance, or 'friendship'). This is one of the ways in which any poems which are 'grouped' have to be made to talk to each other.

Formally, what is common to all the poems in the book is that they all have fourteen lines and are all confined to a single page, but there are many variations in the look of the poems on the page, just as there are variations in rhyme and metrical patterns across a traditional sonnet sequence. Students could be asked to draw up a brief typology of these variations, and data such as the following would probably emerge: most of the poems have a justified left margin and an unjustified right; some have a prose-like and 'wordy' look, others look fragmented and mini- malist; some have a break between octet and sestet, some don't; some are fragmented and impressionistic, while others set a realist scene in a manner that is almost novelistic, such as 'The Engine of Love' (p. 13), which begins:

> Dark drizzle falls & falls the sparkling dark
> rain falls as evening falls on the football pitch
> on the Ex-Servicemen's Club & Social Centre
> where bitter's a pound a pint & where talk too
> is cheap on a Saturday night

Some of the poems muse explicitly about poetry, the nature of the self and of experience, or about love and the passage of time, these being matters which have often been the focus of sequences of sonnets in the past. Some have literary echoes and allusions, for example 'Interrogation Room Remix' (p. 53), which opens with the line 'The pillar perished is whereto I leant' from Thomas Wyatt's sonnet, and quotes five other complete lines from the same sonnet. The note tells us that the poem is 'In memoriam Eric Mottram, 1924–95', Mottram being Edwards' teacher at King's College. Wyatt's line about the pillar occurs again in 'Three' (p. 69) and 'Two' (p. 87), while 'One' (p. 108, the last poem in the book) also quotes a line from the same poem, as does 'Four' (p. 63). This makes 'Four', 'Three', 'Two', 'One' (which occur in the book in that order) a kind of concealed, reversed composite, and since Wyatt's poem is also incorporated into the cover design (printed in Zapf Dingbats), it can be taken as a major thematic vehicle for the whole sequence.[10]

In close-up: 'point' and 'flow'

The sequence seems to accept personal change as natural, including the inevitable and gradual shift from what we used to think, to what we think now. This seems especially so of the poem 'THE POETS GATHER *(Theory of Poetry 2)*', which is one piece which I would look at more closely. For the discussion of a complete poem like this I use (in early sessions, at least) a modified form of a four-stage reading schema for poems, originally devised by myself and Marianne Taylor at Aberystwyth,[11] the aim of which is to help readers to give as much attention to the whole poem as to the parts of it. Thus, the four stages alternate between attention to 'points' in the poem (where we stop the flow of the poem, so to speak, and get off, in order to examine particular parts of it) and attention to the 'flow' or dynamic of the whole poem (where we stand further back, as in a gallery when we want to get a sense of the whole composition of a painting). The whole procedure can be set out in schematic form as follows:

1 ('point')
Read through the poem two or three times, then identify the word or phrase which seems the strangest or most surprising in the poem. Try changing that word or phrase to one which you would consider less surprising. How is the *overall* effect of the poem now changed?

2 ('flow')
Poems have 'stages and phases'. We might identify an 'entry phase', a 'development phase', and an 'exit phase' which may double back, or break off or transpose earlier material in some way. What 'stages' can you see in this poem?

3 ('point')
Poems often have a 'crux', or 'nub', or 'node' or 'vortex' – a section of extra complexity, from which we tend to look away. Find the bit in the poem which has this 'ardent obliquity' (J. H. Prynne's term, meaning, more-or-less, passionate indirectness) – talk back to it and 'negotiate' with it.

4 ('flow')
Poems have *patterns*. Identify some in the poem (for example, those concerning line length, stanza length, rhyme, rhythm, type of vocabulary, angle of view, and so on). Having identified a pattern, look for points where the pattern is broken. Breaks in pattern are usually at points of high significance.

As the course progresses, students supplement or develop the four steps, gradually tailoring their own method, and broadly speaking the intention is that they shift from a passive/contemplative reading stance to one which is more active/interventionist, which is perhaps the difference between *reading* poetry and *studying* poetry. How might this method be used on the poem in question?

THE POETS GATHER
(Theory of Poetry 2)

The poets gather. They, like poetry itself,
want to be, not seem. Which is seemly.
These are their stories, and the summation
of them is this: that they reject story.
Why, they are paralytic with joy: on their plastic chairs
They identify the depth of field of such paradoxes
and exult in it – they presuppose no need
for emotional closure.
That was then. And now?
Well, only you and I are left, and we're engaged
in refutation. Yours is a pint of bitter,
mine's a Guinness. This proposition is true. We raise
our glasses, we refute it.
And refute again.

A fairly close use of the schema might pick out at the first stage the word 'paralytic' in the phrase 'paralytic with joy', since 'paralytic' collocates oddly with the phrase 'with joy'. The more normative 'displaced' word in the collocation might be 'ecstatic': the word 'paralytic' suggests that the poem is suspicious of high theoretical talk about poetry, and perhaps of *all* talk about poetry, wondering whether such talk is actually more inhibiting than enabling. The poets who 'want to be, not seem' echo the ending of Archibald MacLeish's '*Ars Poetica*', 'A poem should not mean / But be' (1976: 106–7). Likewise, the same scepticism about detached intellectual exposition is seen in the lines 'We refute it. / And refute again', which echo Johnson's response to Berkeley's proof of the non-existence of matter, spoken while kicking a stone, 'I refute it, *thus*' (as reported in Boswell's *Life of Samuel Johnson*).

    Secondly, on the idea of 'phases', the poem breaks clearly into two, these being the 'then' of the 'octet' and the 'now' of the sestet. But the latter repeats the former: in the former, something as concrete as a poem is (reprehensibly) made into an abstract concept, while in the latter something as concrete as a Guinness is made into a 'proposition'. The shift between 'then' and 'now' suggests different ways of thinking at different times of life, with the youthful earnestness of theorising giving way to a more relaxed pragmatism later on. At the third stage, we might identify the 'crux' as the lines 'They identify the depth of field of such paradoxes / and exult in it – they presuppose no need / for emotional closure.' Here the poem seems to comment on itself, enclosing the irony of its own 'message' in irony, so to speak, for the 'paradoxes' mentioned are exemplified by its own phrase 'paralytic with joy', and the phrase 'depth of field' mocks any attempt (such as my own) to say precisely what it means. The 'plastic chairs' seem to evoke the seminar rooms in which such futile discussions often take place, and the disregard of the need for 'emotional closure' may gesture towards ideas about the 'impersonality' of poetry. If something like that really is what the 'crux' section is saying, then there is no way out of it which can leave the critic intact.

The final step of the schema (thinking of patterns) is often challenging in the case of open-field and free forms, but this can make it more rather than less fruitful, since it can involve reformulating our notions of what a pattern is. A general proposition for discussion is that all poems have patterns of some kind, and that patterns can be of the fractal type, that is, rough and fragmented, like the pattern seen by looking along the top of a line of trees. In this poem, the 'ghost' of the regular sonnet pattern is also in play (mention has already been made of 'octet' and 'sestet', and the implied *volta* or turn between them). The poem employs a style of vocabulary associated with logic and intellectual argument ('summation', 'identify', 'paradoxes', 'presupposed', 'refutation', 'proposition'), but against that, its own procedures and propositions are defiantly illogical (being is seemly, the story is the rejection of story, the proposition which is true is refuted – a logical impossibility, etc.). Against the scholastic tone, a 'blokey' register asserts itself ('Yours is a pint of bitter, / mine's a Guinness') in a manner which actually seems both blokey and scholastic at the same time ('we refute it. / And refute again.'). The poets refute the theory of poetry, but from intellectually above, so to speak, rather than below – in a word, they refute it *thus*, by actually doing it, that is, by writing poetry about it.

Doing the queen strut

My final text is Jeff Hilson's book *Stretchers*, which takes us from the neo-mod to the neo-rad generation. It was published complete by Reality

Street in 2006, following publication of two of its parts as Writers Forum 'chapbooks' in 2001 and 2002, and the appearance of several shorter sections from it in various magazines. *Stretchers* comprises fifty-four pages of text, followed by a seven-page essay entitled 'Why I wrote *Stretchers*'. The broadest characterisation of the book would be that it is about the experience of living on the Isle of Dogs in the East End of London over a period of fifteen years.[12]

The main pedagogical reason for discussing this text here is that it raises the question of how data about poetic provenance and documentary context can be negotiated by students. The sequence represents a kind of writing which I have elsewhere described as 'content-specific', in the sense that it seems to require the reader's 'participatory engagement' with its materials as well as with the words on its pages.[13] But how should this engagement be fostered? Is there a way of avoiding the off-loading of information in a mini-lecture format, and instead getting students to assemble data themselves? One source of relevant material arises from the enormous growth, from about 1995 onwards, of the academic field now usually called 'Literary London' or 'London in Literature'. 'LL studies', which is strongly interdisciplinary in character, is affiliated to the theorisation of notions of the city and urban space which has been a phenomenon of the past two decades. In the LL field, a range of books of an anthology or survey type is beginning to emerge,[14] there are MA and undergraduate courses on the topic,[15] specialised journals and conferences,[16] and the growth of a new interdisciplinary outlook and methodology which derives from the new urbanism.[17]

A starting point for the 'participatory' approach to this area with the Hilson book would be to ask students to find out which other poets have written about the Isle of Dogs. Using web resources significant progress can be made in a couple of hours: thus, a Google search on '"Isle of Dogs" + poetry' reveals the play *The Isle of Dogs* by Nashe and Jonson, performed in 1597 at the Swan theatre in Bankside and immediately suppressed on the grounds that it was a 'lewd plaie' full of 'slanderous matter'. So a link between the Isle of Dogs and social controversy is immediately apparent, reinforcing the air of social confrontation associated with the place, as if it has always been a locale where the tectonic plates of capitalism grind viciously together, threatening eruptions. In the period during which Hilson lived there, the nature of the district was changing fundamentally: from having been a working-class area servicing the docks and adjacent industries, it became the centre of a gentrified 'Docklands' whose 'industry' is financial and (to a lesser extent) commercial.

Unsurprisingly, the Isle of Dogs is not unexplored territory for contemporary poets and urban scrutineers, and the Google search will also turn up poems by Paul Murphy, and references to Sean Bonney's Salt collection *Blade Pitch Control Unit*, as well as to *The Waste Land*. Iain Sinclair's *Lud Heat* of 1975, and the late Ken Smith's urban sequence 'The London Poems' (in his 1986 Bloodaxe volume *Terra*) are the immediate poetic predecessors of *Stretchers*. Hilson's explicit intertextual link-up (in his end-essay) is with Iain Sinclair's dismissal of the Isle of Dogs at the start of his prose work *Lights Out for the Territory* (Penguin, 1997) as a graffiti-free place, if only because 'there's no surface rough enough to take the pen'. Sinclair's meaning is that the glass and chrome of the newly yuppified terrain has smoothed away and obliterated all trace of character or dissent. Sinclair's title puns, of course, on the last line of *Huckleberry Finn*, in which Huck decides it's time to 'light out for the territories'. Though the poet doesn't mention it, there is a neat intertextual symmetry in the way Hilson takes the title of his riposte from the opening lines of the same book, where the Huck persona says that the book *Tom Sawyer*, in which he previously appeared, 'is mostly a true book, with some stretchers'. Hilson, then, appropriates the 'narratorial fictiveness' of Twain's writing, and his own stretchers, he says, are also 'a barrel of odds and ends', like Huck's stew, and a discourse which 'lives in the gaps of the languages used by grown ups and professionals who use smooth, specialised languages which say "keep out".' The dichotomies set up here are fairly clear: *Stretchers* strives to be the rough graffiti of the terrain which Sinclair sees as wiped away by the smooth professionals with their mouse swipes and their glossy PR-speak.

The foregoing, I hope, gives a kind of contextual and intertextual placing of *Stretchers*. I would, again, ask students to do the intertextual tracking for themselves; the lead questions would be 'What echoes, allusions, references, connotations, etc., do you pick up in the text? Track some of them, and consider some of the effects of writing in this way: for example, does allusiveness make the writing less accessible? Does it imply a *cohesion* between word and world, or does it highlight a *tension* between them?' Library copies of a basic text like Graham Allen's *Intertextuality* (in the New Critical Idiom series) would be available as part of the library resources for the course. Like Ken Smith (whose sequence used twelve-line 'curtal sonnets' throughout), Hilson uses a highly formalised structure for the sequence, but he emphasises what might be called the 'randomness' of the form. By this I mean that the form has no inherent connection with the subject matter, and is not striving to be 'organic' with it (as a Leavisite might have wanted) in such a way that sound, shape, and structure would strive to be an echo of the sense. Thus, the fifty-four 'stretchers' which make up the book, each one of which fills a single page, are all of thirty-three lines. But why that number? Hilson says that 'the decision to use a 33-line form was ultimately banal, based on my age at the time of writing the first set of them', though 'not all the poems are 33 lines long because sometimes I miscounted'. This seems a conscious defiance of accepted notions of literary form, a defiance which could be seen as germane to the neo-rad stance.

At the 'just looking' stage, we note that *Stretchers* is divided into three untitled sections, these being '1–12', '13–33', and 'vol 3'. The three parts are uneven in length, the first containing 12 stretchers, the second and third 21 each. Each of the three parts has an epigraph, which I take to be signalling the bias of the content in each case: the first epigraph is about an island, which can be read as indicating that the first part has a topographical focus on the Isle of Dogs itself. The second is a comment on stretching, taken from poet Maggie O'Sullivan, and perhaps indicating a focus on the arranging of words as cognate with the arrangement of places and spaces. The last is a quotation from architectural theorist Christopher Alexander, author of *The Timeless Way of Building*, and perhaps indicating a focus, again, on arranging, that is, on composing the 'text of the city', so that the parts can live and breathe together. The stretchers are arranged in a column down the centre of each page, with the columns becoming somewhat narrower as the book progresses. The flight from notions of 'organic' form is further underlined by the following remark:

> I have tried whenever possible to avoid the 'effects' which a line ending can produce. Any 'effect' produced by a line ending is accidental. I do not see stretchers as having lines. They are more prose pieces with a frayed right margin. They are tatters, ragged flags. (p. 72)

This too is a strong statement of the rejection of the dominant aesthetics of contemporary poetry. The effects generally admired by those who write about (say) Heaney or Hughes are often highly localised – the apt or expressive word, the phrase which flickers with multiple signification, the line ending which supposedly enacts an added subtlety in the thought, and so on. Neo-mods and neo-rads are less interested in this kind of detail than in overall effects – 'flow' rather than 'points', in the terms used earlier, or in other words the onward 'teleological' drive of the sequence, rather than the local, 'entropic' braking force which seeks to arrest the flow and fix the attention on a single, highly charged 'aestheticised' spot. In this sense, the difference between the two kinds of poetry discussed by Ken Edwards (see note 1) is that one tends to privilege the 'teleological' flow, while the other privileges the 'entropic' point. Hilson draws attention to this dimension when he tells us 'Every stretcher tells a story and each story contains many other stories. The opening (line) of each stretcher is in a way another way of saying "Once upon a time."' This, then, is another strong pedagogical reason for choosing the Hilson text, for it demands head-on debate about the extent to which contemporary modernism has a distinct and separate aesthetic and what some of the important elements of that aesthetic might be. The secondary material for this debate would be the remaining items listed in note 1.

When we look closely at the individual stretcher, the anarchic, surreal juxtapositions of style and material are very striking. This one, for instance, is number 24 (p. 35), and it begins and ends, as they all do, with an ellipsis:

>...on the way to the cleve
> lands and the bloom fields
> (this then the end of long
> division) poe has she has
> been charmed by *please*
> *buy an cat or dog food* for
> what what kind of days
> thinking of our spaniel *kitty*
> *kitty kitty* helps you with 7
> days a week helps you 55
> days in pell-mell helps you
> once upon a time (well do
> you) if not pull if so part
> then you will see the tall
> thin ladies they are lookout
> they are unfinished they
> will make a comeback as
> heart's desire (mainly were
> whispering I am lost in this
> book) and then the flood
> came along which he liked
> (it was my country cousin
> caught up with curtis (doris)

> doris in the dock-road mostly
> aged 5 danced a queen strut
> through the cluster block
> to the lifting bridge its soffits
> gently curved and there
> danced a quarter round with
> the rough-&-toughs (uprights
> of silos) where she sang the
> one about pouring on water
> for a barrel of pears...

What can we make of it? Well, the end-essay remarks that 'The poems incorporate a lot of found material', and the same paragraph ends with the information that 'A number of the stretchers were wholly lifted from a single source' (71). The first sentence is true of this one, but not the second, though the last paragraph of the essay identifies one of its sources as Nikolas Pevsner's 'London Docklands' volume in the *Buildings of England* series. From this Hilson takes the technical term 'queen strut' (a section of wooden roof beam) and imagines it as a kind of funky dance step: the term 'soffits' is presumably from the same source, and denotes the underside of an arch, here suggestive of some kind of decorum-challenging unseemly display. The feisty character so conjured up seems to dance through the whole stretcher in a kind of irresistible in-rush of Bakhtinian urban carnival. The whole piece seems feminised – a parade 'to the cleve / lands and the bloom fields', a kind of anarcho-feminist challenge to the masculinist waste lands of the Docklands ('the end of long / division'), ladies who 'will make a comeback as / heart's desire', country cousins dancing the queen strut along the dock-road with the formerly excluded rough-&-toughs. 'The / one about pouring on water' which is being sung is presumably the song 'London's Burning', again suggestive of the apocalyptic collapse of an era, and an area, but with strong overtones of a regenerative claiming back of the terrain. The starkness of such juxtapositions is enacted in this stretcher, and in *Stretchers* as a whole.

Overall, the kind of course I have discussed here aims to achieve something comparable – the regenerative claiming back of rejected poetic terrain. If at the start of the course the students (in Hilson's words) 'mainly were / whispering I am lost in this / book', it is hoped that by the end they might have 'danced a queen strut / through the cluster blocks' of disjunctive textuality.

Notes

1. Eric Mottram's defining essay 'The British Poetry Revival, 1960–75' is reprinted in Robert Hampson and Peter Barry (eds), *New British Poetries: the Scope of the Possible* (Manchester: Manchester University Press, 1993), 15–45. For an excellent account of some of the differences between 'BPR' poetry and the rest, see Ken Edwards, 'The Two Poetries', *Angelaki* 3(1) (April 2000): 25–36. Also extremely useful is the chapter 'Innovative Poetry in English', pp. 121–38 in *Meaning Performance: Essays on Poetry* by Tony Lopez (Cambridge: Salt, 2006); the chapter 'Linguistically Innovative Poetry 1978–2000', pp. 142–67 in Robert Sheppard's *The Poetry of Saying* (Liverpool: Liverpool University Press, 2005); and for an overview account of the nature of 'BPR' writing see the chapter 'The British Poetry Revival – Some Characteristics', pp. 123–43 in Peter Barry, *Poetry Wars* (Cambridge: Salt, 2006).

2. These include: Andrew Crozier and Tim Longville's *A Various Art* (Manchester: Carcanet, 1987); *The New British Poetry*, ed. Gillian Allnutt, Fred D'Aguiar, Ken Edwards, and Eric Mottram (London: Paladin, 1988); Iain Sinclair's *Conductors of Chaos: a Poetry Anthology* (London: Paladin, 1996); *Other British and Irish Poetry since 1970*, ed. Ric Caddel and Peter Quartermain (Middletown, CT: Wesleyan University Press, 1999); *Foil: An Anthology – Poetry, 1985–2000, Defining New Poetry and Performance Writing from England, Scotland and Wales, 1985–2000*, ed. Nicholas Johnson (Devon: Etruscan Books, 2000); Keith Tuma's *Anthology of Twentieth-Century British and Irish Poetry* (Oxford: Oxford University Press, 2001); and *Poems for the Millennium*, Volume II: *From Postwar to Millennium* (Berkeley: University of California Press, 1998), ed. Jerome Rothenberg and Pierre Joris.

3. A pairing of primary text and secondary text for each of these would be as follows: Allen Fisher, *Gravity* (Cambridge: Salt, 2004) and *The Salt Companion to Allen Fisher*, ed. Cris Cheek and Robert Hampson (Cambridge: Salt, 2007). Bill Griffiths, *The Mud Fort* (Cambridge: Salt 2004) and *The Salt Companion to Bill Griffiths*, ed. William Rowe (Cambridge: Salt, 2007). Lee Harwood, *Collected Poems* (Exeter: Shearsman Books, 2004) and *The Salt Companion to Lee Harwood*, ed. Robert Sheppard (Cambridge: Salt, 2007). Maggie O'Sullivan, *In the House of the Shaman* (London: Reality Street, 1996) and *The Salt Companion to Maggie O'Sullivan*, ed. Lawrence Upton (Cambridge: Salt, forthcoming). Denise Riley, *Selected Poems* (London: Reality Street, 2000) and *The Salt Companion to Denise Riley*, ed. Simon Perril (Cambridge: Salt, 2007).

   The use of recordings of the poets reading can be an enormous help in the classroom: in the case of the above poets, examples are: **Lee Harwood**, *Rockdrill 3: The Chart Table*, Audio Books CD (ISBN: 1 905001 02 9 and ISBN: 978 1 905001 02 6) (Manchester: Carcanet Press 2004); **Maggie O'Sullivan**, online reading from *In the House of the Shaman*, and other material, at: http://www.writing.upenn.edu/pennsound/x/OSullivan.html; **Denise Riley**, *Denise Riley Reading from her Poems*, CD available from The Poetry Archive: http://www.poetryarchive.org/poetryarchive/home.do

4. The list is Robert Hampson's, who emphasises that it is in no way comprehensive, or even representative of this group. All the same, it offers an excellent 'starter pack', and a key book from each is as follows: **Sean Bonney** (poet and academic, born Brighton), *Blade Pitch Control Unit* (Cambridge: Salt

Contemporary Poets, 2005); **Andrea Brady** (born Philadelphia, 1974, poet and lecturer at Queen Mary's, London), *Vacation of a Lifetime* (Cambridge: Salt Contemporary Poets, 2001); **Miles Champion** (born Nottingham, 1968), *Compositional Bonbons Placate* (Manchester: Carcanet, 1996); **Drew Milne** (born 1964, lecturer at Cambridge), *The Damage: New and Selected Poems* (Cambridge: Salt Modern Poets, 2001); **Jeff Hilson** (born Singapore, 1966, poet and lecturer in creative writing at Roehampton University), *Stretchers* (London: Reality Street, 2006); **Ira Lightman** (born 1967), one of four poets in *Vital Movement* (London: Reality Street Editions 4packs, 1998); **Helen McDonald**, *Shaler's Fish* (Devon: Etruscan Books, 2001); **Brigid McLeer** (Irish-born, London-based performance-writing lecturer and text-installation artist); **Peter Manson** (born Glasgow, 1969), *For the Good of Liars* (London: Barque Press, 2006); **Redell Olsen** (performance and site-specific poet, lecturer in creative writing at Royal Holloway, London University), *Secure Portable Space* (London: Reality Street Editions, 2004); **Keston Sutherland** (poet and lecturer at Sussex University), *Neocosis* (London: Barque Press, 2005); **Scott Thurston** (born Surrey, 1973, poet and lecturer at Salford University), *Hold* (Exeter: Shearsman Press, 2006); and **Catherine Walsh** (born Dublin 1964), *City West* (Exeter: Shearsman Books, 2005). Of these poets, Milne, McDonald, and Walsh are in the Tuma anthology; MacDonald, Manson, Milne, Lightman, and McLeer are in *Foil*, and Walsh is in *Other*. Details of these anthologies are given in note 2.

5. For an excellent example of this approach, see Charles Bernstein's essay in this collection and the material for his course 'English 88: American Poetry Modern and Contemporary' at the University of Pennsylvania, http://www.writing.upenn.edu/bernstein/syllabi/88-intro.html.

6. The poem is in *Out of Everywhere: Linguistically Innovative Poetry by Women in North America & the* UK, ed. Maggie O'Sullivan (London: Reality Street Editions, 1996), p. 149. There are several other pieces by Reedy in the same book which would be suitable for repeating this exercise in class. For an essay by Carlyle Reedy on her own poetic practice see Denise Riley (ed.), *Poets on Writing: Britain 1970–1991* (London: Macmillan, 1992), which also has much useful and enlightening material by poets in the 'BPR' orbit. For other material on contemporary women experimental poets see: Alison Mark and Deryn Rees-Jones (eds), *Contemporary Women's Poetry: Reading/Writing/Practice* (Basingstoke: Macmillan, 2000), in which especially relevant chapters are: Chapter 9 by Maggie O'Sullivan, which both describes and enacts some of her techniques; Chapter 16, by Carol Watts, which is on interpellation and the poetry of Denise Riley; and Chapter 21 by Harriet Tarlo, which is on the contemporary avant-garde and the issue of gender.

7. Am I justified in making this assumption? In the source, all the other pieces by this author have a title, in the usual 'title case' form, at the top of the page. Evidence for my assumption is (a) The phrase 'The Bedsits' is centred. (b) It is in 'title case'. (c) It is in a common 'title form', in that it is a short phrase beginning with the definite article, like the titles of three of the other five pieces by this author in the source (though one of these three titles is aligned to left margin rather than centred). (d) It is in a larger typeface than the remainder of the text, in common with all the titles in the source. The evidence against is that the titles of literary works always occur at the start

or top of the piece. This 'mini debate' about titling conventions raises issues about the expectations we have of pages and the way they 'perform' or 'stage' a text, issues which are highly relevant to the discussion of 'open field' poetics. It also makes explicit elements of the semiotics of textuality which are not commonly articulated by readers, and this too is a very useful procedure for students of open field work.

8. For these terms and concepts see Peter Quartermain, *Disjunctive Poetics: From Gertrude Stein and Louis Zukofsky to Susan Howe* (Cambridge: Cambridge University Press, 1992).

9. I have not looked for any structural symmetry or thematic shift between the two parts, but searching for data along these lines would be a useful task for students to undertake.

10. I found the following reviews of *eight + six* very useful: James Wilkes in 'Intercapillary Space' (http://intercapillaryspace.blogspot.com/2006/10/ken-edwards-eight-six.html) (accessed 12 July 2007); Edmund Hardy in 'Terrible Work' (http://www.terriblework.co.uk/eight.htm) (accessed 12 July 2007); in 'Shearsman', as 'Book of the Month', January 2004 (http://www.shearsman.com/archive/bookofmonth/2004/jan.html) (accessed 12 July 2007).

11. For the full version see 'The end is nigh: reading short poems', in Peter Barry, *English in Practice* (London: Edward Arnold, 2003), pp. 14–19.

12. For a useful review of *Stretchers* see 'Intercapillary Space', 2005 (http://intercapillaryspace.blogspot.com/2006/08/jeff-hilson-stretchers.html) (accessed 11 January 2008).

13. See Chapter 8, 'Allen Fisher and "Content-Specific" Poetry' in *New British Poetries* (details in note 1).

14. I have found the following very useful: *Waterstone's Guide to London Writing*, ed. Nick Rennison (Brentford: Waterstone's Booksellers Ltd, 1999); *Thames: an Anthology of River Poems*, ed. Anna Adams (London Enitharmon Press, 1999), with preface by Iain Sinclair; *London in Poetry and Prose*, ed. Anna Adams (London: Enitharmon Press, 2002); *London: a Collection of Poetry of Place*, ed. Barnaby Rogerson (Glendle, Arizona: Elan Press, 2004); *London from Punk to Blair*, ed. Joe Kerr and Andrew Gibson (London: Reaktion Books, 2004); *The Swarming Streets: Twentieth Century Literary Representations of London*, ed. Lawrence Phillips (New York: Rodopi, 2004); and *London: City of Disappearances*, ed. Iain Sinclair (Harmondsworth: Penguin, 2006).

15. For example, the Literary London MA at Greenwich University, and at undergraduate level such courses as 'Literary London, 1666 to the Present' at Goldsmiths, and 'London in Literature' at UCL.

16. For example, the online *Literary London Journal*, based at Liverpool Hope University (http://www.literarylondon.org/london-journal/index.html), and the conferences on Contemporary London at the Museum of London in 2003, on 'Teaching London' at University of Westminster in 2006, and on 'Literary London' at Brunel University in 2008.

17. Covering such concepts as *flaneurie*, situationism, psychogeography, and heterotopia – see Jenny Bavidge's forthcoming *Theorists of the City: Walter Benjamin, Henri Lefebvre and Michel de Certeau* (London: Routledge, 2009). The books of Edward Soja, such as *Postmetropolis: Critical Studies of Cities and Regions* (Oxford: Basil Blackwell, 2000), make an excellent starting point on 'new urbanisms'.

Works cited

Barry, Peter (2003) *English in Practice*. London: Edward Arnold.

Edwards, Ken (2003) *eight + six*. London: Reality Street Editions.

Hilson, Jeff (2006) *Stretchers*. London: Reality Street.

MacLeish, Archibald (1976) *New & Collected Poems, 1917–1976*. Boston: Houghton Mifflin.

McGann, Jerome (1991) *The Textual Condition*. Princeton: Princeton University Press.

O'Sullivan, Maggie (ed.) (1996) *Out of Everywhere: Linguistically Innovative Poetry by Women in North America & the UK*. London: Reality Street Editions.

Tarlo, Harriet (1999) 'Provisional Pleasures: the Challenge of Contemporary Experimental Women Poets', *Feminist Review* 62: 94–112.

7
Modernist Pedagogy at the End of the Lecture: IT and the Poetics Classroom

Alan Filreis

> I dwell in possibility
> A Fairer House than Prose...
> For Occupation – This...
> Emily Dickinson (#657/327)

> They cannot.
> A note.
> They cannot.
> A float.
> They cannot.
> They dote.
> They cannot.
> They as denote.
> Miracles play.
> Play fairly.
> Play fairly well.
> A well.
> As well.
> As or as presently.
> Let me recite what history teaches. History teaches.
> Gertrude Stein, 'If I told him: a Completed
Portrait of Picasso' (466)

Intrigued by what Stein might mean by 'teaches' in the seemingly agencyless phrase 'history teaches' – is 'history' not usually the taught object rather than the pedagogical subject? – I will argue in the end that history *doesn't* teach that history teaches. Modernism is a topic, of course, but it is also a modality – a didactic, or more properly perhaps, an *anti-didactic* mode in which any recitation of what history teaches is ironized. Conventional denotative pedagogy (*teacher points to text and then to an object in the world, implying or saying outright: 'This is what it means'*) is not up to the challenge of permitting the performance of such self-reflexivity, miracles playing fairly well, we might call it in Stein's terms, as an alternative to the historical mode. In modernism's materials must at least implicitly be a meta-pedagogy.

The problem will be to define or at least describe an alternative. Although he was not writing about teaching, Bruce Andrews was imagining a specific practice when he expressed the hope 'for a revived radicalism of constructivist noise or athematic "informal music"' in the world of poetry and poetics. Aligned with the spirit of this, I wonder here if the poetry classroom might be filled with such noise. The 'use' of new technologies to abet the teaching of poetry is not going to make a bit of difference unless some sort of fundamental pedagogical change accompanies it. The quality of that changed environment might indeed sound something like Andrews' athematic informal music (Bernstein, 1998: 73). If it is true that 'An onomatopoetic expression automatically entails the specification of what is being described' (Tawada, 2009: 192), then the teacher of that expression who wishes to describe specifically must to some extent reproduce the non-sense or sound-sense of the verse. Because of the difficulty of effecting such reproduction, most advocates of an historically capacious modernism – the radical modernism that embraces archaic, pre-literate forms, the non-Eliotic mode that defies New Critical analysis – have argued that such poetry simply does not belong in the classroom. If one accepts such a contention, such as that put forward by Jerome Rothenberg in 1975 in his 'Dialogue on Oral Poetry', then one must either remove this poetics from the curriculum or rebuild the classroom space and reinvent the role of the teacher. 'As for poetry "belonging" in the classroom, it's like the way they taught us sex in those old hygiene classes: not performance but semiotics. If I had taken Hygiene 71 seriously, I would have become a monk; & if I had taken college English seriously, I would have become an accountant.' Yet Rothenberg has taught in schools, and so admits to the realisation that 'the classroom becomes a substitute for those places (coffee shop or kiva) where poetry actually happens & where it can be "learned" (not "taught") in action' (36).

A cue from sound poetry

In the preface to *Close Listening: Poetry and the Performed Word* (1998), Charles Bernstein describes the book – a collection of essays on the poetics of sound and performed poetry, the audiotext (including digital forms) in general – as 'a call for a non-Euclidean . . . prosody for the many poems for which traditional prosody does not apply' (4). My argument here begins with a query that is quite simple in this context: Where is the non-Euclidean pedagogy to go along with this new aural consciousness?

Why even seek such a thing? Surely, if it is true, as Bob Cobbing put it in 1969 (pub. 1978), that '[s]ound poetry dances, tastes, has shape' (11), then those of us who have been teaching poetry as printed (poetry on the page, unsounded poetry) would presumably have to add these dimensions to the realms of approach in the classroom. This is perhaps an unnecessarily elaborate way of saying that the experience of having been trained to teach words on a page, no matter how complex, is *not* necessarily preparation of any sort for the task of presenting a language practice as a kind of dance or as an object with a physical shape – the poem as 'dance, gesture & event, game, dream . . . music . . . vocable' (Rothenberg, 1981: 94) that Rothenberg has idealized as poetry's 'blaze of reality' (77). 'When the audiotape archive of a poet's performance is acknowledged as a significant, rather than incidental, part of her or his work,' Bernstein writes, 'a number of important textual and critical issues emerge' (1998: 7–8), and he goes on to name these. Permit me to add another issue to his list. The technology that enables this – our ability to acknowledge such material as significant rather than of additive or illustrative quality – must itself become a part of the story of the poetic art taught to students of that art.

'Leonardo da Vinci,' Cobbing liked to say, 'asked the poet to give him something he might see and touch and not just something he could hear. Sound poetry seems to me to be achieving this aim' (1978: 11). The problem posed by this challenge is similar to the one mentioned above. *Seeing* and even *hearing* we can manage, albeit the latter with special new effort. But *touch*? Enabling such an engagement is next to impossible in traditional poetry pedagogy. And although *seeing* a printed poem – really seeing it as a thing, in William Carlos Williams' sense (poems aren't beautiful statements; they're things) – is a feat we believe is brought off in a close reading; yet looking at a poem, even staring hard at it, is of course not the same as comprehending it. All this strikes me as relatively easy to discuss in theory, but actually doing it, making out of poetics a consistent practice, is daunting.

Of course we can and must broaden the scope of the problem by moving from sound poetry specifically to poetry that is aided generally by (although in the case of sound poetry was never dependent on) new computing media. Yet the contributors to *New Media Poetics: Contexts, Technotexts, and Theories* (Morris and Swiss, 2006) make precious little mention of the impact on pedagogy made by poetic technotexts. To be sure, at nearly every point in this collection an altered practice is implicit, even in the section titled 'Technotexts', which offers examples of computer-generated, programming-dependent, or network-enabled poetry. Stephanie Strickland and Cynthia Lawson (2006), for instance, describe the 'social reading space' required by this work in a manner that suggests rather specifically what a teacher would need to do in the classroom in order to 'teach' such art: while the text is performed through the artist's virtual interaction with the site – which can of course be apprehended without its creators present – 'the audience is also reading while being in a social space' (177). However, the artists add, 'we do not read it *as* they do.' Thus their 'performing new media poetry' is a kind of teaching, assuming teaching to be a dynamic three-way interaction among (1) the technotext itself, (2) the performers/instigators of the site, (3) an audience that reads/looks/interprets within a social space. One of the several innovative contentions underlying such a poetics is that the artists' 'creative process is [itself] an initial model for th[e] interaction' (177) of the sort that can take place in the classroom, so that students can glimpse the creative process and, if the technotext succeeds, can experience it.

As a thought exercise, I re-read each contribution to *Close Listening*, deducing for the arguments a corresponding pedagogical practice. Dennis Tedlock's poetics of polyphony and translatability, for instance, reminds us that 'Writing, like speaking, is a performance' (Bernstein, 1998: 178), and strongly implies that teaching such writing is or can be an enactment as well; that 'speaking' in this special sense can come to entail participating in the intermedia performance of polyphony, or indeed helping to create it. We can conceive of all that speaking as sharing with the audiotext its quality as 'a semantically denser field of linguistic activity than can be charted by means of meter, assonance, alliteration, rhyme and the like (although these remain underlying elements of this denser linguistic field)' (13).

Peter Quartermain's 'Sound Reading' reminds me that such literal 'Unsayability . . . is a central feature of a great number of poems' (Bernstein, 1998: 227) that I have always taught without conceiving of them in such a way. I have in fact been teaching them as if they *were* sayable, and saying it rather well myself; there is an aspect of incorrectness about this. The day after I first read Quartermain's article I was to teach John Cage's 'Writing through Howl' (1984), a poem generated from Allen Ginsberg's 'Howl' (1956); the later work uses the earlier as a source text for words within line arrangements.[1] My students and I had discussed 'Howl' during the previous two meetings and now we turned to Cage's Ginsberg. The result of Cage's relatively strict, mostly determinative procedure of 'writing through' the language of the earlier poem with its canonical status and its easily recognisable line-by-line sound is stark and beautiful, producing a kind of succinct basis or tonally similar but quantitatively dissimilar viscerum of the aurally familiar original that seems to argue for doubt about the notion that one way of saying things can be closer or truer to the original idea than another. The power of Cage's poem is its relative unsayability or, in my view, as a proponent of both artists, the idea that it is itself its best edification. Old pedagogical wine (New Critical focus on the poem as itself) in a new bottle (aleatory verse in a truly interactive – which is to say, non-Socratic – classroom). Usually the hyper-articulate teacher espousing a poetry he always says he 'loves', I performed a deliberate struggle with saying what I had to say about the poem, a stutter. After all these years in which I've taught 'Howl', now the classroom, enjoined by a Cagean enjoining of Ginsberg – a teacher-text teaching history, both the vast public history of the predecessor poem and the psycho-anthropological chronicle of its moment ('mAdness / coLd-water / fLats // thE / braiNs / throuGh / wIth / aNd /academieS / Burning / monEy') – became a site where the poem thrived in its own mode. What happens when the teacher of such works attempts to convey their unsayability through the *form* of the teacher, neologising in order to innovate, and discovering, thereupon, that the new words offer a fresh social history? To what extent is the teacher finding an educational advantage in staging her or his own exit from the realm of semantic verse? Here I believe the claim of imitative fallacy does not necessarily obtain, notwithstanding my own performativity as the consciously avid presenter of the poem, since the derogation of imitation has itself already been called into question by Cage's art.

From Peter Middleton's historical survey of the live poetry reading, we learn a good deal about the dynamics of the reading space. Although again this was not Middleton's concern, one has little trouble imagining the analogy to the classroom as potentially like rather than unlike such a space. Imagine that the following observation was written about the poetry classroom: 'The persistence of the . . . momentary ascendancies of poetry in an everyday world that threatens at every instant to flood back in and reclaim the space for its everyday functions suggests another possibility', namely that 'these intruders', such as unplanned sounds, unconducive ambience, the abruption of non-poetic uses of the space onto the scene of the performed poetry, etc., *'are really participants'* (270–1). Whereas the poet asks, as David Antin actually once did in the middle of a talk poem, 'what am i doing here?' I strive to imagine that the teacher can ask the same question and permit the extra-poetic ambience to be part of the meaning to be studied. Only thus would poetry's constant resistance to and inclusion in what Wallace Stevens called 'the pressure of reality' (1952: 92) be part of the lesson about poetry. Otherwise the teaching space is idyllic and qualitatively different from what happens when the same poetry being taught must submit to Middleton's 'intruders'. A poem gets put into practice in a space of a certain character.

Third space

In the world of teaching poetry, there are conventionally two distinct spaces. There is of course the teaching space (typically, of course, 'the classroom'); secondly, there is a private or semi-private or at any rate a teacherless space (a student's room or house or café or favourite library carrel). For me there has almost always also been a third space, a common but not academic – or at least not curricular – site where teacher and students, but also practitioners and other denizens and citizens of the scattered poetics community can meet, actually and virtually, and make something new out of the work that has been studied in the first space and has been romantically internalised or individually complicated in the second.

This third space really defies generic description, because, for one thing, it can take many forms. Yet I am nearly certain that the successful teaching of modern and contemporary poetry depends on its availability and, crucially, its accessibility in some form, ever more so now that digital audio recordings of the poetry are widely available. Notwithstanding my own fortuitous experience working with students of modernism in a non-curricular salon, a 145-year-old open house, formerly a private residence now devoted to such middle-ground interaction as described above – an intellectual watering hole, a sandbox or aesthetic skunkworks, 'where,' as Rothenberg says, 'poetry actually happens' – I am actually indifferent as to whether the third space I mean is a built, located site, an address to which one can walk, ride, or drive and physically enter (on the model of Rothenberg's coffee shop or kiva where poetry is '"learned" but not "taught"'), or a virtual space (synchronous chatroom, Second Life niche, asynchronous email listserv, social network circle, or multi-authored blog).

But let us for the moment leave this kind of place, the place located between the site of formal learning and that of readerly isolation, and consider the situated state of the poetic text itself. Contemporary poets concerned about the acoustical non-semantic meaning of poetry or more generally the bodily quality or materiality of verse – its actual form but not in the formalist's sense of the term – can somewhat control, or at least participate in, the discourse about how their poetry can be sensually apprehended. Edwin Torres, for instance, insists that to understand his work well one has to be oneself, along with him, somewhat a 'lingualisualist'. The verse of the dead modernists cannot derive this particular advantage. As subjects of their poems they cannot except accidentally anticipate a day when the sound of their voice would be very much more ubiquitous than the poem printed on a page in a book. But in either case – either the live poet alive to the polyphony and interanimations of reception, or the deceased artist whose textual shade cannot perform the present and must leave it to us – the third space in this sense is a site where the eye and ear find common (as it were) ground. Here is Torres, at turns a concrete and a performance poet once affiliated with the Nuyorican Poets Café, writing in an essay called 'The Impossible Sentence':

> Unrecognizable patterns of uttering – the polyglot crying for social affiliation – as we portray our demons with hierarchy, the available workhorse is the lingualisualist . . . Taking notes against the voice falling in the ear, where many ways of understanding stutter into yester-speak. There is a third space, the eye that is the ear in the back of the brain. (2004: 19)

If one can imagine a convergence of these two third spaces – a situation between the lecture and isolation but partakes of neither, where social affiliation is associated with the text and which is also a place in which the eye can function like the ear and hand – then that is the model of teaching and learning implicit in this essay. It is a built poetic environment, a non-figurative house of possibility, to use the Dickinsonian trope, in which the thisness of poetic Occupation (dwelling as both residing and obsessing) is an actual thing, the specific product of communal practice.

Trained to see

I was trained by people – not a single 'lingualisualist' among them, to be sure – who brought texts into the room and presented them to us as images (*as if* they were images). I refer here to writing we were to comprehend visually, poems learned with the eyes. I came to associate the finest readings of poetic texts with the act of looking or seeing. I believed the word 'rhetorical' specifically and exclusively referred to printed language, that rhetorical tools were limited to the alphabetical. I *saw* Whitman and *looked at* Williams and *viewed* Ginsberg on the page. I even learned to *see* Vachel Lindsay's 'The Congo' in an anthology of American literature, and recall sensing even then that an irony had been created that was pedagogically either quite a trick or alternatively a miserable failure – and at least counter-intuitive, given Lindsay's extreme orality and performativity. Yet, I dare say, more often I and the other students were unconscious of the intuition we moved against.

Even such a strange, exciting sound as Lindsay's, a vocable that is indispensable to an understanding of the poem, I did not fully hear then and would not hear for years, well after I was sufficiently professionalised.[2] No, the only thing audible in the room on such occasions was the kindly but unmodulated voice of the professor who was with modest effectiveness insisting that we look (and look again and keep looking) at the piece of mimeographic writing he had given us. To look hard was to master the poem. Until recently it never bothered me that this was a mixed message. The PennSound Vachel Lindsay page – full of sounds seemingly impossible to have made in the classroom of the 1970s – is now commended to students and teachers. The instructional expectation is simple: in William Blake's words, 'Hear the voice of the bard.' The sound of the poet is thunderous, vaudevillian, primitivist, implausible, at times incoherent, and apparently unmasterable, resisting settled close-reading practices, rendering commentary irrelevant and funny. Yet on the anthology page, Lindsay seems nicely to befit a literary-historical moment, marks a spot on the spectrum from Whitmanian proto-modernism to twentieth-century visionary Romanticism. Seeing Lindsay enables a discussion that does not at all resemble the naturally awed response to the wild stagy voice as heard.

In our time, the teaching of poetry was becoming a creature of the twin revolutions of mass-produced anthologies and mimeography, even as we have theoretically distanced ourselves from the critical ideology suited so well to it: formalist classroom practice in its booming post-GI Bill manifestation, alleging its formalism yet unconsciously teaching the poem's arbitrary concreteness. The mode was not revolutionary at all in this special context; it instead marked an adamant continuity out of convention established several centuries earlier by the close association of poetic text with image – I mean, the text of the poem as an image, the text as an image with language written or printed on it. Once again, thus, conventional poetics pedagogy is always at least implicitly the medium of a critical ideology the purveyors of which are half-aware of an even more conventional counter-trend hiding inside the method.

The history of the better part of the literary curriculum in the modern university can be told crudely as follows: The emergence of the printing press, and of moveable type, the techno-genesis of the modern page, coincided with (and partially helped to instigate) the redevelopment of the idea of the university that more or less holds today. This is a story that has been told often and fairly well. In a speech called 'Text and University' (1991), Ivan Illich lamented 'the separation and subordination of the ear with respect to the eye' in higher learning today, and reminded us that before the thirteenth century scholarly reading was an oral-auditive activity, the scriptorium was a noisy place, the tradition of the 'singing page' held sway, and so forth. Then the trope changed. 'A new technique of writing lay-out makes university teaching possible.' 'Visual *ordinatio* replaces contemplative chewing, an oral backing and for-thing, *ruminatio*.'[3] Texts considered worth studying were recopied, and later printed in many copies, and made their way to emergent centres of learning, where apprentice learners gathered literally around scholars who gathered around texts, all of them seeing texts with their eyes. The longer and at that point deeper (and suddenly very separate) history of poetic orality benefited from little to no such convergence with the rise of the modern university as an institution, a new powerful social corpo-ration that bred leaders of the polity and of the economy and, to be sure, those who would go on to lead the universities themselves. Thus the poetry-as-sound tradition went its own mostly unacademic way, contin-uing on, outside sites of visual authentication and accreditation and to this day, even in some of the hippest university poetry communities, is roughly associated with a less rigorous, sometimes sloppily popular or facile Beatnikised or Slam-dominated world, unserious and deliberately untheorised.

Almost a century after the rise of reliable mechanical reproduction of sound, four decades after the recorder-player morphed into devices available and affordable to almost everyone, six or seven years since worldwide super-dissemination of sound files, and a few years into the era of stable widely agreed-upon non-proprietary audio-file formats, we are still, many of us, unconsciously subject to the seemingly benign hegemonic tyranny of the pedagogy of the text as image. It is this tight affiliation of text and university that tends to prevent, as a mode of learning, the 'third space' to which a lingualisualist like Edwin Torres feels he belongs and with which he actively seeks affiliation.

When a poet, in a poem, gives us a visual cue – the line that runs further towards the right margin than others, the widowed phrase, the word suddenly presented in all caps, the use of the incorrect homonym, the unusual extra spacing between words or the three dots of the caesura, the deliberate erratum, the title that enjambs into the first line – we read such a cue and permit it to bespeak evidence of emphasis, irony, tone, playfulness, mental rhythm, etc., and criticism has taught us to consider such moves fair game without the need to worry about intention or other kinds of extrinsic evidence for the reading. Most formalisms accounted well and insistently for these visuals. They were, after all, 'part of the text'. But the sound-text offers the same array of possibilities. A spoken word is stretched or dragged out unusually. Another is mispronounced or surprisingly accented; or the poet alphabetises an accent (Louis Zukofsky renders 'A fine lass bothers me' as 'A foin lass bodders me' in 'A'-9 (2006: 152)) thus leaving a notation or script for later oral performance that might or might not be followed or followed well.[4] Separate sound-senses or phrases from different spoken vocabularies converge and form an oral dysraphism. Silence does not so much imply as presuppose white space. A line is read too hurriedly to be fully understood as sense, thus creating a difference discerned only in the heard experience of the poem. The odd sound of an otherwise conventional word pronounced aloud indicates the way the mouth was once open eccentrically at the moment of utterance. And so on. The critical language for describing these options, a myriad of them, is relatively impoverished. One could satisfyingly imagine now the equivalent (for poems heard) of the old pedagogical cadre of New Critical terminologists, who in the late 1940s and early 1950s revived and in some cases invented a super-language for the poem-as-seen that every college sophomore could use with seeming competence and upon which, it might be said with scant exaggeration, the institution of postwar academic humanities is founded. So perhaps one reason we do not often, if ever, teach poetry through their sound-texts is that we collectively lack the critical language to describe (let alone interpret) what we hear.

If indeed it is so, then perhaps this can be turned to a great advantage, at least for the moment changing the relationship between teacher and student. It is surely the case that when my students and I in class

together listen to sound files instead of reading poem-texts, our vocabularies tend to be on the same plane. I might have a subtler response
to what we're hearing, and certainly I know far more than they about
the sound in literary-historical context, but they are never struck dumb
by the terminology I bring to bear on the point I seek to make about the
specific sound of the words, the poetics of it. The students notice this
difference – between their talk about the poem on the page and their talk
about the sounded or recorded poems – and their discussion of poetics
generally becomes charged with it. If it is true of those who perform spoken poetry that (as David Antin has put it) 'it was my habit to record my
talks / to find out what i[']d said'[5] then similarly, the disorienting and
terminologically disruptive mode I am describing is the means by which
we might find out what we are teaching.

Students in a freshman seminar taught in the spring of 2008 by poet
Julia Bloch were assigned to listen to recordings of several poems by
Amiri Baraka archived in PennSound. One, 'In Walked Bud', was not
available to the students in print. Halfway through the discussion, a student, Andrew, offered a reading of the poem that successfully associated
Baraka's jazz-metrical scatting with the narrative of the speaker's physical
movement:

> So I try to listen and see if the sound tells me the story. Why is this guy
> saying DO DO DEE [*he imitates the scat*]? And then I realize that it's the
> way he's walking into the scene that summer night. He's an African in
> the West with European harmonies. And then he says, 'In walked us.'
> Later the DO DO DEE comes back but it's changed by then. I heard it
> as a story and then [in a writing assignment] did a close reading based
> on the sound of the [scatting]. I never bothered to imagine how it
> would look as language on a page.

From there the discussion among the students was all about the form
of the poem, very little directly about its social content. Bloch had not
pointed out the lit-class anomaly: students assigned to *write* about a poem
they had not seen as writing. She patiently waited for a student to do
so. 'We haven't even seen this written down,' Amy exclaimed (and her
remark then precipitated Andrew's capable formalist reading). She threw
up her arms excitedly and loudly asked, 'How *do* we read this poem?'

What more fundamental question could there be? The noise of Baraka
instigated it. To those who worry, as the anti-modernist conservative
Georges Duhamel once did in a screed against the radio, that 'people who
really need education are beginning to prefer noise to books' (1939: 30),

such student response is a powerful rejoinder. The book has been a medium for arriving at the teacher's goal, which is to teach young people to understand form as an extension of content. 'Noise', as either separate from the book or parallel to it, can similarly be the medium.

When in my course on modern and contemporary American poetry I teach Ginsberg's 'America', my students and I listen together to recordings of two quite different performances by the poet. One, performed live before an ecstatic, sympathetic, and perhaps largely inebriated audience, is dated 1956, introduced by Ginsberg's remark that it's 'an unfinished poem which I'll finish sooner or later'.[6] The second is a professionally produced track from the LP *Howl and Other Poems*, a Fantasy-Galaxy record (#7013) laid down in Berkeley in June 1959; 'America' here is a studio recording done in a sombre, unironic plaintive and vulnerable voice, absent ambient noise of any kind. In the first, as the audience laughs and responds raucously, Ginsberg's voice changes and slows as he recites. 'When will you take off your clothes?' suggests the same meaning to the raucous live audience as it does to my students. Yet lines such as 'I'm trying to come to the point' have varying effects on the students (most interpret it as a serious lament, furthering what they take to be the speaker's sense of his failure), while the live 1956 audience accepts the sentiment as antic and wildly ironic, and they cheer on the poet as if to say, *Don't ever come to the point! The point is not to come to the point, but to wander everywhere in the writing!*

Teaching this poem – or *poems*, really versions of a poem – I merely ask my students to describe differences between the enacted sounds of the words, and to begin to construct a reading based as exclusively as possible on what they heard. I have taught the poem more or less every year for more than two decades, and until recently, when I began teaching the poem as sound, as a recorded performance, I had never successfully been able to shake my students from the conviction, one they seem to have inherited as children of Cold War Americans, that Beat poetics was ultimately meditative, un-antic, angry. The text on the page obviously does not in the same way enact tonal or rhetorical options and alternatives. I would contend that even just one recording does so. But having *two*, to compare, takes discussion of the poem to a realm in which difference and disagreement is not just possible but arguably necessary as a structure of learning. (Two handouts produced to offer the same lesson, I hardly need to add, do not create this *agon*.) In the 1956 reading, Ginsberg himself was clearly reinterpreting how he felt about the poem, as about America, in the act of reperforming it, understood new contexts for it (in a way that anticipates our own context), and responded to live hearers as they began to hear what he was doing inside the fleeting temporal life of the poem-when-read-aloud. Even though Ginsberg's text, the basis of his different performances, is for the most part fixed, an ur-text played out through performed variations, the best way to respond critically to the sound of the performance is to see it as similar to the extraordinarily beautiful and also unpredictable phenomenon of quasi-improvisation that talk-poet Antin describes as 'a dialogue that [as I perform] I also conduct with my material and myself . . . and with a particular audience that I don't know till I get there' (1984: 218). We in my classroom at the Kelly Writers House in Philadelphia were not Ginsberg's live hearers, of course, but we were nonetheless 'live' in a specific and generative sense. We were 'hearers' and succeeded in imagining ourselves analogously, and behaved like the audience whom Antin does not know but with whom his poem nonetheless interacts.

Then something else can happen that is different: that same night, the evening after the class convened to discuss this poem in this quasi-counter-institutional way, there was inevitably a contemporary poet performing live in the same room, a poet not *per se* in the curriculum (indeed unlikely to be in the curriculum). This was a poet of perhaps accidental aesthetic relation to Ginsberg's 'America'. And chances were much greater than before that my students would attend that performance too, thinking of the mode of listening to poems at a reading (famously an experience of listening without the aid of printed texts) as relevant to interpretation rather than irrelevant in the way implied by the convention of seeing 'literature' as a category distinct from 'writing'.

Above I observed that one reason we don't teach poems through their sound-texts is that we ourselves lack the critical language to interpret what we hear. Indeed, as Marjorie Perloff notes, in the supposedly scientific method of prosodic analysis, perfected by linguists and rhetoricians in recent decades, 'the more thorough the description of a given poem's rhythmic and metrical units, its repetition of vowels and consonants, its pitch contours, the less we may be able to discern the larger contours of a given poet's particular practice . . . Then too, conventional prosodic studies cannot allow for the difference individual performance makes, much less for variants of individual and culturally determined reception' (2009: 2). I want to add that among the unaccounted-for cultural determinants Dworkin and Perloff describe, especially in the meaning created by teaching such poetry, is the university as an institution – how leaders of the university identify and then legitimate categories of curricular innovation. Notwithstanding valid observations about the narrowness of prosodic studies, perhaps the most fundamental reason

why our language about sound-texts is relatively poor is that recordings of poems have not until recently been widely available, and this is
essentially a problem of the way resources follow academic ideology.
Curricular legitimacy is attached to tuition dollars and core budgets.
Although its main contribution *within the university* before very long will
be curricular, the vast audio poetry archive called PennSound has been
managed and funded as a boutique operation – edgy, charming, the play-
thing of adored (but also aggressive) innovative faculty. For a 'roundtable
discussion' on 'new media literature' convened by Thomas Swiss in 2002,
I and others were asked to respond to this well-formulated question,
'Since New Media literature typically represents the digital convergence
of words, images and sound, it clearly comes out of a variety of traditions, only some of them literary. Do you agree?' (85). And then this even
keener question: 'What will need to happen in terms of institutional ...
support, education, promotion and so on for New Media literature to be
more widely known?' In my response, 'Kinetic Is as Kinetic Does' (2006),
I noted that funds flow most freely through connections to traditional
curricular structures and for traditionally built and equipped teaching
spaces. The first years of the IT revolution at the university unfortunately focused obsessively – one might even say fetishistically – on the
mere digitalisation of existing courses, a costly (and I think largely waste-
ful) activity that tended to carry over all the conventional values already
associated with the course, typically a lecture course that became no
more dynamic or interactive or intersubjective after the great conversion.
These might easily have been new *kinds* of courses, indeed a new medium
implicit in the promise of the 'new media', but they typically were not.
'Web development' was mostly a matter of putting old visual-text materials online, a vast but poorly conceived media-transfer project that took
little account of the quality of the new medium receiving the transfer.
In most cases students now found course materials on the web and then
printed them out, putting them back on paper. The only innovation was
a sly economic one: instead of the teacher providing paper copies (as
my own teachers had done during the New Criticism-endorsed Mimeo
Revolution), the students were obliged to pay for the traditional format
by way of the new-fangled one. Even such few courses in poetry and
poetics using digital materials as there were tended to take insufficient
advantage of the real revolutions in reading and learning practices that
were – mostly outside the academy – the basis, in fact, of the explosion
of the new forms. A mode that would seem almost ipso facto interactive is remarkably static, a bad modal translation. (Brian Kim Stefans in
Fashionable Noise (2003), noting that 'the most uninteresting cyberpoetry

which has yet been written in our language' (48) simply animates already existing images, implies a parallel to teaching experimental poetry from outside the academy: ironically, poets in this innovative field have been singularly non-innovative. On the contrary, 'I am interested in interactivity, which is a theory about the use of material' (45).)

The traditional departmental and disciplinary categories have presented another major difficulty. The digital poet Loss Pequeño Glazier was thought at first to be 'one of the UNIX guys', an experience he later described as 'suffering ignominy' and always sensing 'dimly veiled rancor'. 'Not only could we not get our early online texts correctly archived,' he remembers, 'we could not even convince the archival site to classify the [work] as poetry' (2001: 37). Although the e-poets explicitly followed in the avant-garde tradition of – to take only Glazier's list of influences – F. T. Marinetti, Charles Olson, Ezra Pound ('Pound's significance lies in his having anticipated the end of "the Gutenberg era"' (35)), Gertrude Stein et al., these were accepted by the department-centric organisation as producers of poems on pages and thus, despite their radicalism otherwise, disciplinarily well defined. The e-poet challenged the historical text-pedagogy of the university in ways that are profound and still not fully appreciated. In the meantime these people are (when they are in the academy) academically scattered – and challenged. Glazier is very much a poet and a literary critic (his book *Digital Poetics* fits squarely in the lit crit tradition) but is housed in a department of Media Study. Martin Spinelli studies and produces sound files in the manner I have been discussing but entered the tenure track (and ascended to the tenured rank) in a department of Television and Radio. As late into the IT era as 2001 the e-poet Katherine Parrish and her fellow graduate students, taking a course in an English department on digital poetry, had to 'close . . . the door when class was in session to protect our professor from the teasing of his passing colleagues who did not think ours was a legitimate enterprise' (2002: 94). We contemplate, sadly, the pre-emption or suppression of new talent within our system as indicated by the fact that (as Adalaide Morris puts it in her book *Sound States*) '[c]ritics with a keen ear tend to turn not to literature but to classical or operatic music, blues, jazz, rock, rap, hip hop and the advance technologies of youth music' (1998: 4). One wants the very same people passionate about art in which meaning is generated by 'What Happens As We Go' to enter the classroom space and urge its transformation on the basis of that updated version of 'It Must Change'. 'What Happens As We Go' was a chapter title and a rallying cry of Michael Joyce in *Of Two Minds: Hypertext, Pedagogy and Poetics* (1995). It has been a long time now since Joyce contended that Charles

Olson's notion of 'the discharge of the many . . . by the one' (199) could and should be applied to pedagogy, transforming the role of the teacher into that of 'learning manager', as Joyce clumsily phrased it. He quickly added that by 'management' he meant 'making do' (121).

I contended above that the main contribution of projects like PennSound *within the university* will finally be curricular, and now, armed with Olson's radicalism of many/one, I need to return to that point because it could be misleading. Overwhelmingly the main effect of PennSound, if it succeeds, will not be felt at the university at all, except in so far as the university consists of people who like any other people want to listen to and own (have for themselves) the sounds of the poet reading the poem. Here PennSound joins UbuWeb and the Electronic Poetry Center and other ventures in the digital gift economy, which deliberately defy the proprietary strategy used by the popular music industry *and* by the intellectual-property-owning research universities – with the music people assiduously tracking ownership of the mp3 file despite its basic nomadic, untrackable quality, while the university people are as of this writing still perfecting their legal tactics. Most readers of this essay surely suspect that the music industry is embarking on a doomed strategy. Since through PennSound – but also, I would say, in the quasi-counter-institutional pedagogy I am describing – we have consciously chosen an alternative, is it not the responsibility of teachers of modern poetry to take some significant advantage of the inevitable victory, of the spread of knowledge and art freely, in whatever direction it wants to go, as an aspect of the university's core mission? And, one is tempted, risking hyperbole, to add: democracy's as well. Liberal pedagogical theory of the 1970s and 1980s formulated such a connection not as an analogy but as a merged category, fending off conservatives who would 'suppress the relationship between learning and critical citizenship' (Giroux, 1990: 120). In 'Dreaming about Democracy', Henry Giroux was explicit: he 'link[ed] the liberal arts to the imperatives of a critical democracy' (121). Giroux insisted on a pedagogy 'that addresses how knowledge is produced, mediated . . . and represented within relations of power both in and outside the university' (123). If 'knowledge' here is the poem, then the critical citizenship that obtains in the poetics classroom requires that the presentation of the poem coincide with the *subject matter* of its making, its changing through performance, its anthologisation, its standing for a movement, etc. When the object of art is permitted its direction, and students are an audience learning to follow its performative dynamism, education finally 'addresses how [the poem] is produced, mediated'; being 'critical rather than "good" citizens' of the classroom transforms the conventional teacher–student master–apprentice practices of *I have/you want, I give/you receive, I am/you're not, I talk/you read* pedagogy. The unintended centrist autocracy of text-as-image-centred pedagogy at the university has contributed to these ratios of dominance. In this sense computing and IT and digital media are on the side of reform and liberation. As one of the alternatives developed within the text-as-image community, the reader-response theorist's old fantasy of a new *I read/you read* mode might be an analogue for what we now have in mind: *I hear, you hear.* Hear what, exactly? If not the sound of the poet himself or herself, then the sounds of the listeners' contemplative chewing: *ruminatio,* an activity that was once said to call for a renewal of learning.[7]

The end of the lecture

At a conference sponsored by the SEI Center for Advanced Studies in Management[8] on 'The Virtual University' in early 1995, the urban sociologist and former university president Martin Meyerson said: 'The best lectures have always been those that deal with "tentative materials" that result from the professor's research. If they cease to be tentative, don't include them in the lecture; print them. The main teaching function has to be interactive.' The World Wide Web was new then, and when Meyerson said 'print them', it was quickly pointed out in the discussion following his remarks, he might have meant, 'digitize them and make them available on the web'. But the pedagogical change these remarks augured was hardly in error. The sociologist's slip about printing suggests that the advent of the web was not required to bring on this reform, but it certainly has catalyzed it. So, too, second-wave postmodern versions of modernism arising since the mid-1990s bear with them methods and even some technical practices that predate digital connectivity by decades, but the emergence of the latter can still be said to coincide with further developments. My point is that teaching has as yet changed only superficially in response to all this. The IT-enabled lecture does not increase the learner's engagement with the material. (Despite great claims made for the introduction of IT into the classroom, and huge expenditures made by colleges and universities, 60 per cent of the undergraduate students surveyed for a 2007 report by the Educause Center for Applied Research said that they disagreed with the statement, 'I am more engaged in courses that use technology.') Technological without pedagogical change is meaningless; the latter, I would submit, is especially difficult for academic historians, for whom the display of 'tentative materials', in the classroom or in scholarly articles and books, is generally greeted with concerns about disciplinary professionalism. This is the classroom in which, as Gerald Graff negatively contended in *Beyond the Culture Wars: How Teaching the Conflicts Can Revitalize American Education* (1992), arguments about the state of the field have already taken place and been more or less resolved by the time the professor walks onto the classroom stage to perform the current state of knowledge and method. Graff writes:

> [A]cademic institutions are already teaching the conflicts every time a student goes from one course or department to another, but they are doing it badly . . . [S]tudents typically experience a great clash of values, philosophies, and pedagogical methods among their various professors, but they are denied a view of the interactions and interrelations that give each subject meaning. They are exposed to the results of their professors' conflicts but not to the process of discussion and debate they need to see in order to become something more than passive spectators to their education. Students are expected to join an intellectual community that they see only in disconnected glimpses. This is what has passed for 'traditional' education, but a curriculum that screens students from the controversies between texts and ideas serves the traditional goals of education . . . poorly.[9]

Historiographers and theorists of history writing, focused as much on method as on content, would rightly call these binaristic generalisations into question, but my point is that the field of modern poetics can be indeed utterly different, for the main idea we want our students to grasp is that contemporary writing modes promulgate tentative materials – that the texts we study are tentative in a very basic sense, that (to take Wallace Stevens' classic modernist formulation) the poem is itself the act of the mind finding what will suffice for the moment.

And so what of the mind of the teacher? The pedagogy of fixed materials is, as I have said, a fundamentally disabling irony. The call to move fixities – for example, informational materials about literary history, the chronological succession of aesthetic movements, etc. – to a shared retrieval space (the web is ideal) literally frees the teaching time and space for a tentativeness that is not just characteristic of the art itself but ought also to be of the manner in which it is presented. Even then there is a pedagogy insisting on the unfixity of the ancillary materials themselves. Such is the view of conceptual poet Kenneth Goldsmith, the founder and curator of UbuWeb (ubuweb.com) who teaches a Creative

Writing course called 'Uncreative Writing'. Because he always teaches in a wired classroom – students typically working away at laptops during the (anti-)lecture, researching mentioned artists and concepts, sending each other messages that the lecturer cannot read – he knows that '[s]hould [he] go off on a tangent about [Jasper] Johns and [Robert] Rauschenberg and their love relationship as expressed in Rauschenberg's bed, an image of that bed is always a click away. From there, we can head anywhere into the non-fixed universe, be it film, text or sound.' Goldsmith's point is that 'the web itself is a non-fixed space', and thus any sharing of the web's qualities with the classroom grants that old space a measure of freedom.[10] 'Because hypertext poetry is something new', wrote Ed Falco in a prose section of his book of hypertext poetry, *Sea Island*, 'there is not yet a body of literature prescribing preferred methods of reading. Pretty much, you're on your own.' C. T. Funkhouser, quoting Falco in his comprehensive book *Prehistoric Digital Poetry* (2007), notes that Falco's statement befits other hypermedia artists' 'liberational' claims. Applying such unmooring to the classroom, Goldsmith and his students discover being on their own, in Falco's liberated sense, yet it is not the lonely process Falco had in mind. What is perhaps 'prehistoric' about Funkhouser's book – that which precedes networked intermedia – is the freedom of artists 'who grant themselves license to appropriate available tools for their own imaginative ends' (195). The effects and values of that imagination extend well beyond the text and are immune to the failure of hardware or network, such as Goldsmith's laptop-crazy students could suffer at any time.

When in *A Poetics* Bernstein described 'the coherence of the "hyperspace" of Pound's modernist collage' he was sure to add scare quotes around the term *hyperspace* so as not to commit an anachronism. Yet of course he meant full well that the Poundian style of cyclonic historical reference performed or at least required a sort of hyperlinking that long before the web became a standard modernist cognitive practice. Indeed, a recent reassessment of the *Cantos* much discussed among the editors of *Poetry* dubs it 'a nut-job blog before the fact'.[11] In any event, before the web such a non-linear version of 'space' was a *metaphor* for unstraightforward connectivity. After the advent of the web the relevance and continued importance of Poundian poetics gives us double the reason to doubt the aptness of delivery-mechanism pedagogy for modernist poetics: first, the mode modernism has long been; and second, the now-enabling actuality (in and near the classroom) of hypermedia linkage. Goldsmith's course is thus itself always another workable instance of the very thing he is teaching.[12] He teaches horizontally, in the manner of hyperlinkage, and since he came to teaching after the coming of the web this concept in his case is not the least bit metaphorical, or for that matter conceptual, but an actual influence.

So Martin Meyerson's progressive understanding of 'research' (those '"tentative materials" that result from the professor's research') refers, in the special context of modernism in the IT era, to some sense of sharing with the orientation to non-narrative process in the writing itself. While the books and articles produced by the college or university teacher as a disciplinary expert (and tenure-seeker) might well eschew the flux and openness and freedom of the texts under study there, my experience in and around the two third spaces – the open learning community beyond the classroom; and the eye that is the ear in the back of the brain – leads me to insist that the practice of teaching there cannot do so. The irony produced by such an abnegation closes off the main avenue by which the student interacts with a kind of writing that seeks inter-animation and is also literally about it. The text and the teaching are what happens as we go.

A few months after the hypertext mark-up language known as 'HTML' had been perfected, I was teaching it to my students – or, rather, requiring them to go out and learn it. This was to enable them to create web projects based on the course materials and as an aid to discussion and disagreement, a sure furtherance of my often rather vague desire to decentre the teacher. (What better means of achieving that decentring than to require the students to learn something about which the teacher knows only a little?) One of the students who resisted all this mightily was Amanda Karsten (now Hirsch). Years later Amanda, based in Washington, DC, is a web consultant, a remarkable outcome given the intensity of her original resistance. She is one of the many creative young people, talented writers, of that moment – the mid and late 1990s – who zig-zagged into information technology, a particular generational bearing out, it seems to me, of Donna Harraway's provocative dictum that 'Writing is pre-eminently the technology of cyborgs' (1991: 176). Now Amanda blogs daily in order to help 'inspir[e] creative living in DC'. She read on my own blog an entry titled 'Patchen, Can't Type, Turns to Picture-poems',[13] and then composed a new piece for *Creative DC*: 'Picture Poems, and How Learning HTML Under Duress Helped Me Lead a More Creative Life, or, Thank You, Al Filreis.' I am flattered by the compliments therein, thrilled in any case to have been Amanda's teacher, but most of all intrigued by the way she has successfully brought together Kenneth Patchen's physical duress, which drove him to a new form of writing, and her own real (though not physical, of course) 'duress' in the seminar where I tossed the students into the cold dark web ocean, from which she emerged with a means of being creative in the then-newest mode. In 1960 Patchen had suffered a series of physical setbacks, including an awful fall from a hospital gurney that resulted in a bad back getting much worse. Unable to stand or even sit up for more than few minutes, he could no longer type. The entry in my blog '1960' reads: 'Here's the good part. Prevented from working at his typewriter any longer, Patchen stopped writing conventional poems. He created letters and poems only in a large hand scrawl. He used pens and a paint brush. He developed his "picture poems".' It was the medium-sense of the picture-poem, not its visual meaning but the fact of its visuality, that drew Amanda's attention back to me as a teacher of would-be cyborgs. While one old move was away from the mechanics of writing, another new move headed further into it – writing as appendaged by it – but I insist that both were and are fresh, and both enable the visual, or, more generally, the concrete. 'Incidentally,' wrote Amanda Hirsch, 'Al [Filreis] is the reason I learned HTML, despite ardent protestations at the time. I was in his Literature of Community class, and our final assignment was to create a website reflecting our definition of community. "But we don't know HTML!" half of us said. This was in '97. "Figure it out," he told us.'

This is the poetics of Figure It Out, Goldsmith's horizontality, Rothenberg's classroom as kiva, Meyerson's space-clearing for tentative materials, Dickinson's possibility, Ed Falco's 'you're on your own', Stein's miracles playing fairly well. I had no more idea of what I was doing just then as a teacher than Patchen did when bodily forced into a new medium – than Amanda did as she grumpily shifted from poetry, which is what she thought the course was about, to programming code and digital culture. One need not be Loss Pequeño Glazier, who writes in *Digital Poetics* about writing as someone who knows the code better than his students, and who I suppose actually *teaches* code as a language – or Brian Kim Stefans who insists that 'A line of javascript scans' (2003: 46) – to know that the 'Occupation' of the teacher in Dickinson's sense is 'This'. 'This' is of course the poem itself, as a poem, the traces left by the activity she is doing when she writes about what occupies her. But it is also its immediate context of conveyance and reception, the place where it enters the house of poetics: the poem we are reading now or dwelling on/in now, *and also the dwelling itself*, the materials presently at hand.

Acknowledgements

I am grateful to Steve McLaughlin, Steve Evans, and Richard Sieburth for permitting me to interview them on this topic. I also wish to thank

Julia Bloch for allowing me to observe her class. Some of the ideas here
were included in a talk, 'Text & University: Working against Conventions of Reading & Listening', given at the International Association of
Word and Image Studies: Elective Affinities conference, 23–27 September
2005, for a panel entitled 'VVV-on-line: Verbal-Visual-Vocal Poetries in
Hyperspace'. I wish to acknowledge the support of the Council on Library
and Information Resources; during several annual conferences at Emory
University hosted by CLIR I gave an evolving presentation on 'The Politics of Scholarship in the Digital Era', including a talk of that title on
13 June 2001. My anti-lecture, 'The End of the Lecture', has been given
several times; I am grateful to Valerie Ross for inviting me to speak on
this subject (for exactly one minute) in 1999.

Notes

1. 'Writing through Howl' was to be published in a *festschrift* for Allen Ginsberg
   on his 60th birthday but the volume was apparently never published. Cage
   himself gave Marjorie Perloff a copy of the text and she reproduced an excerpt
   in *Poetic License* (1990: 9).
2. See PennSound's Vachel Lindsay page: http://writing.upenn.edu/pennsound/
   x/Lindsay.html
3. Illich's 'Text and University' was a keynote address delivered at the Bremen
   Rathaus on 23 September 1991, on the occasion of the twentieth anniver-
   sary of the founding of the University of Bremen. My copy of the English
   translation is a typescript provided by Silja Samerski.
4. Charles Bernstein has performed this poem and recorded it: http://writing.
   upenn.edu/ezurl/5/
5. Quoted by Cabri (2004: 51).
6. Available for streaming (but not download) at poetryarchive.org
7. Illich (1991: 4).
8. http://mktg-sun.wharton.upenn.edu/SEI/
9. Graff (1992: 12). See Filreis (1995).
10. '[T]he web itself is a non-fixed space. Much of what is there on Wednesday
    afternoon is gone or unavailable on Thursday morning. So I must, within
    reason, somehow fix that space for lecture purposes. I PDF like mad and
    archive; I always bring an external hard drive crammed with hundreds of
    gigabytes should the thing I'm looking for not be available. Also, much
    of the stuff I teach is so non-fixed that it never appeared in any sort of
    stable form, rather its nature is ephemeral. So, the teacher becomes an
    archivist (but haven't we always?). The secret, though, is making the mate-
    rials available in a sharable form that can be passed around. Xeroxes can
    only go so far. So in that way, the pedagogical materials need to be truly
    non-fixed, even at the risk of breaking arcane and outdated notions of
    copyright law. The students need things to take away with them, to listen
    to on their iPods, to share, to love . . . to possess' (Kenneth Goldsmith,
    in a blog exchange with the author: http://afilreis.blogspot.com/2007/10/
    new-thoughts-on-modernist-pedagogy.html).

11. James (2007: 271), cited by Christian Wyman and Don Share, podcast, 'When I Fell out of Love with the Cantos', 5 December: http//www.poetryfoundation. org/journal/audio.html
12. Bernstein (1992: 122–3).
13. http://afilreis.blogspot.com/2007/11/patchen-cant-type-turns-to-picture.html

Works cited and further reading

Antin, David (1984) *Tuning*. New York: New Directions.
Bernstein, Charles (1992) 'Pounding Fascism (Appropriating Ideologies – Mystification, Aestheticization, and Authority in Pound's Poetic Practice', in Charles Bernstein, *A Poetics*. Cambridge, MA: Harvard University Press.
——— (ed.) (1998) *Close Listening: Poetry and the Performed Word*. New York: Oxford University Press.
Cabri, Louis (2004) 'Discursive Events in the Electronic Archive of Postmodern and Contemporary Poetry', *English Studies in Canada* 30(1): 31–72.
Cobbing, Bob (1978) 'Some Statements on Sound Poetry', in Steve McCaffery and B. P. Nichol (eds), *Sound Poetry: a Catalogue*. Toronto: Underwich Editions. Cobbing text available at http://www.ubu.com/papers/cobbing.html
Dickinson, Emily (1955) *The Complete Poems of Emily Dickinson*, ed. Thomas H. Johnson. Boston: Little, Brown & Company.
Duhamel, Georges (1939) *Defense of Letters*. New York: Graystone Press.
Dworkin, Craig and Marjorie Perloff (eds) (2009) *The Sound of Poetry / The Poetry of Sound*. Chicago: University of Chicago Press.
Educause Center for Applied Research (2007) 'The ECAR Study of Undergraduate Students and Information Technology, 2007', http://www.educause.edu/ECAR/ TheECARStudyofUndergraduateStu/161967, accessed 11 January 2008.
Filreis, Alan (1995) '"Conflict Seems Vaguely Un-American": Teaching the Conflicts and the Legacy of Cold War', *Review* 17: 155–69.
——— (2006) 'Kinetic Is as Kinetic Does: On the Institutionalization of Digital Poetry', in Adalaide Morris and Thomas Swiss (eds), *New Media Poetics: Contexts, Technotexts, and Theories*. Cambridge, MA: MIT Press, 123–40.
Funkhouser, C. T. (2007) *Prehistoric Digital Poetry: an Archeology of Forms, 1959–1995*. Tuscaloosa: University of Alabama Press.
Giroux, Henry A. (1990) 'Liberal Arts Education and the Struggle for Public Life: Dreaming about Democracy', *South Atlantic Quarterly* 89(1): 113–38.
Glazier, Loss Pequeño (2001) *Digital Poetics: the Making of E-Poetics*. Tuscaloosa: University of Alabama Press.
Graff, Gerald (1992) *Beyond the Culture Wars: How Teaching the Conflicts Can Revitalize American Education*. New York: W. W. Norton.
Harraway, Donna J. (1991) 'A Cyborg Manifesto: Science, Technology, and Socialist-Feminism in the Late Twentieth-Century', *Simians, Cyborgs, and Women: the Reinvention of Nature*. London: Free Association Books.
Illich, Ivan (1991) 'Text and University: On the Idea and History of a Unique Institution', trans. Lee Hoinacki, http://www.davidtinapple.com/illich/1991_text_and_university.PDF, accessed 11 January 2008.
James, Clive (2007) 'The Arrow Has Not Two Points', *Poetry* 191(3): 271.
Joyce, Michael (1995) *Of Two Minds: Hypertext, Pedagogy and Poetics*. Ann Arbor: University of Michigan Press.

McCaffery, Steve and B. P. Nichol (eds) (1978). *Sound Poetry: a Catalogue*. Toronto: Underwich Editions.

Morris, Adalaide (1998) *Sound States: Innovative Poetics and Acoustical Technologies*. Chapel Hill: University of North Carolina Press.

Morris, Adalaide and Thomas Swiss (eds) (2006) *New Media Poetics: Contexts, Technotexts, and Theories*. Cambridge, MA: MIT Press.

Parrish, Katherine (2002) Untitled statement. In 'New Media Literature: a Roundtable Discussion on Aesthetics, Audiences, and Histories', *NC1*: 94.

Perloff, Marjorie (1990) *Poetic License: Essays on Modernist and Postmodernist Lyric*. Evanston, IL: Northwestern University Press.

—— (2009) 'The Sound of Poetry', in Craig Dworkin and Marjorie Perloff (eds), *The Sound of Poetry / The Poetry of Sound*. Chicago: University of Chicago Press, 1–9.

Rothenberg, Jerome (1981) *Pre-Faces & Other Writings*. New York: New Directions.

Stefans, Brian Kim (2003) *Fashionable Noise: On Digital Poetics*. Berkeley: Atelos.

Stein, Gertrude (1993) 'If I told him: a Completed Portrait of Picasso', in Ulla Dydo (ed.), *A Stein Reader*. Evanston, IL: Northwestern University Press.

Stevens, Wallace (1952) 'The Noble Rider and the Sound of Words', *The Necessary Angel: Essays on Reality and the Imagination*. New York: Knopf.

Strickland, Stephanie and Cynthia Lawson (2006) 'Vniverse', in Adalaide Morris and Thomas Swiss (eds), *New Media Poetics: Contexts, Technotexts, and Theories*. Cambridge, MA: MIT Press.

Tawada, Yoko (2009) 'The Art of Being Synchronous', in Craig Dworkin and Marjorie Perloff (eds), *The Sound of Poetry / The Poetry of Sound*. Chicago: University of Chicago Press, 184–95.

Torres, Edwin (2004) 'The Impossible Sentence', *The Poetry Project Newsletter* 19.

Zukofsky, Louis (2006) *Selected Poems*, ed. Charles Bernstein. New York: The Library of America.

8
Reading and Writing Through Found Materials: From Modernism to Contemporary Practice

Redell Olsen

In his introduction to Hannah Weiner's *Weeks* (1990), Charles Bernstein, in gleefully mixed metaphors, asks:

> What do we make of our everyday lives: make of them, make out of them? What do we make of, that is, these materials that we can no where (not anymore) avoid, avert our ears as we do, or, as in poetic practice, hide behind the suburban lawns of laundered lyricism? (Charles Bernstein, introduction to Hannah Weiner's *Weeks*).

Bernstein's question implies a shared, if somewhat ambiguous, community that includes the reader in an invitation to navigate the fault-line between the understanding and the making of poetry from 'these materials' of the everyday, which here refer both to the 'materials' of Weiner's poem and to the 'materials' of the media and its contents. His question raises and simultaneously blurs awareness of the difficulty of making sense of both the representation of events and of the events themselves. His evocation of 'laundered' lyric lawns erects an apparently neat picket fence between the properties of a 'poetic practice' based on sanitation and evasion and a proper (rather than Proper) practice of writing which messily engages itself in both the stuff of language as it is encountered in existing contexts and the topics which it discusses. While this distinction has the potential to re-mark an all too predictable division between lyric and non-lyric strategies of writing in modernist and contemporary writing, his gibe at the rise of the 'laundered' lyric may be justified given that lyric poetry is increasingly synonymous with the types of poetry produced for creative writing workshops both here in the UK and in the States.[1] A different kind of poetic practice and of teaching is necessary if students are to be encouraged to reflect critically on the activity of writing and of the effect of linguistic structures and representations on their own thinking.

This necessary reconsideration of the pedagogical approach to poetry writing is already underway in recent books such as Hazel Smith's *The Writing Experiment: Strategies for Innovative Creative Writing* (2005) and Joan Retallack and Juliana Spahr's *Poetry and Pedagogy: the Challenge of the Contemporary* (2006). These volumes are highly useful in their synthesis of critical, theoretical, and practical discussion around the writing and reading of innovative poetries. Many of the examples of exercises aimed at students in the classroom extend pioneering work by poets such as Ron Padgett and Kenneth Koch, both of whom have produced a range of books since the 1970s, mainly aimed at secondary school students, which are exemplary in their refusal to dumb down the teaching of poetry and commitment to teach the reading of poetry alongside its writing. Such approaches help to reorientate students more familiar with historical or contextual approaches to reading, highlighting modernism's interest in conceptual projects based on experiments in language. Many of the examples of practical exercises contained in Padgett's volumes for the Teachers & Writers Collaborative in New York are clearly rooted in the spirit of Dada and Surrealist word games and are designed to stimulate conceptual and theoretical discussions around the writing of poetry that uses found and chance procedures. The new poetic pedagogy helps to connect practice in the classroom to modernist and late modernist debates surrounding aleatory procedures in writers and artists as diverse as John Cage, William Burroughs, John Giorno, and Joe Brainard as well as to the potential of poetic language to incorporate the everyday materials (to return to Bernstein's phrase) that surround us in popular culture and the media. This strategic approach to the writing of poetry is often obvious in the work of contemporary practitioners but difficult to teach to students who are sometimes conditioned to expect their poetry writing seminars to help them pursue a search for their 'authentic voice'. A politics of pedagogy is implicit in this focus on writing and reading practices that seek to extend the reach of poetry and poetic language through the incorporation of found or ready-made linguistic structures and fragments from other texts and contexts, and that makes connections to traditions of writing and reading in the visual arts and to everyday operations of linguistic register as it absorbs and is informed by the shifting modalities of linguistic environment in which it finds itself.

Such practices also have a history. The use of found materials is one of the most important approaches developed in various forms of

modernist visual art, from synthetic Cubism, which included the incorporation of newsprint and other materials, through Dada and Surrealism,
to the mixed media 'combines' of Robert Rauschenberg. Mina Loy,
writing about Gertrude Stein, provides an early characterisation of the
dynamics:

> Modernism has democratized the subject matter and *la belle matière* of
> art; through cubism the newspaper has assumed an aesthetic quality,
> through Cezanne a plate has become more than something to put an
> apple upon, Brancusi has given an evangelistic import to eggs, and
> Gertrude Stein has given us the Word, in and for itself.[2]

The use of different kinds of found materials is so central to modernism's many currents as to resist summary, and it is important that the
different processes and procedures involved are not lumped together.
Poetry shares in modernism's democratisation of the materials out of
which work can be made, as well as modernism's developing through
tensions with the forms and contents of newspapers and newsprint.
Gertrude Stein provides perhaps the most important early example of a
writer whose poetic practice works through dialogue with the visual arts,
notably the techniques of Cubism, as well as through a new approach
to language as a material.[3] As Gertrude Stein's writing reveals, however,
understanding the consequences of Cubism for writing unsettles conventional ways of reading as well as unsettling conventional ways of writing
about or through art.

Many modernist writers are directly or indirectly informed by modernist visual arts, ranging from literary impressionism[4] to the work
of artists drawn on by poets such as Ezra Pound and William Carlos
Williams.[5] It is possible to read modernist poetry through deft juxtapositions with the visual arts, and there are some analogies to be drawn
between the placing of words on the page and techniques in the visual
arts. Studies by Jerome McGann, Marjorie Perloff, and Charles Altieri
provide a number of helpful angles on such placement.[6] Along with the
diffuse dialogue between poetry and painting, modernism often tests
what can be understood at the limits of art and poetry.[7] Rather than generating stable methods or conventions applicable to reading modernist
poetry, the visual culture of modernism provides many examples of col-
laborations exploring difference and differentiation. It is often difficult,
accordingly, for students new to modernism to avoid the temptation to
produce readings which are too simplistic or too schematic. The visual
appearance of modernist poetry – what is sometimes known as 'mise en

page', 'concrete poetry', or, more simply, 'visual poetry' – can provide useful ways into modernist poetry's dialogue with visual art.[8] The analogies often drawn by modernists and critics between poems and paintings, or between the page and the canvas, are sometimes only superficial, however, even if there are shared sensibilities. As imagist poetry reveals, there are many critical differences between visual images and the literary image. Even for the work of writers who are also artists, such as Wyndham Lewis or David Jones, there are difficulties reading their texts in the light of their visual art works. Some of the most important dynamics are less obviously visible and concern the reworking of the materials taken up by visual artists and poets, hence the importance of found materials. One way of introducing students to different ways of reading modernist poetry through its dialogue with visual arts, then, is to focus on different ways of using found materials still being developed by artists and poets. By looking at the reworking of modernist techniques in contemporary work students can be introduced to some of the ethical and aesthetic decisions in play, and develop a fresher sense of poetry as a practice in dialogue with visual culture, a dialogue in which there are also critical differences.

This chapter will present a number of examples of contemporary poems as starting points from which to reconsider the teaching of poetry in a creative writing context, a context which is not seen in isolation from approaches to reading modernist and contemporary work. These examples are drawn from the Poetic Practice course module that I teach to undergraduates at Royal Holloway, University of London, which attempts to set in dialogue approaches to writing and reading. The course is taken both by students who are engaged in traditional literary critical study, and students more focused on creative writing: the course seeks to show how an understanding of poetic practice can inform and guide both approaches. Each of the poems in the following examples uses a variety of procedures and processes in its construction that correspond directly to the writing exercises that the students are asked to engage in. The aim of this course is to present a parallel approach to the reading and writing of recent innovative poetries. These poems demonstrate how a recognition of the materialities and processes of practice as they are articulated in paintings and collage of the modernist period can become a useful starting point for addressing the visual semantics of a range of contemporary poetries on the page. Discussions of the way in which an art work generates meaning through its scale, its juxtaposition of materials, and its contexts of production and reception can offer students alternative models for reading and writing about practice which make explicit connections between process and meaning, and reveal the potential for a politics of form that forges connections between the art work and wider contexts. These poems can also be made to demonstrate that a contextualisation of poetry in relation to the visual arts need not be confined to a discussion of the visual aspects of language on the page. These poems can all be usefully situated in relation to conceptual art and its apparent turn away from pictorial representation, a move which could be paralleled by traditions in poetry that favour a found or process-based aesthetics and which eschew historical categories of poetic form in order to explore the already fraught object status of language as it exists. The exercises do not stand alone but work through juxtaposition with the poems discussed, and are designed as much to provide reading strategies as to stimulate writing and discussion.

Hannah Weiner, *Weeks*

Hannah Weiner's *Weeks* is a poem which cannibalises and spits back a collage of sound bites and overheard fragments from the TV news and was written by Weiner page by page for fifty weeks. In book format it is presented alongside grainy photographs taken from the TV by Barbara Rosenthal that often feature close-ups of heads or crowd scenes with subtitles such as 'More Violence' or 'Exclusive'. Each page of *Weeks* is outlined within a square black box which forces an analogy between the pages of images where the rectangle clearly refers to the TV set and the pages of text which are also presented inside a frame. This bracketed presentation works as a kind of screen which creates a distance between the identification of the poet with her images and her use of personal pronouns. The poem presents a tension between the disappearance of a coherent subject (the news reader) and an emergence of a mutated and fragmented series of what Bernstein calls 'tellers' through which the shards of found debris fluctuate in and out of focus. In *Weeks*, the media itself becomes a new form of lyric subject, a marker of collective unconscious which is mobile and transitory. Two portraits of Weiner and Rosenthal that have been taken from a video monitor appear like ghostly mediums at the end of the book. The book presents a double-sided representation of the poet, and indeed of the reader of the poem, as receivers of information transmitted by some outside force over which they have no control and as shapers of the existing language that is already all around us in the fabric of the everyday. This latter description of the practice of the writer positions *Weeks* in the tradition of American poetry which includes Charles Reznikoff's *Testimony*, Ronald Johnson's

Radi os, and the poetry of Jack Spicer, as well as the traditions of writing and art practice by groupings of practitioners as diverse as Dada, Surrealism, Oulipo, Pop-Art, $L=A=N=G=U=A=G=E$ writing, and conceptual artists such as Lawrence Weiner.[9]

This dual conception of the poet's role as potentially involving both Romantic and conceptual attitudes towards practice is a useful departure for discussion with students who are embarking on a course which will involve the practice of writing poetry and it also offers a model for a project which can be easily translated from a discussion based on reading a poem to one involving their own writing projects. For example, following a reading of *Weeks* students might be given the following instruction:

Exercise with Found Material I

Write a poem over a period of a week which contains only found writing/images overheard from the radio or TV. Consider the implications for the role of the writer and reader raised by your project.

The setting of such a project clearly has pedagogical implications for the teaching of both poetry and creative writing. It is an approach which does not fit what Michelene Wandor has aptly described as 'the Romantic/therapy axis' of creative writing teaching in which students bring poems that they regard as finished to the seminar or workshop to have them criticised by their peers and by their tutor in what by her account often turn into 'brutal and patronising exchanges' (2008: 131). She terms this mode of teaching 'the workshop as a House of Correction' which is 'built around *re-writing*, rather than *writing*' (131). The rewriting that takes place in the seminar involving the use of found material is of a very different kind and foregrounds the activity of writing as a conceptual and discursive enterprise which explicitly directs students away from the production of poems as uncritically motivated vehicles of self-expression.

The student who has arrived clutching her dog-eared sheaf of poems about her latest failed relationship is, according to this very different model of poetic practice, encouraged to recombine her original poems with a range of other found materials such as junk-mail, manuals, natural history guides, ephemera from her grandmother's attic or even her recycling bin. The aim is to introduce such a student to an understanding of the elastic and absorptive potential of what a poem might be. The student is attuned to a practice of writing generated by strategies that juxtapose various chunks of found material. This will necessarily involve the development of a range of different reading and critical practices associated with poetry. By extension, becoming attuned to registers already at work in different contexts of language use will expand her approach to lyric and confessional modes of writing and reading because she will be encouraged to recognise that writing in these modes is as circumscribed by tradition and artifice as any other apparently natural form of expression, including automatic writing. Similarly a student who is assigned to give a seminar presentation on Roland Barthes' 'Death of The Author' on Tuesday and one on Sylvia Plath's *Ariel* on Wednesday will need to be supported in her explorations of how the potential tensions inherent in this juxtaposition of influences might be translated into the activity of writing in addition to writing about writing.

[interjection I]
   Teacher: How do you set about writing a poem?
   Student: I put on some music, tidy my room and wait for inspiration to strike.
   Teacher: What if it doesn't?
   Student: I go out.

Bernadette Mayer, 'X ON PAGE 50 at half-inch intervals'

Bernadette Mayer's list of writing experiments (1984: 80–3) provides a welcome and useful antidote to the myth of the writer in his garret waiting for inspiration. In many ways they are themselves a conceptual art work with affinities to the lists and installed texts of Lawrence Weiner, Sol Le Witt, John Baldessari, and more recently Douglas Gordon. Students are often shocked and then excited by the permissions and starting points that the 'experiments' offer them. What is consistently foregrounded is the process of writing as an activity in itself rather than aimed at an end product. Amongst other things the experiments involve: deletion, substitution, accrual, duration, failure, and considerations of the material technologies of writing in relation to the making of poetry out of the substance of language. Techniques make manifest a potential relationship between process and meaning as the basis for the practice of writing poetry.

   The following is an exercise, in the spirit of rather than copied from her list, which students are asked to undertake before reading her poem

'X ON PAGE 50 at half-inch intervals':

Exercise with Found Material II

Using a marker pen divide a page of your newspaper into a grid of approximately 12 squares. Record the word or phrase that falls on each of the cross-points of the grid. Adapt, leave or rewrite your poem to suit.

'X ON PAGE 50 at half-inch intervals' is published in the *Bernadette Mayer Reader* (1992) as an 'early poem' and is the companion piece to Mayer's 'Definitions At The Center of The Newspaper, June 13, 1969' which was first published in the journal *0 To 9* that Mayer edited with Vito Acconci between April 1967 and July 1969. Contributors to the journal included Hannah Weiner, Adrian Piper, Sol Le Witt, Jasper Johns and Robert Smithson, and it was unique in bringing together writers and conceptual artists whose convergent projects used language as a medium of critique and investigative thinking.[10] Like 'Definitions At The Center of The Newspaper, June 13, 1969' the title of this poem, 'X ON PAGE 50 at half-inch intervals' is a description of its content:

> upper left corner to lower right corner: (in the margin), (at a line), (inside a photograph – at hair), (inside a photograph – at a bridge of nose), (inside a photograph – at left jaw), (in an empty space above *agonies*), (in an empty space between *been* and *not*), (at *Los*), [. . .]. (Mayer, 1992: 27)

The poem does not call for the type of close-reading usually associated with tackling a poem in a classroom situation. Instead its existence raises a number of questions about reading and the role of the poet. Nevertheless we can begin with some discussion of its process and how this might relate to our 'reading' of it. The blocks of text record the tracking of the X on page 50 of a newspaper that contains articles about Senator H. Dodd and space travel. Dodd was a Democrat senator censured for financial impropriety in 1967. The poem clearly isn't about Dodd or a trip to the moon but there is a correspondence set up between the methodological process of making the poem, space travel (the tracking of the X), and the 'evasion' of different forms of laws, referential and social. The poem effectively presents a flawed translation of the space of the newspaper page which points to the inadequate systems of representation already in operation in language.

[interjection II]
  Student 1: But these aren't poems are they?
  Teacher: Why not?
  Student 2: Because we just sort of found the words and put them together.
  Teacher: That's interesting, so what do poets do then?
  Student 1: This just isn't poetry.
  Teacher: So where do we find poetic language?
  Student 1: In poems.
  (General laughter)

Clearly Mayer's poem positions itself as far away as is possible from the expectations of a confessional poem. It can be contextualised in relation to the contemporaneous emergence of conceptual art. Joseph Kosuth's 1967 work *Titled (Art as Idea as Idea (Idea),* presents the viewer with a dictionary definition of the word 'idea' photostatted and mounted on board.[11] A student of poetry who approaches the practice of reading in the light of this work might be encouraged to consider the object status of language. She might begin to consider the way in which the dictionary is already a sculptural object that is itself a representation of the time in which it was constructed. She might also begin to address the apparently invisible force of poetry as itself a context which generates meaning and ask how designating something as being composed of poetic language can alter its signifying potential. She might consider how doing so echoes modernist debates surrounding the phenonomena of the ready-made and the ability of the space of an art gallery to generate meaning.

For many conceptual artists the use of language in place of paint seemed to provide an apparent alternative to the commodity status of the art work and to privilege the idea of the work of art above its material status. The writer and critic Lucy Lippard documented this phenomenon as the 'dematerialisation' of the art object (Lippard, 1997). In terms of an art market, modern poetry has never really had much of a commodity status to reject but this has clearly not stopped it commodifiying itself. The rise in creative writing courses is part of this trend. In poetry, however, it is often through chance and process-based operations that the submerged ideologies of power and control are rematerialised in the language of poetry. Kristin Prevallet and Jena Osman have both cited Tina Darragh's poem 'Adv Fans' as an example of a poem which does just this.[12] The poem uses dictionary definitions of new words recorded in 1968. As Osman notes 'Whereas "cultural revolution" may be the key-phrase that most think of when the year 1968 is evoked, it was a particularly nonrevolutionary vocabulary that was being generated at the time' (Osman, 2002: 265). Rather than providing an index of radical social change the etymologies documented by the poem relate to the rise in new technologies available to the domestic consumer.

> *[interjection III]*
> *Student 1: I just don't think that this is poetry.*
> *Teacher: How do we know what one (a poem) is?*
> *Student 1: Well, it has poetic language in it.*
> *Teacher: How does it get there?*
>   *Silence*
> *Student 2: From outside.*
> *Teacher: Where is that exactly?*
> *Student 2: I suppose it is just there. It's just there naturally.*
> *Teacher: That's interesting. So is all language natural?*
> *Student 1(Glumly): This poetry isn't.*

As Darragh's avowedly 'unnatural' poem demonstrates, language 'naturally' soaks up such tensions as it renews and adapts to historical circumstance. Rather than providing a transparent interface through which to transmit the sufferings of the poet these poems demonstrate how it might be used for different ends and complicate both the confessional poet's and the conceptual artist's apparently uncomplicated acceptance of language as a simple medium of transmission. Reading Darragh's poem requires attention to the vocabularies on the page but also to their visual layout. At various points she uses torn pages from the dictionary which are collaged together in a way which alters the surface of the poem and encourages the reader to view the page as a conceptually meaningful whole as well as a series of individual syntactic units. Darragh's pages are designed to be both read and looked at, and their use of juxtaposed fragments emphasises the poems' own material status and the history of their constituent parts in relation to other objects of definition such as the dictionary. Darragh's visual use of language inflects the more apparently conventional passages of her poem so that a reader is encouraged to reconsider her reading of the object nature of language and its visual signifying potential in other less obviously visual passages – an effect which is echoed by the procedural narrative of the poem as a whole.

Joan Retallack argues that 'at its best' literature 'enacts, explores, comments on, further articulates, radically questions the ethos of the discourses from which it springs' (2003: 11). Potential writers and teachers of writing need to be directed to examine the apparently naturalised borders of their discipline and to raise the question of what kinds of practice might lie beyond it. Darragh's work is an example of poetry which is potentially helpful in raising these questions, concerned as it is to develop a conceptual project over a series of pages that tests the limits of its medium by interrogating the signifying potential and history of language.

My approach to teaching poetry has much in common with established models of making and pedagogy in the visual arts. Visual arts students often work on a series of increasingly self-directed projects which assume a developing engagement with notions of practice-based research. Research might involve experiments with form and materials, study of the history of the visual arts and also reading in subjects other than their own, for example if the student decides to make environmental or site-specific art. By contrast, practice-based research is a term that is often difficult to justify in relation to many of the poems produced for conventional creative writing workshops where levels of 'research' can often only be gauged according to levels of narcissistic engagement commonly dressed up in the identity politics so fashionable in the 1970s and 1980s. Other art practices such as architecture, painting, performance, or music offer invaluable expanded conceptions of writing that allow the student to position herself within a wider field of related cultural production and to consider poetry in an expanded field of writing practice.

This expanded field of reference need not in itself necessitate an interdisciplinary practice. For all the current talk of hybridity and interdisciplinarity the production of such work might well have the effect of rendering the work of the student invisible within the culture of literature both in the academy and in the publishing industry. How the academy both generates and responds to the cultural climate in which it finds itself is of real concern to teachers of creative writing, many of whom seem poised to simply replicate market trends. For the most part, writing students are encouraged towards the production of writing that conforms to rather than challenges the allotted slot on the shelf of a high street store. By contrast, the pedagogical model adopted towards students of Fine Art is often one which encourages students to insert themselves within a tradition of both making and reception which they might seek to alter.

Exercise with Found Material III

Collate a series of one-sentence summaries of five news items chosen at random from today's newspaper. Swap lists with your neighbour. Write a lyric poem which takes as its starting point each of the summarised stories and synthesises them into one whole.

Kristin Prevallet, 'Lyric Infiltration'

This exercise has much in common with the processes and methodologies undertaken by Kristin Prevallet, whose book *Scratch Sides* (2002b) is subtitled *Poetry, Documentation, and Image-Text Projects*. Like Mayer, Prevallet's work can be approached through considerations of writing as text, the form of which intersects poetry and the visual arts rather than precluding the contextual field of either one or the other in its construction and subsequent reception.[13] *Scratch Sides* has an appendix entitled, 'Notes on Composition a.k.a. "demystifying the process"' (69) and includes a methodology for each of the poem series in the book. The sequence 'Lyric Infiltration' she describes as a 'cut-up technique' which reassembles fragments of her existing lyric poetry alongside 'one-line descriptions' of news stories. These synthesised lines are then used to 'infiltrate' another 'news story' (71). This happens successively over the sequence whose titles include, 'Synthesis A (lyric + source)', 'Synthesis B (lyric + 2 sources)', 'Source + Lyric Infiltration no. 1'.

The use of the term 'cut-up' places Prevallet's procedural work in relation to the strategies of previous writers such as Tristan Tzara, Brion Gysin, and the Oulipo founder Raymond Queneau, and can also be related to the chance-based operational writing of John Cage and Jackson Mac Low. The work of Prevallet is unusual in that it does not dispense with either the term 'lyric' or the process of lyric writing but uses it as a basis for her procedural work. She foregrounds the intuitive 'jamming' of found (public) and lyric (private) material (71).

This intuitive juxtaposition of found materials which are reworked and recontextualised as part of an art practice also has affinities between Prevallet's processes and the visual art tradition of collage, or *papiers collés*, as pioneered by Pablo Picasso and Georges Braque in 1912. The materials utilised by these two artists in their early works (wallpaper, fake wood grain, and musical scores alongside paint and pastel), are at first glance very different from Prevallet's range of examples of found material which move from political discussion ('Continuing unofficial counts reveal the full extent of Al Gore's lead and the massive abuses that have put George W. Bush into power.' *The Observer*, December 24th, 2000), through mundane reflections of our consumer-led society; 'Glossary of Terms: A Collection of terms useful for shopping Gap online store'), to the quirky and the absurd ('Family feud may doom brown dwarfs', *Rocky Mountain News*, July 7, 2001). In his discussion of Picasso's early collages, Brandon Taylor describes how these were 'constructed things: outside the category of *beaux arts* representations . . . intrusive new entities with

a hybrid ontology all their own' (Taylor, 2004: 19). He draws attention
to the significance of the choice to include scraps of wallpaper in the
composition, suggesting that 'they were intended to hang (framed or
otherwise) against the very wallpaper of which they were made' (19).
Prevallet's poem, patched as it is from scraps found on the internet
and newspapers which have presumably found their way into Prevallet's living space, is a comparable use of the fabric of domestic daily life.
Prevallet's lyric writing is presented in relief against this fabric and as the
series progresses is radically fused with it into new wholes which merge
lyric and found material.

In her essay, 'Investigating the Procedure: Poetry and the Source',
Prevallet uses the term 'sampling' to describe the poetry of Ed Saunders.
She argues that his poem '1968: A History in Verse' incorporates 'chunks
of information from his files of anarchist magazines, FBI files, letters, and
photographs' to present an alternative 'narrative history' of the period
and that the authority for this alternative account comes from the range
of its cited material (Prevallet, 2002a: 125). She is keen to distinguish his
procedural work from collage:

> Unlike collage, which decontextualizes and removes the reference
> from the object by forcing a cohesion with other objects, sampling
> preserves the reference by presenting it as a chunk of information,
> rather than as a fragmented cutup. Both recontextualize the origi-
> nal reference – but whereas collage consumes the reference, sampling
> allows the seams, and the points of convergence with other references,
> to show. (125)

In Prevallet's own poetics these 'seams' and 'points of convergence'
between references are also made manifest in ways that are not dissimilar from the X that Mayer tracked through her newspaper. As well as
the inclusion of a procedural methodology alongside her poem she frequently includes footnotes which are integrated into the poem and not
extraneous to it. These footnotes invoke the conventions of academic
citation and scientific investigation and map a processual path of activity through the poem. At the same time they playfully allude to and
document the ultimate failure of both the official systems of representation to provide a scientific basis for the empirical analysis of data from
the world around the lyric subject and of the poetic process to be bound
to any such formulaic and reductive account of reality:

1. 'Texas' deadly deluge,' *New York Post*, June 11, 2001. 2. source lost.
3. 'Dying for water in the Promised Land: 14 Mexicans are left to perish

as Arizona heat hits 46C,' *The Guardian*, May 25, 2001. 4. 'Survey offers a look deep into cosmos,' *New York Times*, June 6, 2001. 5. Accidental verso of clipping: source lost. (2002b: 21)

For Prevallet it is not the presentation of factual data clusters that will determine the veracity of the politics of her writing – instead it is there in the procedural obliterations and messy logics of process-based narrative which the lyric subject subjects herself to and then documents in her methodologies. As she writes: 'Poetry will not raise mass consciousness, although it will articulate new systems in which sources, language, lyric, document, collage, and process come together in alternative logic' (Prevalet, 2002a: 128).

Jena Osman, 'Dropping Leaflets'

> In the spirit of Marianne Moore, who often incorporated what she was reading into her poems, I'm going to read a piece made of words I found when I read transcripts of press conferences given by Bush, Ridge, Rumsfeld, and Cheney in the last few days. I read the transcripts, printed them out, I tore them up, and then I stood on a chair, and then I bombed the office floor with them as if they were leaflets and the leaflets told me what to do. So this piece is called 'Dropping Leaflets'. (Osman, 2001)[14]
>
> **Exercise for Found Material IV**
> Write a score for an action/performance of no more than three minutes which will involve a deconstruction and reconstruction of today's news.

Osman's poem 'Dropping Leaflets' is the residue of an apparently inconsequential yet highly resonant action carried out in response to the events of 9/11 and the subsequent launch of the war in Afghanistan by UK and US forces. Her procedure echoes the thousands of propaganda leaflets dropped by allied forces in Afghanistan which sought to persuade ordinary Afghanistan people of the legitimacy of the war against them. Osman recontextualises a quote from US Representative Cynthia McKinnny in November 2001 as the poem's epigraph: 'Help me come up with a strategy to get through this white noise.' The white noise of misinformation, propaganda, and lies that surrounds the war becomes a plea on behalf of the poet who struggles to find a direction in which to continue to write in a way that can engage with such terrible events. There is a deeply understated pathetic and fragile quality to her privately acted

but publicly recounted gesture which is integral to the poem. The procedure underscores an obvious frustration with what use a poetics and even
a politically motivated action might be at this time ('I tore them up, and
then I stood on a chair, and then I bombed the office floor'). Nevertheless
the obvious irony of 'the leaflets told me what to do' offers the fragile
possibility that the poem will have the effect of destabilising, at least
momentarily, the pervasive and insidious rhetoric with which it engages.

Her poem raises the question which she also recently asked in essay
form: 'Is there a way to have a poem do political work without preaching,
monologuing, speechifying, shutting down dialogue, or making use of
absolutes and essentialism?'[15] She cites artist Alfredo Jaar and poet Cecilia
Vicuna (both of whom work with found materials but in very different
ways) as practitioners whose work might begin to approach such a position. One practice, however, is all too easily co-opted or 'made palatable'
by the spaces which it seeks to critique (Jaar by advertising), whereas the
other proposes a 'reciprocity, recycling, participatory recognition and
reconnection' (Vicuna) through its representation of found materials.
For Osman it is the textual experiment that makes a 'conscious agreement to lay bare its own devices', as she herself does in the poem above
and which Kristin Prevallet does also, that comes closest to an adequate
attempt to 'do political work' in poetry.

The use of found, or source, material in the classroom provides a useful
distancing device between the writer and his/her material, and creates
gaps and spaces in which to begin discussions about assumed definitions of poetic form and of the role of the poet. Students can begin to
make work which through its rewriting of source texts has the potential to become part of what Craig Saper has termed a poetry of 'intimate
bureaucracies'. He cites mail-artists, concrete poets, and fluxus artists
all of whom reconfigure existing materials around them, such as junk
mail and office stationery, to 'shift the use of and tone' of bureaucratic
images and language 'from signalling authority to participation in ironic
satire, parody and inside jokes' (2001: 16). Through the use of procedural
approaches to writing, students can be encouraged to view their work as
conceptual and project-based explorations of the possibilities of poetic
thought rather than as a permission to lift the sluice gate on their emotional torrents of sensitivity. This does not mean that this approach to
writing practice is designed to give students a series of recipes for how
to write poetry but rather to present them with a demystification of the
poetic process which will detach it from models of creativity based on
the cultivation of the potential genius within and will reconnect the
actual process of writing to conceptual and ethical considerations of the

relationship between methodologies of practice and the production of meaning.

The approach that these writers I have discussed take in their treatment of found material has similarities with what Joan Retallack calls a 'poethics' of practice, which she defines as 'the ethos of making something of one's moment' which intertwines poetry and thinking in dialogue with the 'historical-contemporary' (Retallack, 2003: 11). At the same time their writing demonstrates the diversity of such a poethics and an expanded range of strategies for working with found materials, strategies clearly not reducible to simplified terms such as collage and cut-ups. As this essay has revealed there are a number of tensions and subtle variations in the strategies and outcomes of the various types of poethical writing which involve found materials. A poem that incorporates found materials often operates as a lens through which to review this material and therefore the choice of source text is crucial in determining the focus of the work. Writing through the television news is quite different from sampling from one's own lyric writing as a source text. Durational writing which collates materials according to a predetermined series of parameters and arranges them in paratactic juxtaposition is not the same as a poem which synthesises lyric and found materials over a sequence of pages. A poem that is the residue of a specific action or performance carried out at a particular time is quite distinct from a poem which continually reworks and resamples its original source texts. A poem which foregrounds multiple strategies of writing through found materials over a number of pages requires a comparable range of attentive and elastic approaches to reading, and such strategies can often be developed through the student's own writing projects. These strategies can also be directed by readings of the traditions of modernist poetry back to Gertrude Stein and Ezra Pound. Connections to the visual arts offer students alternative ways of conceptualising language as a medium. Encouraging students to recontextualise, write through, remake and recombine found materials helps them to develop as readers of modernist and contemporary poetry who are sympathetic to the complexities of language use by poets for whom lyric is only one approach to writing. Through creative attention to the reading and reuse of found materials students can be offered roles as writers who are conceptually engaged in the continual reflection on and redefinition of what constitutes poetic practice.

Notes

1. For an overview of the different practices associated with the term 'workshop' see Wandor (2008).

2. Mina Loy, *The Last Lunar Baedeker* (Manchester: Carcanet, 1982), p. 298.
3. See, for example, Majorie Perloff's discussion of Gertrude Stein in *The Poetics of Indeterminacy: From Rimbaud to Cage* (Princeton: Princeton University Press, 1981); and Randa Kay Dubnick, *The Structure of Obscurity: Gertrude Stein, Language and Cubism* (Champaign: University of Illinois Press, 1984).
4. Jesse Matz, *Literary Impressionism and Modernist Aesthetics* (Cambridge: Cambridge University Press, 2001).
5. See Richard Humphreys, *Pound's Artists: Ezra Pound and the Visual Arts in London, Paris & Italy* (London: Tate, 1985); and Rebecca Beasley, *Ezra Pound and the Visual Culture of Modernism* (Cambridge: Cambridge University Press, 2007); Henry M. Sayre, *The Visual Text of William Carlos Williams* (Urbana and Chicago: University of Illinois Press, 1983); and Peter Halter, *The Revolution in the Visual Arts and the Poetry of William Carlos Williams* (Cambridge: Cambridge University Press, 1994).
6. Jerome McGann, *Black Riders: the Visible Language of Modernism* (Princeton: Princeton University Press, 1993); Marjorie Perloff, *The Futurist Moment: Avant-Garde, Avant-Guerre, and the Language of Rupture* (Chicago: University of Chicago Press, 2003); Marjorie Perloff, *The Dance of the Intellect: Studies in the Poetry of the Pound Tradition* (Evanston, IL: Northwestern University Press, 1996); and Charles Altieri, *Painterly Abstraction in Modernist American Poetry: the Contemporaneity of Modernism* (Cambridge: Cambridge University Press, 1990)
7. See, for example, J. D. McClatchy (ed.), *Poets on Painters: Essays on the Art of Painting by Twentieth-Century Poets* (Berkeley: University of California Press, 1988).
8. See, for example, Willard Bohn, *The Aesthetics of Visual Poetry, 1914–28* (Chicago: University of Chicago Press, 1993).
9. See the following for further information on each of these groups of poets and writers: Elza Adamowicz, *Surrealist Collage in Text and Image: Dissecting the Exquisite Corpse* (Cambridge: Cambridge University Press, 1998); Brandon Taylor, *Collage: the Making of Modern Art* (London: Thames & Hudson, 2004); Harry Matthews and Alastair Brotchie (eds), *The Oulipo Compendium* (Atlas Press, 1999); Bruce Andrews and Charles Bernstein (eds), *The L=A=N=G=U=A=G=E BOOK* (Carbondale: Southern Illinois University Press, 1984); Peter Osborne, *Conceptual Art (Themes and Movements)* (London: Phaidon Press, 2002).
10. See also: *The Ubu Web: Anthology of Conceptual Writing*, ed. Craig Douglas Dworkin. UBUWEB, accessed 6 May 2008 (http://www.ubu.com/concept/). *0 To 9* has recently been reprinted as *0 To 9: the Complete Magazine: 1967–1969*, ed. Vito Acconci and Bernadette Mayer (Brooklyn, NY: Ugly Duckling Presse: Lost Literature Series, 2006).
11. See Morley (2003: 145).
12. See Prevallet (2002a) and Osman (2002).
13. See Roland Barthes, 'From Work to Text', *Image/Music/Text*, ed. and trans. Stephen Heath (London: Fontana, 1977), 155–64.
14. See Osman (2004: 28) for text of the poem.
15. Osman (2007).

Works cited and further reading

Andrews, Bruce and Charles Bernstein (1984) *The L=A=N=G=U=A=G=E BOOK*. Carbondale: Southern Illinois University Press.

Bernstein, Charles (1990) 'Introduction' to Hannah Weiner, *Weeks*. Madison, WI: Xexoxial Editions.

Darragh, Tina (1992) *Adv Fans: the 1968 Series*. Buffalo, NY: Leave Books.

Lippard, Lucy (1997) *SIX YEARS: the Dematerialization of the Art Object from 1966 to 1972*. Berkeley: University of California Press.

Mayer, Bernadette (1984) 'Writing Experiments', in Bruce Andrews and Charles Bernstein (eds), *The L=A=N=G=U=A=G=E BOOK*. Carbondale: Southern Illinois University Press.

——— (1992) *A Bernadette Mayer Reader*. New York: New Directions.

Morley, Simon (2003) *Writing on the Wall: Word and Image in Modern Art*. London: Thames & Hudson.

Osman, Jena (2001) '"Dropping Leaflets" read at the Kelly Writers House, November 7, 2001', PennSound (http://www.writing.upenn.edu/~afilreis/88v/osman-leaflets.html), accessed 6 May 2008.

——— (2002) '"Multiple" Functioning: Procedural Actions in the Poetry of Tina Darragh', in Mark Wallace and Steven Marks (eds), *Avant-Garde Poetics of the 1990s: Telling It Slant*. Tuscaloosa: University of Alabama Press, 255–80. New York: Teachers and Writers Collaborative.

——— (2004) *An Essay in Asterisks*. Berkeley: Roof.

——— (2007) 'Is Poetry the News? The Poethics of the Found Text', *Jacket* 32 (http://jacketmagazine.com/32/p-osman.shtml), accessed 6 May 2008.

Padgett, Ron (2000) *The Straight Line: Writing on Poetry and Poets*. Ann Arbor: University of Michigan Press.

Padgett, Ron and Christopher Edgar (eds) (1994) *Educating the Imagination: Essays and Ideas for Teachers and Writers*. New York: Teachers and Writers Collaborative.

——— (1995) *Old Faithful: 18 Writers Present Their Favourite Writing Assignments*. New York: Teachers and Writers Collaborative.

Prevallet, Kristin (2002a) 'Investigating the Procedure: Poetry and the Source', in Mark Wallace and Steven Marks (eds), *Avant-Garde Poetics of the 1990s: Telling It Slant*. Tuscaloosa: University of Alabama Press, 115–30.

——— (2002b) *Scratch Sides: Poetry Documentation, and Image-Text Projects*. Austin, TX: Skanky Possum Press.

Retallack, Joan (2003) *The Poethical Wager*. Berkeley: University of California Press.

Retallack, Joan and Juliana Spahr (2006) *Poetry and Pedagogy: the Challenge of the Contemporary* (Basingstoke: Palgrave Macmillan).

Saper, Craig (2001) *Networked Art*. Minneapolis: University of Minnesota Press.

Smith, Hazel (2005) *The Writing Experiment: Strategies for Innovative Creative Writing*. London: Allen & Unwin.

Taylor, Brandon (2004) *Collage: the Making of Modern Art*. London: Thames & Hudson.

Wandor, Michelene (2008) *The Author is not Dead, Merely Somewhere Else: Creative Writing Reconceived*. Basingstoke: Palgrave Macmillan.

Weiner, Hannah (1990) *Weeks*. Madison, WI: Xexoxial Editions.

9
Experiment in Practice and Speculation in Poetics

Robert Sheppard

Like many teachers of creative writing I was a practising writer before I was a pedagogue of the subject, although I was a teacher of English in Further Education for many years. During this time my literary work developed outside of most academic contexts, but within the groupings of poets sometimes called the British Poetry Revival or Linguistically Innovative Poetry. As a critic I had some responsibility for the propagation of the second cumbersome term, and also some responsibility for the polarising of these groups of writers against a mainstream which I dubbed the Movement Orthodoxy. By this I meant not just the kinds of poetic conservatism associated with Philip Larkin, but the default style of British poetry as it had developed into an unexamined and largely unconscious regulatory poetic mode.[1] Since beginning to work in higher education as a lecturer in creative writing in 1996, I have always expected the associated 'poetry wars' to break out, to experience the equivalent of the hostility from conservative quarters towards writing that is formally innovative that I have experienced as a poet and critic, but beyond the odd distant gunshot, I have heard nothing. A plurality of approaches to teaching writing practice seems available and acceptable and while I am doubtful about claims for a rainbow alliance in contemporary poetry – the notion that there is now a charmingly plural pantheon where an apparently radical poet like Denise Riley is enthroned alongside the more orthodox Andrew Motion with equal status, for example – something like love seems to have broken out in the creative writing world, as writers of very different kinds, from professional writers such as journalists, through to 'mainstream' poets traditionally antagonistic to the poetics of an extended modernist tradition have become close colleagues. In this chapter I reflect upon what my own pedagogic experience, with reference to both radical poetic practice and the speculative discourse of poetics, signals in this contemporary context.

Of course, such optimism is necessarily cautious. I do not want to downplay the continued existence of purely traditionally formal work-shop orientations that insist that students must profoundly know the 'rules' (of which the tutor is in privileged possession) before they may break them – but at least there is a sense that they *may* break them. I could be cynical about a module which features free verse in week eleven and concrete and pattern poetry in week twelve, but they are at least repre-sented, and students may make rich use of their permissions, as well as of more authorised forms. In my research for the English Subject Centre on what I called 'supplementary discourses' in creative writing teach-ing in higher education,[2] I found that, rather than a commitment to self-expressive or therapeutic modes of writing, tutors emphasised craft and technique in ways which often allow for the kinds of experiment I would recognise in my own pedagogy and practice.[3] In short, many of the tenets of the writing that I practise are to be found embedded in various workshop situations as elemental parts of general pedagogy. The greatest apologia for Creative Writing *as an academic study* is not that it produces writers and writing, but that it poses questions of literariness in a conjectural way, and that includes the production of original creative writing and both the production and reading of poetics. As such, poetics has the potential to heal the creative–critical split of some creative writ-ing programmes, render the boundaries between them porous, or – most radically – erase the distinction entirely.

My own teaching materials were designed without reference to extant creative writing materials or courses. Nothing offered itself as a model in 1997, when first I designed the poetry components of the degree pro-gramme at Edge Hill. Perhaps if Hazel Smith's *The Writing Experiment* had been published a decade before it was in 2005, I might have borrowed from her working through of innovative writing strategies. My own undergraduate teaching is based on the modernist and postmodernist inheritance in Anglo-American poetry and may be simply described in summary form (I will deal with poetics later). For first-year students I cautiously set graded exercises in haiku, imagist, objectivist, projectivist and collage writing, aware that students come with preconceptions and fears about poetry writing. With the exception of the exercises in collage, these teaching materials have been adapted for publication in a conven-tional textbook of creative writing, where I present them as elements of a hygiene of writing, indeed as lessons in concision, compression, and imagistic (observational) outwardness appropriate to many forms of imaginative writing (Graham et al., 2005: 207–16). For second- and third-year students, I devise readings and exercises drawn mostly from the poems contained in the second volume of the Jerome Rothenberg and Pierre Joris (1998) anthology *Poems for the Millennium: Post-War to Millennium*, based around concepts of writing for the eye, the ear, and sense (a development of Pound's taxonomy of 'phanopoeia', 'melopoeia', and 'logopoeia' in his *ABC of Reading* (Pound, 1951: 63) and of Zukofsky's 'test of poetry' which assesses 'the range of pleasure it affords as sight, sound and intellection' (Allen and Tallman, 1973: 250). I use performance (both oral and aural, listening to tapes and CDs) as an extension of Pound's second category, with a literal look at visual poetries, such as concrete poetry and also forms of writing such as Susan Howe's, where the visual disposition of the poem on the page is a major part of its poetic artifice, which is an extension of the first. This is an emerging mode of writing which interests an increasing number of students each year, as their digitised sense of text and image interface becomes more complex. In other words, I offer particular techniques which students can use in a variety of ways. There are specific experiments in fundamental poetic procedures such as repetition and change, and particular exercises in thinking of collage as a basic structure of experience and perception as well as a major modernist art practice. Concepts of the (free verse) line are continuously re-examined, nurturing a permanent sensitivity towards, a constant crisis about, line, so that any freedom of choice in lineation that students experience is coupled with a sense of the responsibility of using the form, and perhaps a little of the anguish of choosing between variants of lineation and spatial disposition. This last aspect involves a consideration of what Marjorie Perloff calls the 'non-linear poetries'. Indeed, her two chapters, 'Lucent and Inescapable Rhythms: Metrical "Choice" and Historical Formation' and 'After Free Verse: the New Non-linear Poetries', in her *Poetry On and Off the Page* are vital resources for class discussions of these issues (Perloff, 1998: 116–67).

I am not sure that tutors who lack my commitment to modernist and postmodernist poetic forms have many problems with these kinds of experiments, as *experiments*. However, unanimity between creative writing teachers may start to crack around the nature and function of this experiment. While most creative writing teachers encourage experiment as a mode of writing process or *practice* – collage or spontaneous modes of writing, for example, may be in their loose-leaf collection of learning strategies – they might be less willing to accept it as a product, as a learning outcome. They may be unwilling to accept a cluster of techniques that point towards an exploratory practice, that is articulated with – and through – a poetics that foregrounds modernist and postmodernist insistence on experiment in its own right. To produce a text inspired by Tom Phillips' *A Humument* (1980), by the deletion and obscuring of a found text, is not a classroom game, but a legitimate literary investigation in releasing the potentiality of a new 'saying' into that which is assumed to have been already completed and 'said'. In other respects I recognise my teaching does not transfer the implications of experimental writing into experimental modes of learning, and I am not as sure as others that I could achieve this within curriculum and institutional constraints. Alan Golding's description of Juliana Spahr's ideal classroom as a 'utopian, dissident space', analogous to certain conceptualisations of the language poem, seems too utopian for the situation I find myself in (Golding, 2006: 24).

It is at the level of reflection upon practice, rather than at the level of practice as such, that the difficulties may arise. The practices of the radical poetries imply the active production of poetics not merely as a reflective reaction but as a speculative function recognising poetry as a paradigm that may be shifted permanently and continually by such work. This emphasises the difference between accepting experiment as an incremental element in personal writerly development, and demanding experiment as the precondition for writing's survival. For the first sort, poetics is necessary to the student. In the second it is necessary to the vitality of the work and its tradition, as well as to the student. As I shall show, poetics is an important part of this pedagogy with the most radical implications.

Poetics is a speculative writerly discourse. It is speculative because it is defined against the various modes of 'reflection' on works already written; its orientation is towards the next job, as Ezra Pound says somewhere. That does not deny a reflective component, but poetics is primarily, in a definition of American poet Rachel Blau DuPlessis that is often picked up by students, 'a permission to continue', beyond the self-evident and the already achieved (DuPlessis, 1990: 156). It is writerly because it is not a literary critical activity; critics may speak of constructing a 'theory of poetry' – Harold Bloom uses this term – but that is distinct from a poetics which will remain the concern of writers or of groups of writers. It is not impossible for critics and creative writers to discuss the same issues, but for writers, the questions will be as practical as they are theoretical. Poetics is a paradoxical theory of practice *and* practice of theory. Thirdly, it is a discourse with a history and rules of its own. While its history is demonstrable – but beyond the remit of this piece – the 'rules' are less so, because the discourse is mercurial and writers' speculations appear in a variety of guises (Sheppard, 2002). The poetics of American language poet Charles Bernstein manifests in a number of different 'genres': from formal essays, lectures, speeches, scattered aphorisms and slogans, in reviews of other writers' works, and – here is the most para-doxical – in the poetry itself, such as his 1,000-line essay-poem 'Artifice of Absorption' which plays essayist voice against poetic enjambment. Readers of modernist and postmodernist poems will have noticed how many are about poetry itself – they are metapoems – and sometimes they 'speculate' their own existence and future into being. Bernstein's poem is particularly hard to reduce to paraphrase, but that is part of its argument (Sheppard, 1999). As this example shows, the discourse of poetics can also appear in hybrid forms between recognisable genres. This is some-thing I encourage students to explore, although it has its own danger of authorising obfuscation in lyrical afflatus or collage 'theory buzz'.

At PhD level, various research students of mine, in addition to their creative work and a 'critical' essay, have incorporated 'poetic' structures of reflection, usually fragmentary and collaged, into their theses: ranging from a series of Wallace Stevens-like aphorisms to a drifting associative weave of ideas relating to the creative component, and miming its style. What is less than encouraging is the fact that during the viva exam-inations, the poetics have seldom been discussed, despite the central position of the poetic thinking they contain to the project as a whole. We might suppose that the lack of institutionalisation of poetics – with which I will deal – suggests that there does not yet exist a language to describe, evaluate, and assess such a discourse. Oddly, at MA and undergraduate levels, the discourse in these experimental forms has been encouraged by external examiners for enabling exploratory investigation of textuality.

At MA level, poetics is central to the philosophy of the currently val-idated programme – this displaced a model which had attempted to combine literary theory with creative production – and the dissertations have been accompanied by poetics that range from accounts of gestation, process, and realisation, to more speculative essays on the completion of, or the future of, their writing projects, through to playful forms that play with form itself, like Bernstein's poem: a script that animates the characters of a novel to speak 'for themselves' in a metadiscourse, for example. One poetry-narrative hybrid text written for the course is pub-lished, with its poetics more or less complete, Alice Lenkiewicz's *Maxine* (Lenkiewicz, 2006).

At undergraduate level, students are introduced to poetics, specifically and by name, in the third year only, but because 'reflection' in various

modes is a given of all writing modules, they are not completely inno-
cent of its function in earlier years. However, even a cursory glance at the
'Art of the Manifesto' section of volume II of *Poems for the Millennium*,
with its hybrid pieces – speeches, lectures, diagrams, poems, performance
pieces, notes, manifestos, etc. – is enough to encourage experimental
responses, mostly using (or miming) the same techniques that students
have developed in their creative work (Rothenberg and Joris, 1998:
408–51). As a counter-balance to effusiveness and stylistic proliferation,
I offer them Rosmarie Waldrop's brilliantly lucid survey of her career:
'Why Do I Write Prose Poems When My True Love Is Verse' (Waldrop,
2005: 260–4).

If its intermittent and mercurial nature causes it to take such strange
forms and to hide in so many genres, including creative work itself, how
can I prove that such a discourse as poetics exists and that it is effective in confirming and subsequently changing artistic practice, and in
shifting poetic paradigms? One answer is that I recognise the impulse
in my own writing practice, which derives from modernist and postmodernist sources. Innovations of any creative writing teacher are often
little more than transferences of his or her own experiences: poetics was
simply what many of the avant-garde London poets – including myself –
who emerged during the 1980s under the banner 'linguistically innovative', found themselves producing (or at least reading) as a matter of
course. Allen Fisher, for example, in his brilliant but convoluted *Necessary Business* weaves speculation between fact-finding interviews with
Eric Mottram and cris cheek and reactions to the work of J. H. Prynne
to create a poetics of 'pertinence' (Sheppard, 1999). This was a major
inspiration for one of my PhD students, Scott Thurston, in the design
and execution of his thesis which largely consisted of annotated interviews with poets, including Fisher himself! (Thurston, 2002).[4] In the
1980s the influx of continental critical theory promised philosophical
definitions of some of the techniques we were applying. Lyotard's definitions of postmodern knowledge, for example – 'The artist and the
writer . . . are working without rules in order to formulate the rules
of what will have been done' – seemed to speak to us as practitioners
of works that explored modes of discontinuity and indeterminacy and
that saw paradigm shifting as necessary to poetic development (Lyotard,
1984: 60). Additionally, the influence of a generation of American poets
who also fed off this theoretical moment, the language poets, cannot be
overestimated. Their theoretical musings, particularly from 1978 onward
in *L=A=N=G=U=A=G=E* magazine, encouraged poetics in hybrid forms.
Reviews of books that were collages of its contents, collage poems that

were also reviews of books, suggested that the expressive modes available to the reflective and speculative poet were capable of limitless extension, and thus of facilitating fresh ideas about writerly potentiality. During this time I was keeping my own poetics discourse alive outside of the academy: in poetics statements, in criticism, in my littlest of magazines, *Pages*, in the editing of an anthology, in the poetry itself, and in the simple keeping of notebooks. It seemed natural, therefore, to encourage students to simulate these activities, along with these influences.

The growing importance of poetics occurred at the same time as the rapid development of creative writing as an academic subject during the early 1990s, although I was outside the academy. I was sceptical about creative writing, not for the usual writers' fearful reaction that 'you can't teach people to write', but because I had studied the subject on the well-known MA at the University of East Anglia in the late 1970s, and it seemed antithetical to the kinds of explorative poetry and poetics I was writing and writing about, in favour of what is known in the US as the 'workshop poem', a neat formulaic (and often formalist) lozenge of experience, lightly spiced with epiphany or leavened with moral, the stateside equivalent of the Movement Orthodoxy. More importantly to my argument in this chapter, early creative writing also seemed to downplay the function of poetics. (Indeed, in my MA thesis, there was no reflective component, save that which I wove into the poems themselves.) To a great extent this was an unfair prejudgement, and my English Subject Centre research on supplementary discourses reveals a variety of reflective and speculative practices, some of which generally accord with my notions of poetics. Indeed, the research strengthened my sense of its specificity and its use, both specifically to teaching the writing and reading of linguistically innovative poetry, and more generally to the modalities of reflection being developed by the creative writing community as a whole.

While the most developed forms of poetics, that is, poetics which takes on the formal characteristics of the writings it calls into being, are found in the area of modern and postmodernist practice, and in its more avant-garde and experimental modes, poetics is a discourse appropriate to all forms of writing, and all forms of writing have a poetics (explicit or not). Poetics also has a promising pedagogic future within creative writing generally, and, as creative writing is making an impact upon English as a developing academic subject, poetics has wider import for literary studies as well, although not yet acknowledged. We must know not only how we recognise poetics, but why we need to read and teach it, and how to teach it.

One unfortunate effect of the comparatively obscured or hybrid nature of poetics is the misreading of it as though it were a variety of literary theory or literary criticism, and it is necessary for students, particularly those undergoing literary studies alongside creative writing, to recognise this. Contributions to Jon Cook's anthology *Poetry in Theory*, a recommended textbook for teaching ideas about mainly modernist and postmodernist twentieth-century poetry that I suspect is used both in creative writing and critical contexts, fall into three broad (sometimes overlapping) categories: literary theory (written by philosophers and theorists, which is constructed at a high level of generality and, it has to be confessed, a low level of specific textual reference; it is alarming how much Lacan squeezes from one line of Mallarmé (Cook, 2004: 315–22)); literary criticism (which is usually textually specific around themes or authors, such as Barbara Hernstein Smith's 'Closure and Anti-closure in Modern Poetry' (Cook, 2004: 399–407) or excerpts from Thomas Yingling's *Hart Crane and the Homosexual Text* (Cook, 2004: 538–46); and poetics written by creative writers themselves, often in forms which evade formal academic discourse, such as Charles Olson's seminal and expressive 'Projective Verse' essay (Cook, 2004: 288–95).

The field of creative writing is saturated by handbooks, textbooks, or even workbooks that claim to instruct the creative writing student how to write, while usually coyly disavowing such an intention. I am sceptical of these (even though I have contributed to one) and they seldom rise to poetics (nor do they aim to). To stay with the example extracted from Cook's anthology: to misread Charles Olson's essay 'Projective Verse' as a 'how to' guide – to fixate on its emphasis on the line as breath, the use of the typewriter as a scoring device, for example – can work only if one is content to remain a second- or third-generation Olsonian. Fortunately, much poetics (including Olson's essay) resists being read in this way. Part of the attraction of poetics to fragmentary and hybrid form is to evade the totalising certainty of a manifesto, which, although it is a classic modernist genre, often elides the speculative with the prescriptive.[5]

Denise Riley's edited volume *Poets on Writing, Britain 1970–1991* (1992) is an exemplary volume that collects poetics prose writings of various kinds (as well as some poems) and, like the Cook volume, such a collection should become central to the development of creative writing, if we accept that the discipline's primary aim is the exploration of states of literariness, as I have conjectured. In Peter Riley's careful consideration of 'The Creative Moment of the Poem', he asks: 'How, then, does the writer transmit through his body? How does he create something at a given point which is recognisable from elsewhere after 2000 years?'

(Peter Riley, 1992: 99). These are questions which sweep off into the most general issues. On the other hand, Roy Fisher's eschewal of abstract theorising in favour of empirical process in his flatly entitled 'Poet on Writing', results in him reflecting only about his 'physically making a creature of blackish marks on whitish paper' (Fisher, 1992: 272). Whereas Peter Riley speculates that 'The poet writes into the poem. World factors pass through him to a scripted heart and on to the new heart', Fisher is content to leaf the pages of his deliberately non-literary notebooks, and tell us that, in the activity of writing, 'this mass of observations, sensations and introspections is inchoate, and undeveloped except by the movements of its own tides . . . I've come to think of it, rather than the poems, as my work, my central occupation' (Fisher, 1992: 273). Peter Riley offers a more public account of the singularity of poetry as techni-cal and ontological unity, emphasising that poetic artifice *is* a battery of meaningful devices:

> Images, sense-gaps, line-endings, syntactical relations, sonance, rhythm, rhyme, music, metrics, numbers, do not just carry meaning in the poem, they are meaning. How are they meaning? By being all there is, by being the intellected world of the poem. How do they bear hope? By showing that a world brought to this constituency makes sense and is complete and necessary and beautiful. The whole of that construct then leaps through the mind towards the future, is borne into it as a possession, like a talisman almost, held against wide harm. (1992: 106–7)

Riley leaps from the technical to the cosmic, a conjectural move that students could debate most profitably. Reading Fisher would bring them back to actual processes of writing, since Fisher feels compelled – one almost feels like saying *merely* – to explain his method of composition: 'When I judge there's enough heterogeneity, so that more material would cause the work to fissure and buckle in on itself, then I stop' (Fisher, 1992: 275). The artisan has downed tools with a resounding thud. Stu-dents could contrast the *macropoetics* of Peter Riley's speculations about the function of poetry in general with the *micropoetics* of Fisher's descrip-tions of actual creative process.[6] Riley's sense of textual completeness and Fisher's pursuit of a certain textual complexity and unfinish reveal much about debates within the poetic community called the British Poetry Revival.

These documents, and similar ones, including the 'Art of the Mani-festo' section of the Rothenberg and Joris anthology of course, speak to the student writer in a spirit of *provocation*. Writers often read poetics with this sense of having been provoked or challenged and I would wish creative writing students to experience this too, to educate them away from the expectations of the answers and models of 'how to' books, to the questioning of conjectures, which requires an active response, one that could either result in further poetics or in more creative work.[7]

In addition to teaching writing students how to write poetics, poetics – from whatever source – should be read and studied in the academy, and we must learn to read and use it in ways not yet developed, or only partially developed. This is quite distinct from the calls one can still hear occasionally for creative writing to be regarded as an adjunct to English literature teaching, to promote literary-critical reading through so-called 'creative' exercises. As English studies in the UK becomes more affected by the presence of creative writing, with a growing student body alert to the potential mobility of text and to *speculative* ideas about textuality, then it will have – perhaps unforeseen – effects. Poetics should therefore be at the heart of creative writing, of all kinds, which in turn should be at the heart of a reoriented English Literature, which might rediscover questions of literary value and resistances to what Derek Attridge calls 'instrumentalist' readings of literature (Attridge, 2004: 6–10). We need poetics journals, not least of all as a venue for research students to publish poetics. We need centres, conferences, networks, poetics research groups, teaching modules, and further academic study to explore poetics and how to write it and to read it.[8] Practice-based research in poetics and academic research into poetics (both of which are in their infancy under those designations) need to acquire a language to talk to one another.

Experiment in practice and speculation in poetics are two major inheritances from modernism. While the experimental is valuable in its own right, and produces exploratory work, pushing at the paradigm of what poetry is and can become, poetics (the powerhouse of this particular experimentalism as well as its speculative vanguard) also has much to offer many other kinds of writing. It may also prove that a poetics – even one, or even especially one, that grows out of experimental practice – may turn against any particular mode of experiment (particularly if repeated endlessly as a mere creative writing 'exercise') in the cause of unceasing poetic development. I insist on that openness – for my students and for myself.

Notes

1. This is the theme of my critical work *The Poetry of Saying: British Poetry and Its Discontents* (Liverpool: Liverpool University Press, 2005).

2. The full report, *Supplementary Discourses in Creative Writing Teaching in Higher Education*, which was written by myself with research assistance from Scott Thurston, may be found in full on the English Subject Centre website, at: www.english.heacademy.ac.uk/archive/projects/reports/supdisc_cwrit.doc, and in summary form as 'Reflections on Reflection', a contribution to a forth-coming fraternal volume to this, entitled *Teaching Creative Writing in Higher Education: Anglo-American Perspectives*, edited by Heather Beck.

3. As a shorthand for 'experiments', I am thinking of those devised by Bernadette Mayer and supplemented by Charles Bernstein, now available at epc.buffalo.edu/authors/Bernstein/experiments.html, accessed 6 November 2004.

4. See Thurston (2002: 10–27), for a short version of this interview and its accom-panying piece on Fisher's work (28–33), and for some of Scott Thurston's poems from the thesis itself (34–9).

5. I remain sceptical about the role of manifestos. There is something inimi-cal to the speculative quality of poetics as I conceive it in the tub-thumping modernist manifesto. At best, such manifestos contain poetics. The post-modern manifesto is, by contrast, more teasing. In Cook (2004) compare Pound's imagist manifesto 'A Retrospect' (83–90) with Frank O'Hara's 'Per-sonism: a Manifesto' (367–9). See also Sheppard (2007) for a fuller account of the relationship between poetics and manifestos.

6. In *The Necessity of Poetics* I define the concerns of this pair thus: '*Micropoetics*: whose domain is the text and its technique; everything below the level of the text', and '*Macropoetics*: whose domain is the text and the world: everything above the level of the text' (Sheppard, 2002: 4). The distinction is also found built into the structure of the MA Writing Studies at Edge Hill, where the two modules between the introductory and the dissertation preparation ones are called 'Text and Technique' (a time to look at technical issues from Bakhtin to Oulipo) and 'Text and Context' (which looks at many of the contemporary 'isms' in contemporary culture, particularly postmodernism).

7. I would like to acknowledge Cliff Yates, a member of the Poetry and Poetics Research Group that has met at Edge Hill since 1999, for emphasising the term 'provocation' in his poetry and poetics PhD.

8. I am increasingly teaching the reading of poetics, as well as the writing of it, on the MA. I have validated but not yet taught an English Literature BA module, entitled 'Contemporary Poets and their Ideas', which will feature poetics as a distinct discourse and which will make use of Riley (1992).

Works cited

Allen, Donald and Warren Tallman (eds) (1973) *The Poetics of the New American Poetry*. New York: Grove Press.

Attridge, Derek (2004) *The Singularity of Literature*. London and New York: Routledge.

Cook, Jon (2004) *Poetry in Theory*. Oxford: Blackwell.

DuPlessis, Rachel Blau (1990) *The Pink Guitar: Writing as Feminist Practice*. New York and London: Routledge.

Fisher, Roy (1992) 'Poet on Writing', in Denise Riley (ed.), *Poets on Writing: Britain, 1970–1991*. Basingstoke: Macmillan.

Golding, Alan (2006) ' "Isn't the Avant-Garde Always Pedagogical?" Experimental Poetics and/or Pedagogy', in Joan Retallack and Juliana Spahr (eds), *Poetry and Pedagogy: the Challenge of the Contemporary*. New York and Basingstoke: Palgrave Macmillan.

Graham, Robert et al. (2005) *The Road to Somewhere*. Basingstoke: Palgrave Macmillan.

Lenkiewicz, Alice (2006) *Maxine*. Bristol: Bluechrome.

Lyotard, J.-F. (1984) *The Postmodern Condition*. Manchester: Manchester University Press.

Perloff, Marjorie (1988) *Poetry On and Off the Page*. Evanston, IL: Northwestern University Press.

Phillips, Tom (1980) *A Humument: a Treated Victorian Novel*. London: Thames & Hudson, 1980.

Pound, Ezra (1951) *ABC of Reading*. London: Faber & Faber, 1951.

Rothenberg, Jerome and Pierre Joris (1998) *Poems for the Millennium*, Volume II: *Post-War to Millennium*, Berkeley: University of California Press.

Riley, Denise (ed.) (1992) *Poets on Writing: Britain, 1970–1991*. Basingstoke: Macmillan.

Riley, Peter (1992) 'The Creative Moment of the Poem', in Denise Riley (ed.), *Poets on Writing: Britain, 1970–1991*. Basingstoke: Macmillan.

Sheppard, Robert (1999) 'The Poetics of Poetics: Charles Bernstein, Allen Fisher and "the poetic thinking that results"', *Symbiosis* 3(2) (April): 77–92.

—— (2002) *The Necessity of Poetics*. Liverpool: Ship of Fools.

—— (2005) *The Poetry of Saying: British Poetry and its Discontents 1950–2000*. Liverpool: Liverpool University Press.

—— (2007) 'Public Poetics: the Manifesto of the Poetry Society (1976)', in Tony Lopez and Anthony Caleshu (eds), *Poetry and Public Language*. Exeter: Shearsman Books.

Smith, Hazel (2005) *The Writing Experiment*. Crows Nest: Allen & Unwin.

Thurston, Scott (2002) 'Method and Technique in the Work of Allen Fisher'/'Allen Fisher: the Necessity of Change'/six poems, *Poetry Salzburg Review* 3 (Autumn): 10–39.

—— (2003) 'Rescale', *Mantis* 3 (Spring): 159–73.

Waldrop, Rosmarie (2005) *Dissonance (if you are interested)*. Tuscaloosa: University of Alabama Press.

10
Wreading, Writing, Wresponding
Charles Bernstein

Writing

Laptops are open and everyone's online and chattering away at the same time. I pass around a yellow pad and it circulates from one person to the next, in zigzag order, for the length of the seminar. The participants are writing an ongoing serial collaboration and will continue to work on this, during the class, for the full fourteen weeks we meet. Each week one student takes the pages home and posts a verbatim transcription and an edited version. From my laptop I project, on the large LCD display screen, the index of the class listserv, to which everyone has posted their work for the week.

Each week students write works based on the experiments list (http://writing.upenn.edu/bernstein/experiments.html), a set of constraints and procedures, which has served as a foundation for much of my undergraduate teaching over the past twenty years. You could call this class 'creative writing', but I resist the label since it comes with all the weight of the prototypical poetry workshop, which is often focused on content-based exercises rather than experiments in form. *Write a poem about the first time you saw your Dad shaving*: 'the blood dripped down his face / and I trembled in the corner, / unseen, whimpering'. Not being particularly interested in sincerity, description, or traditional craft, I've long made a point of teaching modernist and contemporary poetry classes rather than writing classes, but the twist is that these literature classes – what I call 'creative (w)reading' workshops – are run as if they were creative writing classes (students write creatively in response to the readings, but the focus is entirely on poems assigned).

Over time, you see, I've become more interested in small seminars devoted just to the students' experiments and so, through a kind of trap back door, which I've fallen through, tripping up my apparent prejudices, I've ended up in a very common space of creative writing (poetry), which I simply call 'Writing Experiments Seminar' – or English 111, after the number of the room in which we meet.

My phobia of creative writing poetry workshops, like all phobias, is exaggerated and no doubt unfair to the eccentric range offered under the rubric; but I cling to it as an untrustworthy friend. But then again I know what I don't like. I am so stubborn that I am sure if someone advised me on how to improve a poem I'd probably do the opposite, just out of sheer contrariness. From the get-go I tell 111 participants that writing good poems, or learning to write better poems, or learning the craft of poetry, or improving your work, is not the focus or goal of the seminar (but it may happen as a by-product). I think of 111 as a non-expository writing class, or a course in anti- or para- or pluri-composition, something, if I had *my way* (and not just a book by that name), I would require as an antidote to Freshman Comp. The class has its value not for budding poets, only, or primarily, or exclusively, but also for all writers. It's less a workshop than a lab, with experiments in mutant forms conducted on the textual body of the living language. (I play the role of a kinder, gentler Frankenstein.) Still, as an elective course, the students who enrol in it think of the class as a poetry class, since that is the only academic slot associated with what one of the students likes to call abnormal writing, but I prefer to think of as r&d (research and development). I figure the more you know how to take words apart and put them together, the more aspects of language you've turned up, down, left, right, inside out, and outside in, the better you will be able to respond to the many contingencies, screw balls and curve balls, and monkey wrenches that language will inevitably throw your way. Like my main man says, Whose in control, me or the words? (*Whose* is, that's who.) And then – I am slowly getting around to the subject of teaching modernist poetry – an approach like this makes for pro-active readers by potentiating pro-active approaches to writing. So, yeah, busted again: this is just another kind of lit'r'ture class, a reading workshop not so much in disguise as in drag.

Let me circle back to the question of craft and improvement. The scene: my grossly caricatured creative writing workshop, led by a teacher who (unlike me) knows good from bad and (also unlike me) prefers the good. A teacher who's not afraid to tell a student what she's doing wrong and how to fix it. I have my tastes too but am wary of legislating them, since I know they are minority tastes, particular and eccentric tastes, and I don't expect students to share them, much less adopt them. I try as much as possible to steer discussions away from good or bad and don't, as a rule, give my opinions about quality or improvement. I do the best I can to direct attention to what is happening in the work, alternative means of construction, and the possibilities of the form.

And I encourage distractions and digressions. Something reminds someone of a cartoon on the web so they turn their laptops around and play that. That reminds me of my boyhood in ancient Greece, so I carry on about etymologies. And I do tend to wax aesthetic and philosophical about any or all of the forms employed; and have a trigger finger ready to fire off examples from modernist and contemporary poetry, many of which I have linked to the web syllabus. Someone laughs, after reading something funny on the yellow-pad collaboration being passed around, or maybe in a text message sent from one class member to another, or maybe just at one of my innumerable, problematic jokes. Laughter is the necessary yeast of good class conversation and opens the possibility for listening, not just hearing.

The best advice I can give to the student in a conventional creative writing workshop is that if your peers or teacher tell you not to do something, because that something doesn't make sense to them, appears as a blur, then probably the thing you need to do is *not cut it out* but pursue it: develop. Something germinal in a young writer isn't necessarily, or even usually, going to make sense even to the most open-minded teacher or generous classmate. Often the most problematic things about a germinal work has the greatest potential for development. That is why the typical workshop environment, with cross-comments towards creating a 'better' piece of writing, that is, one that a group will agree is 'better' (more fluid, less awkward, clearer, more logical or expressive, more direct) runs counter to poetic invention and aesthetic process, which will more likely (but not necessarily) produce work that is not legible by such workshop criteria. But you can rely on something: the quizzical, puzzled, and overtly negative responses are signs you are on to something.

How many creative writing workshop members does it take to change a well-crafted light bulb? Three – One to screw it in (the student), one to hold the ladder (the peer), and one to block the light (the teacher).

I block the light too. But I try to use that as a point of rhythmic oscillation, as I move in and out of the rays.

The Writing Experiments seminar focuses on transformation, metamorphosis, substitution, and deformation. It has a typical order (you can see a recent example of the syllabus at http://writing.upenn.edu/

bernstein/syllabi/111.html), starting with a reading of Raymond Queneau's brilliant variations of the 'same' story in *Exercises in Style*:

1. Substitution
2. Homolinguistic translation
3. Recombination
4. Homophonic & dialect translation
5. Ekphrasis
6. Chance operation & the aleatoric
7. Without rules, (n)not!, or is free writing free?
8. Short lines / short poems (attention)
9. Memory
10. Novel forms
11. The art of constraint
12. Flarf & conceptual poetry: web-generated poems, found poems, appropriation
13. Digital & visual poetry
14. Performance
15. Class anthology / chapbooks / website

The syllabus itself is subject to deformative performance; as a final assignment, Kimberly Eisler (a Penn freshman) did a set of substitutions for the experiments, making something of a bestiary of possible modernist forms. Here's my edited version:

• Homolinguistic transduction: Take a pretence (someone else's or your own) and traverse/rewrite/rate it by substituting warp for word, phase for phrase, load for line, or 'free' troupe as repose to each phantom or sentence. Or: traditionalise the poem into another, or severely other, illegitimate style.
• Recombination (1): Write a piece and crack it somewhere in the middle, then recharge with the 'best' part following the enjoyable part.
• Reposition (2) – Doubling: Starting with ominous sentence, write a series of penitentiaries each doubling the number of sexes in the punitive paragraph and including all the words used previously.
• Homophonic translation: Take a poem to a foreign country that you can pronounce but not necessarily understand and never make it back. Take the sound of their lips before the clouds.
• Use the wet dream engine.
• Acrostic charades: Pick a book at random and use the title to feather your pinkie nails and scratch off your wings. For each letter, create a pore and cover every faucet in your multiverse.

- Poem is made according to the order in which it swells like icicles. Solo: pick a series of ferns or vines from your closet to put in the vat.
- Dream work: Use the moon to sweep every fur coat under the couch for 30 days. Double the length of each diamond. Borrow a friend and apply these techniques to him or her.
- Write a poem just when you are on the verge of being forced into the back of a police car.
- Read the Bible with a stranger's chapped lips.
- Bring your brain storm into a bomb shelter.
- Fertilize your pipe dreams.
- Write a poem in which all the events never happen.
- Write a poem made up entirely of hydrogen.
- Let the morning come and tell each of your addled minds a lie.
- Do something five times, then pray.
- Create a blueprint of the way thoughts speak like tiger lilies at the center of gravity.
- Bite your tongue until it bleeds.
- Write a poem in the form of the future.

and the moral of that is: ideally the syllabus is an imaginary map to a constantly transmogrifying place: the process begins with the readings and assignments but ultimately engulfs every aspect of the class and perhaps the psychic spaces beyond. The syllabus (like the pronouncement of the teacher) is subject to its own mandates to question and reorder. And the moral of that is: leave no turn unstoned.

Reading

Modernist poetry projects futures, even if that means concatenating the present as if it were a future. The modernist poem is always in the future because that's where you catch it, just beyond the poem, in Wallace Stevens' 'what's after' ('Thirteen Ways of Looking at a Blackbird'). And once you catch it, it dissolves into air; the butterfly net is empty. In other words, the more I try to pin the poem down, the more it eludes me and elates me. I come to the poems I know best as an enigma comes to a weigh station. I'm the enigma, the poem's my grounding.

In the 1970s, many of us, batty as hornets in a bee's nest, spoke of reader's response, the reader not the poem makes the meaning. This was true in a deliciously technical sense of 'makes', as in my favourite Lenny Bruce joke, where the kid comes into the candy store, where the genie is behind the counter while the owner's out: 'Make me a malted'. 'YOU'RE

A MALTED!' But as readers, and teachers, we all know that every reading is not equally good; that for all the range of readings some can be entirely off-base, while others, off-beat, offer new horizons for interacting with the poem. In the end, the poem makes malteds of us all.

But even so, there is no one meaning to a poem and the poems I know best, like Stevens' 'The Plain Sense of Things' have no plain sense. It's less the heresy of paraphrase than the paraphrase of heresy.

I remain mystified by the culture of testing in modernist and contemporary poetry classes. I couldn't pass a multiple choice test of one of my own poems. A friend once sent me a passages-identification quiz and I couldn't quite remember if the passage in question, which the written record will show that I wrote, was by David Antin, Moses Maimonides, Madonna, or me. Confusion can be more productive than adjudication. If we ask the mind to wonder in reading the poems, let's accept some collateral drift too.

'The student is always right'. No that's not quite an adoption of the corporate ethos for the classroom, where we don't teach but offer client services. I mean if a student says something, within the context of the classroom, she can't be wrong about her perception, though it may not correlate with the poem at hand. So the question is: what about this poem evoked this apparently unsupported response? And how does *that* relate to what is going on in the poem? A misperception can be just as generative for engaging a poem as a supposedly correct perception, especially one grounded in schooling, in rational analysis. The first thing to learn (you can't quite teach it) about modernist and contemporary poetry is that you have to get the hang of it, trust your intuitions before your analytic faculties come into (and try to keep it in) play.

A poem is a work of art using words (or related verbal materials). New poems often challenge prior definitions or understandings of poetry. Another way of saying this is that a poem is any verbal construction that is designated as a poem. The designation of a verbal text as poetry cues a way of reading but does not address the work's quality. Disagreement over the nature of what poetry is, or what constitutes a poem, is as much a part of the history of poetry as disputes about what makes a good poem. The most contentious of these disputes are fundamental to poetry's continuing social and aesthetic significance.

At the University of Pennsylvania, I teach two basic undergraduate twentieth-century poetry classes: one focused on US poetry (http://writing.upenn.edu/bernstein/syllabi/88.html) and one focused on poetry outside the US (http://writing.upenn.edu/bernstein/syllabi/62.html). I've become increasingly agitated about the Anglomania of our literature classes. I see no problem with actively reading poetry in other languages, working through our own translations in class, or reading multiple translations, together with the originals, where possible. Listening to the sounds and rhythms of the poem, even in the absence of knowing the language, can be exhilarating.

The web syllabus is a key part of the course as I have moved away from photocopied course packs and anthologies and towards greater reliance on web materials, many of which I have compiled for this purpose. I do use print anthologies, but I see these more as background information and further readings than at the centre of the class. Wherever possible, I make available sound files of the poets reading their work (together with texts of the poems), something that has been a central focus for Al Filreis and me in starting PennSound (http://writing.upenn.edu/pennsound), our huge sound recording archive. (And we are working on developing select recordings of non-English language poetry.) The Electronic Poetry Center (http://epc.buffalo.edu), which I edit with Loss Pequeño Glazier, provides additional digital resources for many of the poets in the syllabi. And fundamental to the project is to make as much of this material as possible available not just to the students registered in the class, but to anyone who accesses our web pages (all free of both charge and advertising).

I developed the Poem Profiler (http://writing.upenn.edu/library/Bernstein-Charles_Poem-Profiler.html) to expand the range of possible responses to the poems, so I use that to generate the first-order response.

Second, I ask that each week students do 'creative wreading' experiments on the poem – a set of deformations, transformations, and imitations that involve doing things with the poems rather than analysing them (http://writing.upenn.edu/bernstein/wreading-experiments.html). These exercises are designed to provide interactive engagement with the assigned reading. I also ask that for each experiment, the student provide a short commentary on the process, the results, the relation to the original, and an assessment of the value of the experiment. The point of these 'wreadings' is not to create 'original' poems of value, though that may well happen. Rather, these exercises are designed to create a greater engagement with the assigned reading and a greater understanding of the structures of, and possibilities for, poetic composition. Indeed, before you can discourse about a poem you need to think *with* it, get it inside your ears; for that, typing it, or hand writing it, or reciting it over and again, or putting the poet's reading on our I-pod playlist, might be a better first encounter with a poem than a thematically unified composition explaining it. The poem cries out: *I don't want to be understood just listened to!* For a last class, there is nothing better than having students recite memorised poems from the syllabus. Imitation and memorisation are as old-fashioned, and future-directed, as poetry itself.

Third, I ask students to keep an intensive journal of their responses to the readings. I emphasise that these journals are to be informal and, as far as possible, integrated with the flow of everyday life. Often students include the comments of their roommates or the responses of their friends. At Penn, reading a poem out loud or playing a sound file of a poem is bound to seem odd and provoke quizzical responses; these too become part of the journal. I ask the students to consider a specific set of questions and instructions:

> What do you think of the poem? Give as much detail as you can as to why you feel the way you do. What does the poem sound like, what does it remind you of? Quote specific lines or phrases that seem relevant. Being specific is the hardest part of this assignment and I almost always request descriptions of the form and style of the different poems: which can be as simple as a description of the visual shape of the poem, its length, the type of lines (long, short, metrical, enjambed), the sort of style or rhetoric or vocabulary (unusual, common, pastoral, urban, urbane, fast-paced, slow-moving, pictorial, bombastic, introspective, descriptive, narrative, fragmentary, etc.).
>
> The point is not for you to analyse or explain the poem but rather to try to react to it. Cataloguing the features of the poem won't explain it but it may enable you to enter into the poem more fully.
>
> Of the poems read for this week, which is your favourite? Why? Which is the best? Why? Are favourite and best the same? Rank the poems in your order of preference.
>
> Of the poems read for this week, which did you like least? Why?
>
> Of the poems read for this week, which is the worst? Why? What are your criteria for deciding the quality of poems? Can poems that you don't like or understand still be good poems?
>
> If you have heard the audio performance, describe the performance and how it extends or contradicts the written version of the poem.

Issues of quality are foregrounded while remaining provisional. The point is not to compare my judgement, or literary history's, with those of students perennially new not only to the difficulties of poetry but also to the pleasures attendant on these difficulties.

As with the Wreading experiments and the poem profiler studies, I ask that all student work be posted directly to a common class listserv or web log. In this way, everything that I see as the teacher is also seen by all students. Nothing is private. The most radical result of the public postings is that students direct their comments to each other, rather than the professor/authority figure. The class discussion extends and intensifies online; it might even be more accurate to say that class discussion is an extension of the online discussion.

I emphasise to students that the responses are meant to be spontaneous, informal, and unedited. The journal entries are not drafts for papers, nor are they necessarily expository. Fragments, lists, incomplete thoughts are fine – in the service of noting reactions and thoughts. The purpose of the writing is to encourage interaction with the poems and also serve as a record of individual reading. The responses to the poems might be mixed with a list of things to do (as in Ted Berrigan's 'Things to Do in New York'), with dream entries, with comments on other classes, or with more typical diary entries.

So, what then of the class meetings? Student discussion is central but, with the online forum, I pick up themes, concerns, interpretations and take off from there. I try less to lecture and more to be a respondent to the stated (and unstated) responses of the students, as expressed in their journals, wreading experiments, and poem profiles. My motto as a teacher comes from Dominique Fourcade's 'tout arrive', which he, in turn, found on Manet's stationery. The class time is a blank page on which a composition takes place: *everything happens* (which Fourcade takes from Manet's insignia 'tout arrive'). Like an upside-down Boy Scout, Fourcade coins my pedagogic method in a phrase: 'Be ready but not prepared' (Fourcade, 2000). This stands for nothing less than the multi-track improvisation of possibility. 'Let, and not force to happen' (Fourcade again) is not the idea but a method played out in each class. 'The light is in the dark'.

A few weeks into the class, after a spirited discussion of Mallarmé's *Un coup de dés*, one of the students half asked, half interjected – 'So you're saying this is art?!'

Or, better (as Carolee Schneemann put it in an email): 'a perfection of the unexpected'.

Works cited

Fourcade, Dominique (2000) *Everything Happens*, trans. Stacy Doris. Sausalito, CA: Post Apollo Press.

11
Conclusion: the History and Interpretation of Modernist Poetry

Peter Middleton

'Now you understand what we feel when we are studying *The Waste Land.*'

The speaker is a student at a day school seminar on modern poetry where I have been teaching a sequence of poems by the contemporary poet Wendy Mulford, and several students have picked me up for missing allusions to lyrics and song titles from punk rock music and therefore misinterpreting lines in the poem. I have just admitted to a momentary and uneasily public disorientation. Here I thought that I had come to the class well prepared and now it turns out I may have been deceiving myself. The result is a defining moment for me, not just because it reminds me that poetic difficulty is no respecter of age and experience; it also helps me start thinking about the issues raised by the contributors to this volume, issues that cluster around the uncertain relations between early and late modernist poetry, and especially the many ways that poems both elicit and resist interpretation. Juxtaposing a classic of high modernism with a contemporary poet and punk rock is a reminder of the potential extent of modernist poetry. Our contributors range across a history of poetry that spans more than a century, and now comes with sometimes contradictory labels whose proliferation can be confusing both as chronology and as theory: modernism, high modernism, avant-garde, late modernism, second-wave modernism, postmodernism, experimental, and innovative. At the centre of these categorisations is the historical divide marked by the Second World War and the actual waste lands it brought to the world. Talking about poetry and music is a reminder that modernist poetry often bridges different media. Several contributors talk about how important it can be to discuss poetic sound, performance, and graphics in modernist poetry, and the challenges to pedagogy these material features of the text create. In this concluding chapter I want to explore further why these two issues are so important for the teaching of modernist poetry.

My argument will be that these two seemingly distinct issues, the divided history of modernist poetry, and the meaningfulness of material textual strategies, are closely intertwined, and that understanding this can help us formulate methods of teaching modernist poetry to meet the sort of problems encountered in my opening anecdote. Some of these problems arise from the ingenuity of the poets themselves; some from the difficulties of demonstrating them in a classroom space alien to the poems; some from this split history of modernist poetry that has at least two acts; and some from the resistances that derive from the concepts of language and subjectivity that dominate our current literary theories. My examples are drawn from American poetry, but similar examples can be found in British poetry too.

Two modernisms

The history of modern poetry now extends for considerably more than a hundred years, reaching back at least a couple of decades into the nineteenth century and extending for nearly a decade into the twenty-first, a span of literary history that is beginning to be too long to teach or research as one continuous endeavour. Not surprisingly communities of literary scholars and university syllabuses increasingly coalesce around either the period 1880–1940 or a less calendrically well-defined postwar era, treating the Second World War as an inevitable division. The Second World War not only suspended literary activity to a considerable degree, though less in North America than in Europe, Asia, and Australia, it also changed social, political, and economic landscapes so utterly that new aesthetic and literary movements emerged and many older forms disappeared, and yet the widespread sense that modernism was an unfinished project inspired new generations of poets. The 1950s were as a result as fertile for new modes of writing as were the 1920s, possibly more so, although we rarely talk in these terms. Our resistance to such terms may have something to do with the contrast between the earlier decade of manifestos and literary shocks, and a postwar decade of chastened pragmatic innovation. As far as modernist poetry is concerned it also has to do with a persistent uncertainty amongst literary historians about whether poetry written after the Second World War, yet still strongly engaged with earlier modernisms, pushes forward an existing genealogy, or marks a complete break, or is an unstable modernist renaissance sometimes called an *arrière garde* (the recovery of suppressed and marginalised poets has had some of the character of a minor renaissance, as has the rediscovery of a series of modernist poets such as Gertrude Stein and Mina Loy), or might even be better described as a self-conscious, sometimes parodic re-enactment of the earlier period as pure style. Irresolution is only reinforced by consideration of the length of the careers of the significant number of long-lived poets who span both eras, and by an associated tendency to think of poets more in terms of the coherence of their authorship than in terms of their changing alignments with short-lived literary movements. Are there, we might therefore ask, two modernisms or only one? And we might add, quietly, that as teachers of modern poetry, two would really be more convenient than one.

This question of the two modernisms is not going to be resolved by finding more accurate names (second-wave, postmodern, late modernist, continuing modernist tradition, experimental, underground, radical, linguistically innovative, and avant-garde have all been proposed by some and dismissed by others), nor is it likely that more history or better theory will, on their own, help. The problems are more fundamental, concerning what might count as a modernist poetics, and how to think about a division that is somehow integral to what we mean by modernist poetry and its poetics. The First World War and the threat of a recurrence of global warfare shaped the outlook of all the modernist poets writing after 1914. War was therefore both a historical backdrop and a possible horizon for the modernist poets writing before 1939, and when it happened it played out much of what their poetry projected in its fragmented forms, themes, and moods. Yet although war could be viewed as the fulfilment of modernist poetic prophecy and therefore its moment of closure, it was also a disruptive shock to many unfinished projects that demanded difficult readjustments of aesthetic priorities, so that after the war modernist poetry regained momentum both by recalibration of sustained modernist strategies and by sheer reinvention. Modernist poetry's bisection is integral to the character of its history.

One answer has been to call the new era postmodernist, but postmodernism has proven a critically unstable term in a way that modernism has not. As Steve McCaffery writes in a review of Jennifer Ashton's book *From Modernism to Postmodernism* (which claims that the two periods are wholly distinct): 'Few if any practitioners would call themselves postmodern. "Formally innovative" or "investigative" or "inventive" are the preferred descriptions precisely because these terms relate to praxis across periods and disciplines, not exegesis' (513). Nor, he might have added, do these substitute terms he is proposing depend on periodisation.

Not all poets have resisted such self-designations, however. In an autobiographical statement written in 1955, Charles Olson admitted that he found it hard even to use the conventional terms 'poet' or 'writer' to describe himself, and then attempted to explain the problem by calling his era 'the post-modern, the post-humanist, the post-historical' (1997: 206), a time after modernity and history that demanded new cultural discourses (a few years earlier, Robert Lowell was described by Randall Jarrell as the author of 'a post- or anti-modernist poetry' (Jarrell, 1950: 164)). This usage, though seeming idiosyncratic, could be associated with Jean-François Lyotard's concept of a postmodernism latent in certain advanced modernist work, but most critics have preferred more straight-forwardly periodising usages, though even George Butterick's attempt to classify such 'New American Poets' as Olson as 'postmodern' in his re-edited version of Donald Allen's key anthology *The New American Poetry* called simply *The Postmoderns*, has not been widely endorsed. Fredric Jameson offered by far the most sophisticated concept of post-modernism by treating it as form of collective cultural consciousness aris-ing from a socio-economically defined historical moment, and ignored entirely Butterick's selection of 'postmoderns' when looking for a poem to exemplify his concept of postmodernism, choosing instead the poem 'China', written by Bob Perelman, a poet linked to the later and almost wholly distinct school of poets, the Language Writers, who are not rep-resented at all in Butterick's anthology. That description did not stick either, as McCaffery indicates, and Perelman himself disowned it.

How then might we teach histories of modernist poetry that do justice to this doubleness if the terms, at least for describing the later phase, are still so volatile? This is not the only challenge facing the teacher. As con-tributors to this collection show, researchers have greatly expanded our understanding of the history of modernist poetry and made us aware of diverse histories of overlapping modernisms in different countries and regions, modernisms both esoteric and populist, employing con-tent ranging from hermetic language to documentary, and in histories always deeply engaged in struggles for recognition that have marked the politics of gender, ethnicity, and class. The difficulty of teaching a chronologically extended modernist poetry is compounded by the lack of consensus about the genealogies and even the literary value of the experimental poetics associated with the various modernisms that fol-low later in the century. There is also still something of a disconnection between our increasingly nuanced histories and the critical terminology for the techniques, aesthetics, prosodies, and subjectivities that char-acterised the modernist poets. Is the doubleness of modernist poetry a further layer of complexity to add to a curriculum that already risks overload?

Firstly, I think we have no choice as teachers of modernist poetry. We have to recognise that separating the two states of modernism risks losing sight of central features of whichever period we select. This doesn't mean that we have to compress more than a hundred years of poetry into one syllabus, however. Concentrating on one or the other periods of modernist poetry separately probably makes more sense today than attempting to cover both at once, as long as we acknowledge that neither is self-contained. Secondly, acknowledgement of the doubleness of modernism can help students grasp aspects of modernist poetry that are hard to convey in the classroom: the character of the intense commitments common to otherwise very different poets that justify the label 'modernist' at all, and the intended impact of the still not properly mapped, large, and changing repertoire of modernist poetic strategies for creating meaning and significance.

One classroom approach to these issues is to include in a course some instances of poetry and poetics that highlight the transitions from one moment of modernism to the next. One place I would start is Donald Allen's anthology *The New American Poetry* (1960), which was one of the most influential anthologies of later American modernist poetry of the twentieth century, and remains a highly readable collection of poems whose idealistic energy and delight in language are likely to engage students. It announced the emergence of a new generation of poets who saw themselves in a continuing modernist lineage, including Charles Olson (whose poems open the anthology), Allen Ginsberg, Robert Creeley, Amiri Baraka, John Ashbery, Barbara Guest, Frank O'Hara, Denise Levertov, and Gary Snyder; it also represented the key poetry movements of the time in what to many readers has seemed a triumph of farsighted inclusiveness: the Beats, the Black Mountain poets, the New York School and the San Francisco Renaissance are all here. In reality, this inclusiveness, the result of deliberate editorial decisions, was achieved at the cost of making it appear that these poets had no mentors, models, or predecessors, and were not part of any continuing traditions or schools. The process of inclusion and exclusion is revealed in a discussion initiated by Allen himself as he was compiling the anthology that could provide a framework for classroom discussion of the continuities and discontinuities of modernist poetry.

Allen corresponded in 1959 with Olson as one of the intellectual leaders of this new generation of poets, on the vexed question of who to include and who to omit. Should the anthology begin with sections

presenting an 'older generation' and then 'continuers', before presenting the new generation? After all, William Carlos Williams, Ezra Pound,
Marianne Moore, H.D., e. e. cummings, and Wallace Stevens had all
continued to publish in the 1950s (and much of this poetry is now considered major work), and the anthologist could not assume that readers
who were not 'insiders' would 'have the key works of the older generation
at hand' (Maud, 2003: 59). The slightly awkward terminology (what is a
'continuer' continuing?) points to an uncertainty about the ascription of
poetic commitments that might variously be identified by cultural eras,
movements, styles, gender, ethnicity, or geography. Allen's dilemma is
familiar to teachers of postwar modernist and avant-garde poetry: do you
teach the modernist poetry of the 1950s and later decades as a continu-
ance of the work of earlier decades, or do you set it apart? Either decision
has large consequences. If you emphasise continuity then poets whose
work spans the period may become more prominent than others who
remain confined to earlier or later periods, and if you focus on what is
new about Allen's generation of poets then the long-lived poets whose
career awkwardly spans otherwise convenient pedagogic divisions will
likely be relegated to an afterthought. Should you, for instance, teach the
pioneering modernists such as Ezra Pound, Mina Loy, and William Carlos
Williams at the start of the course, and what is your position towards the
relatively long-lived generation that straddle the middle of the century
such as Louis Zukofsky, Hilda Doolittle (H.D.), or George Oppen, poets
who were too young to form part of the great generation of the 1920s,
and too old to be one of the Beats? What about a neglected figure such as
Muriel Rukeyser, whose poetic career also spanned the period from the
1930s to the 1960s (her great poem about silicosis in West Virginia, 'The
Book of the Dead', was published in 1938, while her much anthologised
'Poem', beginning 'I lived in the first century of world wars', appeared
in book form in 1968)?

Olson is quite unsympathetic to Donald Allen's queries, and it is not
difficult to imagine why. He wants his own work and that of his peers
to have the stage to themselves; he had been writing for nearly fifteen
years by this point, and had very little public recognition as a poet other
than from a small circle of friends. So he begins his reply bluntly: 'I
wldn't myself add either of those two units: either the "aunties" or the
grandpas' (Maud, 2003: 59). This familial rhetoric manages to admit that
there are connections while simultaneously distancing them by identifying potential sources of influence with the categories of relative who
didn't directly engender the new generation. The justification is that
there has been a 'change of discourse' (presumably their poetics), because

the postwar generation is a historically distinct 'group' with its own 'character'; adding these connections to the past would entail 'smudging the point' of the anthology (60). Newness must be emphasised at the expense of tracing indebtedness. Allen followed Olson's advice with fateful consequences for the reputations of many of those 'continuers' such as H.D. and Louis Zukofsky, whose work continued to be neglected by most of the leaders of opinion amongst the innovative poets. Live interconnections between different generations were also obscured and perhaps more credit for innovation went to this generation than it quite deserved.

But the lesson to be learned from this editorial history is not simply that we should always value continuities in poetry. Allen's anthology was enormously successful and went through many editions as well as providing a vital stimulus to succeeding generations of emerging poets. Would the same have been true if he had carefully emphasised legacies and filiations the way we might now wish? These are questions worth putting to students. Most writers, readers, and critics have treated the so-called 'New American Poets' as part of a second wave of modernist poetry rather than as an extension of the earlier high modernist moment in poetry, and from this standpoint poets such as Zukofsky and Oppen remain forever late arrivals in the first wave of modernist poetry.

Olson's somewhat clumsily expressed conviction that there had been a 'change of discourse' deserves attention too, since he himself had been partly responsible for the change. His essay 'Projective Verse', first published in 1950 in *Poetry New York* alongside a selection of British as well as American poets, rapidly became a manifesto for his generation and was widely reprinted over the next three decades. Many of the ideas in this essay were taken, unacknowledged, from Muriel Rukeyser's book *The Life of Poetry* (as well as from the modernist poets such as Pound and Williams) and translated into a discourse for this new era. Rukeyser wrote: 'Exchange is creation. In poetry, the exchange is one of energy. Human energy is transferred, and from the poem it reaches the reader. Human energy, which is consciousness, the capacity to produce change in existing conditions' (1945: 185). Olson turned this to a more materialist process: 'A poem is energy transferred from where the poet got it (he will have several causations), by way of the poem itself to, all the way over to, the reader' (Olson, 1966: 16). Rukeyser had written a biography of the greatest American scientist of the late nineteenth and early twentieth century, Willard Gibbs, a chemist and a pioneer of statistical mechanics, and she borrowed his ideas about dynamic systems to describe what happens in a poem because she thought that New Criticism offered a model of the poem that was too static: 'In poetry, the relations are not formed like crystals on a lattice of words, although the old criticism (which at the moment is being called, of course, the New Criticism) would have us believe it so' (Rukeyser, 1942: 177). Instead the poem is a dynamic entity: 'Truth is, according to Gibbs, not a stream that flows from a source, but an agreement of components. In a poem, these components are, not the words or images, but the relations between words and images . . . All of these words were known, as the results leading to a scientific discovery may have been known. But they were not arranged before the poet seized them and discovered their pattern. This arrangement turns them into a new poem, a new science' (1942: 178). Olson replaces the terminology of statistical mechanics from chemistry with language that echoed both the nuclear physics that had had such notorious success with the atomic bomb, and the new science of group psychology that was then known as 'field psychology' and studied the 'constructs' or working models of experience, by which individuals interact with group. A poem we are told should be a 'high-energy construct and, at all points, an energy-discharge' (1966: 16) (syllables are equivalent to nuclear particles). One of the most striking changes that Olson makes to Rukeyser's metaphors while keeping her underlying concepts, is to abandon cinema as an aesthetic role model. She had direct experience of film-editing and made comparisons between the use of cutting to create speed and complexity in film and the rapid shifting of focus in modern poems which similarly 'moves in terms of quick, rhythmic juxtapositions' (17). Olson wants to retain the idea of rapid transitions, but makes no mention of the art of film, saying instead that he learned from the novelist and essayist Edward Dahlberg that 'ONE PERCEPTION MUST IMMEDIATELY AND DIRECTLY LEAD TO A FURTHER PERCEPTION' (17) if the poem is to do justice to the process of shaping its compositional energies. His slightly puzzling deletion of the film analogy (he was keen on art films) may have been the result of his desire to claim the status of knowledge for poetry (hence the association with the sciences through the field and energy metaphors), and the suspicion that film was overwhelmingly associated with pure entertainment in the public mind.

What we are seeing here is the process of converting the first state of modernism into the second state, a process begun by Rukeyser that in Olson's eyes did not go far enough. His extensive borrowings (there are many more) undergo a change of rhetoric in order to achieve several aims: to give prominence in his analogies claiming significance for poetry to newer sciences than the mechanics used in chemistry; to restore a masculine character to poetry; and to occlude any suggestions that poetry is a form of entertainment, however high. Behind all his guidance on how to write a poetry for the new decade is a simple admonition learned from Pound: 'make it new'. Newly ascendant sciences of nuclear physics and psychology that rely on discourses of fields and particles help support this message. Both Olson and Rukeyser want to emphasise the dynamic character of poetry but Olson doesn't want to be tied to an older science, nor does he even want to be tied to a modern art form, film, that might seem rooted in commercial entertainment of earlier decades. Like Rukeyser, Olson realises that the use of the scientific analogies is not just a means of claiming another break with the past of the kind that is defining for what it means to be genuinely modernist; he also sees the power of this rhetoric to secularise poetry by avoiding another set of terms of the kind that many poets and critics influenced by Eliot were then employing – imagination, spirit, soul, mystery, symbol, heart and faith. In place of the rhetoric of poetry as a mode of faith both Rukeyser and Olson want to emphasise the rhetoric of 'discovery' (Rukeyser) or inquiry, or as Olson puts it, an ability to be a good observer of nature not distracted by subjectivity or 'the lyrical interference of the individual as ego' and capable of revealing 'secrets objects share' (25).

James Breslin begins his useful study of *From Modern to Contemporary: American Poetry 1945–1965* (1984) by echoing firmly Olson's belief that 'the history of American poetry forms not a "continuity," as Roy Harvey Pearce had argued, but a series of discontinuities, eruptions of creative energy that suddenly alienate poetry from what had come to seem its essential and permanent nature' (xiii). Breslin knows this is an over-simplification of the history, so he quickly acknowledges that the poetry of Pound, Williams, and Stevens, that they continued to publish until their deaths in the 1950s and 1960s, continues to inspire and inform the new generation of poets. The instability of the discussions of poetics by Rukeyser and Olson centres on the difficulty of insisting on a new modernist poetry capable of demonstrating its credentials with the all-important impact of modernity on readers, the shock and surprise so integral to what it means to be a modernist poem, and can be so difficult to convey in the classroom. Rukeyser and Olson use their topical metaphors as subtly as possible to suggest the importance of this shock of breaking with tradition (Olson seems to imagine something quite literally like an electrical shock, the high-energy discharge). They both emphasise discontinuity while actually acknowledging continuities as well, especially an enduring feature of modernist poetry that is also hard to address for similar reasons, the centrality of inquiry. Modernist poets have been keenly interested in experimentation that might lead to discovery and the creation of new knowledge, while also acutely aware of

their marginal status as researchers in an age when science has the absolute hegemony over the legitimate methodologies for the production of
knowledge. Aligning the new poetry with the latest scientific inquiry
amounts to reaffirming the capacity of poetry to take its place at the
cutting edge of new understanding and possibly new knowledge.

Their problem in understanding and representing the onrush of
modernity has its counterpart in teaching modernist poetry. I have often
found it helpful when teaching modernisms to reflect with students
at the start of the course on the social transformations modernity has
brought over the past 200 years, and go on to consider the various poetic
modernisms as cultural contributions and responses to these changes. It
is important to convey that there is no one set of correct answers to
the question of what constitutes modernity, and although I have found
most helpful those summaries offered by Anthony Giddens in *The Consequences of Modernity*, and Robert Pippin's *Modernism as a Philosophical
Problem*, others would work as well, for what matters is just to keep
open the question of what makes a literature *modern*? This also helps to
remind students that the concept of the modern is inherently temporal
and historical (I find Peter Osborne's work helpful here).

There are many seemingly good reasons for thinking of later modernist poetry as extending, amending, or challenging the projects of
earlier modernism: shared interests in pushing the boundaries of expression; shared experimentation with mixed media; shared convictions that
poetry can be a cultural and political force through its formal experimentation; and a commitment to poetry as a scene of inquiry as important
as those of the sciences. Poems, careers, and allegiances that reach across
the century appear to reinforce the reasonableness of this, and yet poetic
and critical opinion is divided about the validity of thinking in terms of
continuity as we have seen.

The case for thinking of a long modernism has been well made in a
series of ground-breaking studies of modern poetry by Marjorie Perloff,
who has consistently argued that we should see continuity between the
modernist poetry of the early twentieth century and the new avant-
gardes of the latter half of the century. In *21st-Century Modernism* (2002)
she laments the 'unfulfilled promise of the revolutionary impulse in so
much of what passes for poetry today – a poetry singularly unambitious
in its attitude to the materiality of the text' (6). Through readings of
Eliot, Stein, Duchamp, and Khlebnikov presented as mentors to contemporary poets she makes her case that 'as we move into the twenty-first
century, the modern/postmodern divide has emerged as more apparent
than real', and there is 'a special relationship between the early twentieth

century and the early twenty-first' (164). The materiality of the text is crucial: 'there is now an impressive range and production of poetry in which language, sound, rhythm, and visual layout are, in Pound's terms, "charged with meaning"' (200). What Khlebnikov said in 1920 is still being explored: 'The word leads a double life. Sometimes it simply grows like a plant whose fruit is a geode of sonorous stones clustering around it; in this case the sound element lives a self-sufficient life . . . At other times the word is subservient to sense' (200). This perspective on the history of modernist poetry implies that to research or teach it we not only need to find ways to acknowledge the continuities of modernist poetry, we must also give great attention to the materiality of the poem. This makes considerable demands on the teacher. Teaching students how to think about the sound, visual forms, and performative dimensions of poetry is a formidable task demanding the sorts of innovative pedagogy described by many of the contributors to this volume. Some critics disagreee about the significance of materiality in modernist poetry, and their arguments are worth listening to, because they can help us clarify just what our interest in materiality entails for the classroom. What are the skills and knowledge that students require to read the material text?

The meaningfulness of the material text

Literary historians will probably always disagree about whether the two modernisms are broadly continuous or, despite some common concerns, largely disjunct in their poetics, depending on how the historians select historical details to make their case. One recent literary historian goes further. Jennifer Ashton asserts unequivocally that 'the modern/postmodern divide remains intact' and insists that this is true 'both historically and theoretically' (2), calling into question the whole idea that there can be an 'open' or 'material' text that extends meaning beyond the words as signs. Her book is a useful challenge to the pedagogics proposed in this volume, because it invites us to consider whether we think it is valid to treat poetic strategies around performance, visual layout, and the materiality of publication, as integral components of the meaning of the text.

Jennifer Ashton's book, entitled *From Modernism to Postmodernism: American Poetry and Theory in the Twentieth Century*, offers a revisionist history of modernist poets and their critics, including Stein, Laura (Riding) Jackson, the New Critics, and several contemporary poets. She argues that the indeterminacy of the open text (in which the reader can participate in the construction of meaning) celebrated by postmodernist poets, especially the Language Writers, is the reverse of the poetics of key modernist poets, especially poets they have claimed as forerunners, such as Stein and (Riding) Jackson. In fact, argues Ashton, these earlier modernist poets thought the poem was autonomous as far as the reader's response or experience of it was concerned. The reader had to accept the meaning given (intended) by the poem. Poets such as William Carlos Williams, Louis Zukofsky, and the New Critics paved the way for postmodernism by rejecting any idea that intention played an integral role in the meaning of a poem, while at the same time being 'committed to the idea that the poem's meaning inheres in its rhythm, measure, and shape – what [John Crowe] Ransom calls the "tissue of irrelevance" that separates poetry from prose and makes it unparaphrasable' (Ashton, 2005: 27). What was latent in their work then became explicit in the poetics of the Language Writers, the avant-garde poets who emerged in the 1970s led by poets such as Bruce Andrews, Charles Bernstein, Lyn Hejinian, Ron Silliman, and Barrett Watten. Ashton is in the end less worried about a misleading history of modernist poetry than about the allegedly misleading principles on which this history appears to be based. She believes that once we start claiming to find meaning in non-signifying sounds, contingencies of visual appearance, and the auditory dramas of performance, features of modernist poetry that several contributors to this volume discuss in detail, we misrepresent the character of early modernist poetry, and misunderstand the meaning of meaning. Another proponent of this view, Walter Benn Michaels, thinks for example that Susan Howe is wrong to criticise the decision by the editor of Emily Dickinson's poetry to ignore the visual evidence of her writing in the manuscript fascicles, on the grounds that the 'irregular spacing between words and even letters is "a part of the meaning"' (2004: 2). Howe, like many other contemporary poets, is supposedly confusing marks and signs.

Jennifer Ashton avoids basing her analysis solely on the axiom that only language can communicate meaning because she is more interested in the history of different beliefs amongst modernist poets and their critics about the role of what she calls 'intention' in the composition of a poem. Running through this history is a fundamental opposition between the idea that a text has causes that might include not only the actions of the author but also the environment in which it is produced, and the idea that a text results solely from authorial intentions (a poem requires a determining act of linguistic creation or *poeisis* to be called a poem). Susan Howe offers such a causal account in her book *Pierce-Arrow*, where she describes her visits to the Sterling Library at Yale to read the papers of C. S. Pierce, and vividly recounts such features of the library environment as the noise of the air-conditioning and the red illuminated lettering that says 'hello' on the microfilm readers. Ashton interprets this scene-setting as an argument by Howe about the way 'such sights and sounds of place . . . are essential to the process through which the writing takes form', because Howe allegedly believes in a mode of agency that is 'purely causal, for it requires no intention at all when poems are effects of . . . that sound she hears in the room where she writes' (24). This somewhat implausible interpretation of Howe leads Ashton to a more compelling argument, that does not I think depend on our acceptance of this causal rather than intentional model of composition. The 'open' text which requires a reader's active collaboration does not therefore depend solely on the intentionality of the text for its realisation, if 'the work is imagined to consist of the effects the reader experiences in her encounter with the material presence of the words appearing on the page or issuing from the mouth of a speaker' (24). It is this apparent invitation to readers to read into the poem *whatever they wish*, that she questions.

Further evidence of the replacement of intention by causality is provided by an essay written collaboratively by several leading Language Writers and published in *Social Text*, where they say that their work offers 'new possibilities of agency for the poet'. They are producing poetic texts for which (in Ashton's words) 'readers and poets are equal agents in the production of the poem' (25). This is quite simply a misconception according to Ashton:

> the texts they imagine being produced through such agency consist precisely of effects that (unlike the poet's own intention) vary from person to person in ways that the poet herself cannot control: how, for example, the letters and words and lines will look, sound and feel not just to her various readers but even, from one reading to the next, to herself. The reader . . . will inevitably experience a whole host of effects that could not have been intended by the author. (25)

In a later discussion of the way Language Writers allegedly misread Stein as an advocate of the poetics of indeterminacy, Ashton insists that these poets make the mistake of 'conflating experience with meaning'. They assume that the sensations, perceptions, and affects elicited in the reader by an encounter with a material instance of the poem (silently reading a printed text or listening to a performed one) create what I shall call a scene of meaning. What they forget (and here she silently echoes Michaels), is that 'when words become *marks* (or incantatory syllables), we have no choice but to experience them because – if we want to continue *to apprehend them as material objects* – we can no longer think of ourselves as *reading* them' [my italics] (92). To read is to read words as signs in a language, looking past the material contingencies of the text without 'experiencing' them, and moving instead via the linguistic code to the meaning of the words. You can't have your words and read them; you must choose to behave linguistically or non-linguistically, you cannot do both at once. Ashton's idea of what is wrong with trying to read the marks that Emily Dickinson used in her handwritten fascicles of poems, or the materiality of a late modernist poem, is that in all these cases we have abandoned the connection between intention and the sign: 'when our interpretation of an utterance no longer concerns its intention, we are led inevitably to a consideration of its effects' (167).

How serious are these concerns (which are found widely if rarely as clearly articulated)? How do we distinguish between relevant and irrelevant features that we might discern when reading the modernist poem? If we start interpreting the visual layout of a Susan Howe poem where lines are skewed across the page in a crisscross, or the oral performance of a poet such as Steve McCaffery, are we reading the poem as if it were a Rorsach blot? Could we go on forever finding meanings that are entirely subjective, peculiar to oneself only? This challenge to a laissez-faire programme of interpretation of poetic strategies is worth listening to. Even the most radical of open poems operate within demarcated language games, and failure to recognise this will lead to failure to understand the poem at all. Is teaching the material text merely a monstrous act of self-indulgence as these arguments seem to imply, or is Ashton importing that old fallacy, the intentionalist fallacy, once again into literary studies? Surely, we might say, intention has no place in literary interpretation?

One form of answer to these questions can be seen in Ruth Finnegan's comprehensive account of how humans communicate by using a vast range of bodily gestures and other media, in modes – linguistic, kinesic, and visual – that range from the highly systematic to the most improvisational. Nor are these merely fixed resources that we have to rely upon; we have the capacity to innovate, 'both to create new resources and flexible ways of using them, *and* to share them with others' (Finnegan, 2002: 261). This capacity for innovation, so prominent in the writers we have been discussing, is evidence that the argument that only legitimate linguistic signs can be meaningful misses something important about language arts. Finnegan's account of writing acknowledges the importance of the sign, but insists that the range of what can count as a sign is very wide, extending far beyond the alphabetic; writing is a 'multimodal source' (229). Counter to the strictures of Michaels and

Ashton, she reminds us that 'written poetry is always partly conveyed through explicit or assumed visible appearance' (229), and that 'a multiplicity of shapes, colours, spatial relations, materials and artistries can be interwoven together in the apparently simple process of communicating through writing' (231). Communication integrates both verbal and non-verbal processes, and in Finnegan's view it is a mistake to think that the non-verbal is ontologically different, not least because 'gestural and vocal actions are often integrated rather than autonomous, and verbal and non-verbal communicating "usually produced in a highly coordinated fashion": they are not distinct domains' (37).[1] Language is not always 'linguistic'. Finnegan doesn't have much to say about intention, and so we also need to look at what contemporary thinkers have said about it.

The line of reasoning used by Michaels and Ashton ultimately depends on the acceptance of a model of how linguistic reference works, especially how it depends on the intention of the speaker or writer. Are they right? What is their understanding of language and does it match with current understanding amongst theorists and philosophers of communication and language? Neither critic gives extensive attention to what they understand by language or intention, but it seems clear that both depend (Michaels more explicitly) on a structuralist theory of language as a system of internally differentiated signs. Such a theory is weak when it comes to explaining intention, however. As I said earlier, many of us have been taught to be wary of intention when studying literature, because it was sometimes used by critics who compared the avowed intentions of writers with their literary productions, and found them wanting. This is not what is meant by intention in Ashton's argument or when contemporary philosophers use the term. For them, intention is a part of ordinary activity and especially of language use.

The starting point for anyone working in literary studies trying to understand intentionality is likely to be some version of structuralism, because this has dominated literary theory, usually as a part of some other form of theory: deconstruction, psychoanalytic, cultural. The American philosopher Robert Pippin, who has written about Henry James as well as the Hegelian legacy, provides one of the most succinct and well-argued accounts of why such structuralist literary theories may not help us understand intention in his aptly named collection *The Persistence of Subjectivity*: 'a structure of possible differentiability or articulability, a language or cultural code, an episteme, a discourse field, the system of forces of production, does not and cannot do anything to make possible intentional or semantic or symbolic content' (2005: 183). Such theories neglect 'the ineliminable role of reasoning, inferences, commitments, entitlements, proprieties, and the offering and considering of reasons in the original possibility of mental and semantic content' (184). He is saying that a *signified* is not the same as a *meaning* unless its signifier is offered in the context of some sort of intentional reasoning. Although dictionaries appear to assign meanings to words, what they actually do is offer some approximate possibilities for what a word may mean when used in a context of reasoning, inference, or belief that you are checking up on. Another way of saying this is to say that words only *make* sense in sentences, and sentences are not just strings of sounds that are different from other sounds, nor even strings of words that are specifically differentiated from other words, as a structuralist analysis proposes. Sentences always assert something (although in special cases the assertion may be partially suspended in some way, or turned into a command). If Michaels had treated the use of language in speech and writing as inescapably bound up with 'reasoning, inferences, commitments, entitlements, proprieties, and the offering and considering of reasons in the original possibility of mental and semantic content', he might have been able to think about the materiality of texts as extending this range, rather than being excluded from it. Materiality is not a denial of service to the utterances in a poem. A better response to Howe, and a better way of understanding the ever 'ghostlier demarcations' at work in modernist poems, than that offered by the critics of materiality, is to identify how poetic texts can invite such reasoning, inferences, and reflection on the commitments to meaning displayed in such materiality. The text of a poem, with all its multi-modal channels, does not simply present a solipsistic experience to an individual reader. Interpretation emerges from a complex shared web of historically formed intentions that might include the writings of the author, her social space, and the assertions and counter-assertions of readers in their social spaces.

There are, we might say, two kinds of indeterminacy in a material text. One is simply a value-loaded name for what may be a long process of making explicit the commitments and ascriptions that encircle any poem, sometimes giving early or new readers the appearance of almost irreducible indeterminacy in the poem. The other is a name for materials and responses that could *never* elicit such an exchange of reasons. Critics such as Ashton are right to foreground the importance of language, because as the American philosopher, Robert Brandom says, 'inferring should be understood as an aspect of an essentially *linguistic* practice' (1994: 158). Some material features of a text may lack such inferential dimensions; they may be subjectively significant but they are poetically irrelevant features. An inkblot spilled onto a few words of a single copy of a book of poems might be such an example, or a pattern made by the letter T as it occurs across a page of poetry. A grid of words on a page of Susan Howe's poem in which the position on the page carries intimations of above and below that are homologous to the relations of earth and sky in a landscape, does carry meaning, though it may take considerable inferential work by a community of readers over time to establish anything like a stable consensus.

I have shown that it is perfectly possible to treat all sorts of features of the so-called material text as communicative and not simply governed by the whims of individual readers, without simply celebrating all acts of interpretative ingenuity as equal. When Language Writers call for more active readers, they could (and have sometimes) been thought to be saying that the open poem is free space over which any meanings can be written. This distorts their aim. They can be more convincingly understood to be saying that readers often approach poems with their capacities for reading severely curtailed by the socio-political conditions of a culture that doesn't want close scrutiny of its ideological discourses. A poem that awakens responsiveness will actually require a heightened commitment to the space of reasons on which interpretation depends, as well as a greater awareness of the multi-modal nature of communication. As teachers of modernist poetry we need to reflect on the implications of these arguments because we want to help our students understand what made these poems 'modern'. I shall now spell out what these ideas mean for the classroom.

How to listen to illegibility and visualise cacophony

Early in my career at the University of Southampton in the 1980s, I taught a year-long course on cultural studies and there was time enough for each of the ten or so students to give an extended presentation of any cultural work of their choosing. One student chose to talk about the Sex Pistols. After playing a generous selection of their songs he turned to the class to invite questions, and a 'mature' student (though probably only in his late twenties) noisily pushed back his chair and said in a tone that combined both surprise and dismay, 'I never thought I would be sitting in a classroom discussing the punk rock I used to hear in clubs.' By drawing attention to the utilitarian classroom chair and the desk in front of him he sharply underlined his point. He wasn't just expressing surprise at the transition from cultural immersion to academic scrutiny, he was also implicitly asking whether it was possible to study these songs at all.

What happened to the shock of their strangeness and provocation, and therefore what most mattered, when he heard them again in a seminar? Most of us are probably not teaching punk rock lyrics, but as teachers of modernist poetry we recognise the problem. How can a teacher help students understand what it meant for a modernist poem to be modern when it was freshly minted? After all, modernist poetry once created at least as much mayhem as Punk.

I think there are two answers to this. One is understandable resignation. We can't fully recapture the experience of reading the modernity in a modernist poem that has been around for decades, and no amount of historical reconstruction or thick description will fully do the job, though both can help point to where the punk ghost may still be glimpsed. A second answer is more optimistic. We can also do what forensic archivists do and increase our sensitivity to the traces that remain, and teach our students to see and hear more of what happens in the poem. To do so we need to re-examine some of our most rooted assumptions about the teaching of close reading in the light of the foregoing discussion of intention and the meaning of the material text.

Sooner or later almost all classroom discussions of a poem are likely to recur to that familiar issue of whether the author intended some meaning or other in a text, and the teacher will usually offer two rejoinders to sceptical student questions. Firstly, most of us will say that the students should concentrate not on a writer's avowed intentions, because these can only be known through the text (even if the writer has written about what the text is supposed to say, we can reasonably be wary about treating this knowledge as exhaustive and reliable), and instead think of this as a choice that we readers make to infer such meaning, based on our unfolding grasp of the poem as a whole, our knowledge of the poet and her or his times, and the history of its reception. So far, so good. Unfortunately, some teachers also see their own role as that of quality controllers of interpretation. They will offer a second rejoinder in reply to proffered interpretations that they deem inappropriate, replying that these suggestions are, as it were, outside the spirit of the poem. Puns, homonyms, etymologies, or idiomatic usages that jar with the main drift of the poem are to be ignored, as is the shape of the book or the colour of its paper. Learning to read the poem properly is learning to distinguish between the good quality interpretations and those that are irrelevant.

Reasonable as all this sounds I think it can be unhelpful to students and obscure part of what constitutes the poem, especially its less salient materialities. A disjunctive etymology or discrepant usage may appear to be throwing students off track, but the problem with telling students to ignore dissonant effects is that it undermines their trust in their own immersive experience of a poem, and even more importantly it can subtract too much of the graininess from the poem's overall effect. Just as painters use rough brushstrokes, or musicians may deliberately include the mechanical sounds of the activity of instruments, so poems do work with a mass of para-verbal effects, not all of which are aligned with the poem's overall drift. Some of the acoustic, semantic, and visual effects may loudly interfere with this overall impression; some may just not contribute anything to it. Every poem has at least a few under- or even unemployed words. To tell students to ignore these may be to steer them away from developing a responsiveness of the kind that poetry requires. Modernist poems can be misread and become partially invisible to readers whose attention in reading poetry has been habitually directed towards certain features (perhaps tone, metrical prosody, self-conscious expression) and have tended to ignore other features (syllabic sounds, the unfolding changes in the meaning of a line of words if interpreted incrementally as Robert Creeley for instance does, or the use of visual placement on the page as a mode of spatial mapping as Susan Howe does) that can be mediated through almost any feature of reception. In any printed poem an overall blend of information, melody, signs, blur, and cacophony gives it a characteristic and often unique texture.

None of this is to deny that articulating some features of one's response in a manner that makes possible dialogue and reflective writing is an important part of the learning process. Habitual methods of teaching poetry assume that it is essential to improve the students' awareness of the differences between those effects of the language and material culture of a poem that are interpretatively relevant, and those that are just background noise. Take these opening lines of *Burnt Norton*. Despite their abstractions and the way the lines turn back on themselves they seem to present little ambiguity or poetic intensity:

> Time present and time past
> Are both perhaps present in time future,
> And time future contained in time past.

Some verbal effects, such as the two subtly different meanings of 'present' (as chronologically contemporaneous, and in the sense of one substance being 'present' or constituent of another), or the homonyms 'past' and 'passed', or even the slight pause on the word 'perhaps' that hints at the way both present and past are provisional, even uncertain in some manner, converge with the explicit meanings of these lines to deepen and enrich their effect. So too does the unusual inversion of the phrases 'present time' and 'future time' that results in a semantic roominess to the concepts since we don't quite recognise them. Other possible inferences, associations, sound patterns, or acrostics, are however likely to be considered irrelevant to a reading of the relatively straightforward movement of the verse: the homonyms 'time' and 'thyme'; the concept of a 'pastime'; 'present' meaning a gift; the association of 'present' with 'correct' in the military phrase 'all present and correct'; the acrostic effect of the capitals read downwards that say 'taa', or a vernacular thank-you; the homonyms 'R' and 'are'; and various meanings of 'contained' such as 'self-contained' and the idea of 'containing' an enemy force. It is important to recognise that there is no obvious limit to how many of these effects, no doubt increasingly contrived or attenuated, that we could spin out if we tried. If students propose that some part of this verbal lint is significant in their written or verbal interpretations teachers will quite reasonably discourage them. Yet should they? One could argue that the slight 'flatness' or anti-poetic cadence of these lines derives partly from the allowance of such noise within the information, but this is not my main point. Even where almost no informed reader would attempt to elicit significance that converges with the main directions of the poem, the background texture generated by these myriad effects will still form part of the experience of reading.

All the discarded options I mentioned in connection with *Burnt Norton* represent types of effect that *are* sometimes significant in other modernist verse, so at the least we hope that readers would be open to their impact and ready to interpret them. As teachers we understandably want our students to discern clear patterns within the haze of meanings radiated by a poem. Students taught to ignore such impressions as irrelevant, however, may inadvertently learn partial interpretative blindness when it comes to experimental verse by turning away from seeing, hearing, and feeling these discordances and rustlings in the undergrowth of the poem. The result for the reader can be a poem with too few shades and, as it were, too much contrast. Imposing selective responses to modernist poems can also interfere with our attempts to convey some hint at least of the modernist impact of the poetry in its time.

Policing of interpretative relevance stems from commonplace assumptions about what happens in the mind of a person reading a poem. Immersive reading of a poem is readily conflated in the polysemy of the word 'reading' with articulation based on self-reflection and dialogue. If we consider non-language arts for a moment this point becomes clearer. Gazing at a painting, listening to music, or watching ballet: these are all activities that can require intense concentration of thought and feeling, and yet such responsive immersion in an art work is not primarily conducted through extended internal articulation. Indeed, the attempt to provide a simultaneous linguistic commentary may impede reception and distract from full attentiveness even though engagement with such art works is cognitive (which may include affect, and sensuous perception, as well as reasoning), and this cognitive capacity can be trained to be more observant and intense. It is helpful to remind ourselves of these commonplaces when considering how we read poetry, because the linguistic medium can lead us to assume tacitly that reading a poem involves a coeval verbal interpretation that, however compressed in actuality, could be subjected to the illuminating magnification of a slower, critical reflection which would make explicit the entire cognitive activity of the initial act of reading (I remember a cartoon which showed a pop singer on stage with a man sitting at the side with a microphone and a sign reading something like 'Continuous critical commentary by the Department of Cultural Studies'). It follows from such an assumption that to teach students how to read poetry one should be encouraging them to strengthen their muscles of interpretative articulation so that they too can generate such verbal responses as they go.

My earlier metaphors of noise, background texture, and undergrowth were meant to suggest that much of what goes on, even when we read a poem effectively with close conscious attention, remains below the level of conscious awareness, and can remain so without loss. Even the most thorough analysis will leave some features apparently unexplained, and in a sense illegible. Craig Dworkin calls our attention to the importance of 'illegibility' in much modernist poetry, especially from the latter part of the twentieth-century in his paradoxically titled *Reading the Illegible*, where he points out that some poems offer resistance even to a limited interpretative paraphrase; uncertainties about the integration of parts into even local wholes, plus the sense of puzzlement, may be key elements of a poem. The teacher of poetry can help students attune their minds to the myriad goings on within poems so that they can have as full as possible a cognitive engagement with a poem – they can hear its sounds, absorb its visual appearance, evoke the sensory experiences it recounts, imagine its tones of voice and the demands of its speech acts, catch the receding echoes of the etymologies, synonyms, homonyms, and registers of its lexis, trace its affective contours, and imagine its career as a historical phenomenon extending out into reading communities – without requiring that they make this process fully conscious and ready to be articulated. Explicit recounting of the process by which an interpretation is reached may be helpful; it isn't essential nor should it be the primary desired outcome.

Should we worry about the students in my opening story about T. S. Eliot, punk rock, and Wendy Mulford, who feel disoriented when they are reading *The Waste Land*? My answer has been that behind this question lies a hinterland of other difficult questions about what counts as meaningful when we experience a modernist poem, and that how we decide on the answers then inflects our view of the divisions and continuities in the history of modernist poetry. The discordant histories of modernist poetry are a fascinating if difficult subject to teach. By exploring why modernisms are divided into two broad currents, and why critics argue about whether one continues from the other, we can gain a better understanding of the achievement of modernist poetry, especially its enormously inventive approach to form and meaning, as well as its insistence on the value of novelty and shock. This can help students to develop sensitivity to the range of textual evolution, and help them learn to understand innovative strategies and sometimes even to interpret them, or grasp why they are to an extent uninterpretable. If we reflect further on our aims as teachers, and treat modernist poems as forms of significant cultural work we can include all those aunts, continuers, mothers, and fathers in our curricula for the teaching of modernist poetry, and we can also contribute to a better understanding of the 'social substance' not only of poetry, but language itself.

Note

1. She is citing A. Sheldon, 'Approaching the Future', in K. Tracey (ed.), *Language and Social Interaction at the Century's Turn*, special issue of *Research on Language and Social Interaction* 32(1–2) (1999): 157.

Works cited and further reading

Allen, Donald (1960) *The New American Poetry*. New York: Grove Press.

Ashton, Jennifer (2005) *From Modernism to Postmodernism: American Poetry and Theory in the Twentieth Century*. Cambridge: Cambridge University Press.

Brandom, Robert (1994) *Making It Explicit: Reasoning, Representing, and Discursive Commitment*. Cambridge, MA: Harvard University Press.

Breslin, James E. B. (1984) *From Modern to Contemporary: American Poetry 1945–1965*. Chicago: University of Chicago Press.

Butterick, George (1994) *The Postmoderns: the New American Poetry Revised*. New York: Grove Press.

Dworkin, Craig (2003) *Reading the Illegible*. Evanston, IL: Northwestern University Press.

Eliot, T. S. (2002) *Collected Poems 1909–1962*. London: Faber & Faber.

Finnegan, Ruth (2002) *Communicating: the Multiple Modes of Human Interconnection*. London: Routledge.

Giddens, Anthony (1990) *The Consequences of Modernity*. Cambridge: Polity, 1990.

Hejinian, Lyn (2000) *The Language of Inquiry*. Berkeley: University of California Press.

Jameson, Fredric (1992) *Postmodernism, or, The Cultural Logic of Late Capitalism*. London: Verso.

Jarrell, Randall (1950) 'Robert Lowell's Poetry', in John Ciardi (ed.), *Mid-Century American Poets*. New York: Twayne.

Lewin, Kurt (1939) 'Field Theory and Experiment in Social Psychology: Concepts and Methods', *American Journal of Sociology* 44(6): 868–96.

Maud, Ralph (2003) *Poet to Publisher: Charles Olson's Correspondence with Donald Allen*. Vancouver: Talonbooks.

McCaffery, Steve (2007) 'Autonomy to Indeterminacy', *Twentieth-Century Literature* 53(2): 212–17.

Michaels, Walter Benn (2004) *The Shape of the Signifier: 1967 to the End of History*. Princeton: Princeton University Press.

Olson, Charles (1966) *Selected Writings*. New York: New Directions.

—— (1997) *Collected Prose*, ed. Donald Allen and Benjamin Friedlander. Berkeley: University of California Press.

Osborne, Peter (1995) *The Politics of Time: Modernity and Avant-Garde*. London: Verso.

Perloff, Marjorie (1973) 'Charles Olson and the "Inferior Predecessors": "Projective Verse" Revisited', *ELH* 40(2): 285–306.

—— (2002) *21st-Century Modernism*. Oxford: Blackwell.

Pippin Robert (1999) *Modernism as a Philosophical Problem*. 2nd edn. Oxford: Blackwell.

—— (2005) *The Persistence of Subjectivity: On the Kantian Aftermath*. Cambridge: Cambridge University Press.

Rukeyser, Muriel (1942) *Willard Gibbs*. Garden City, NY: Doubleday, Doran & Co.

—— (1949) *The Life of Poetry*. New York: William Morrow.

—— (1978) *The Collected Poems of Muriel Rukeyser*. New York: McGraw-Hill.

Index